Hope in the Main Street

Rob Cotton

To Anna
with thanks for your
partnership in the Gospel

Rob

5th Oct 2021

Onwards and Upwards Publishers

3 Radfords Turf, Cranbrook, Exeter,
EX5 7DX, United Kingdom.
www.onwardsandupwards.org

This first edition published in the United Kingdom by Onwards and Upwards Publishers (2018).

ISBN: 978-1-78815-639-4
Typeface: Sabon LT
Editor: Holly Bird
Graphic design: LM Graphic Design

Printed in the United Kingdom.

About the Author

Rob Cotton is the Superintendent Minister at a large Methodist church in Knutsford and also the village of Plumley in Cheshire. He has previously served in Arnold, Nottingham and Ingol, Preston. He is known as being passionate about mobilising the church to meet needs within local communities and to bring hope into the lives of individuals.

Prior to his current appointment, he was the Senior Campaign Manager at Bible Society, working on citywide media campaigns relating stories in the Bible to soap stories, and also on the leadership teams for national campaigns such as Hope 08, Biblefresh and The 2011 Trust (celebrating the 400th anniversary of the King James Bible).

Endorsements

Rob Cotton is the real deal and as such is constantly provoking the church to take our message of hope out to where it's really needed. He's learnt so much over the years and anybody who is serious about mission will love this book.

Andy Hawthorne OBE
Founder and CEO of The Message Trust

Great to see first-hand a dream, once just a spark – spoken of and prayed about so faithfully for so many years – come to fruition and into being. This is a timely book with a message downloaded from the realm of expectation to a season of realisation; where many will without doubt be blessed by the unflinching arrogance of hope in the face of devastation; a book that will leave you not a moment longer without the beautiful fragrance of hope.

Rob Cotton is a great pastor, leader, author and even greater friend!

Freddie Kofi
Singer/Songwriter

Rob, as a Methodist presbyter engaged in circuit ministry and with his many years working with Bible Society, has encountered people who needed to hear the good news of Jesus Christ. In this book he shares his rich experience of mission and ministry while trying to bring hope and healing in seemingly hopeless situations. I hope this book will encourage each of us to share our stories of hope and faith, bringing hope into the lives of others.

Loraine Mellor
President of the Methodist Conference, 2017-2018

Rob Cotton's book invites churches to take hope into public places, and to be the presence of Jesus on high streets and in town halls, at bus stops and school gates. I warmly commend *Hope in the Main Street* for study and as inspiration for mission.

Andrew Lunn
Chair of Manchester and Stockport Methodist District

I first met Rob Cotton when he inspired Bristol church leaders with his presentation *Engaging Contemporary Society,* the story of his Arnold Church in Nottingham meeting need in the local community after the tragic murder of Marian Bates. As a result, I commended him to other church leaders as he then helped to develop Bible Society's citywide media campaign in Bristol, and became his friend. More recently, I have been pleased to return to my childhood home of Knutsford and to support Rob's ministry in that context. I now commend his book *Hope in the Main Street* as he seeks to inspire the wider church with his story.

Rt. Rev. Bishop Mike Hill
Bishop of Bristol

I regard highly the ministry of Rob Cotton and this book will help many who are seeking to see their ministry and mission both widen and develop. He writes as a genuine practitioner who has a love for God and people.

Keith V. Garner
Superintendent, Wesley Mission, Sydney, Australia

Dedicated to my wife Carol Cotton in
appreciation of her partnership in
life, love and ministry.

With thanks to our children Sarah,
Steven and Timothy for their
encouragement and inspiration.

Written in memory of my parents,
Charles Frederick and Edith Mary Cotton.

Contents

Foreword by Roy Crowne

I would call Rob a good friend and colleague. We had the privilege of working closely together on the leadership team of Hope when he was seconded by Bible Society to help develop the Hope 08 campaign.

Rob brought to our team the experience of leading a local church and of enabling many churches to work together in unity. He believes in the spiritual principal of synergy, that churches and organisations working together in unity are capable of achieving far more than they could possibly do individually if each were working in isolation on its own agenda. I was pleased to have Rob working alongside us because of his experience of developing campaigns with Bible Society in Nottingham, Bristol and Greater Manchester, as well as his passion for both the Bible and the mission of the local church.

Hope Together is a year of mission for the whole Church, seeking to reach the whole nation. I believe that Rob has written *Hope in the Main Street* as his way of sharing both his missional experience and something of his passion to see the local church engaging their community in credible ways to share something of the hope in Jesus practically and tangibly.

Hope in the Main Street is based on stories of individuals and churches that have seen God at work; they will build faith and inspire you to share God's love in your villages, towns and cities.

Roy Crowne
CEO, Hope Together

Hope in the Main Street

Foreword by Chris Blake

I am very pleased to have been invited to write the foreword for *Hope in the Main Street* as a friend, ministerial colleague and contemporary of Rob Cotton.

I have known Rob for some years now since we worked together as line managers at the Easter People event with the late Rob Frost. I got to know more about him through our mutual friends Mark and Janet Dunn Wilson when I was serving as Chair of the Cornwall District of the Methodist Church, but it was when I accepted an invitation to preach and lead the Bible Studies at Summerfire (formerly the Southport Methodist Holiness Convention) that my wife Joy and I shared with Rob and his wife Carol at a much deeper level and we became firm friends.

As Rob shared with me something of his ministry as senior campaign manager at Bible Society, I knew that few of our contemporaries would have had such significant opportunities to engage in the public square as he had in that time. He was working in an almost unique position, but he brought to that role his experience of being a local church leader, his entrepreneurial creativity and his real passion to see the church engaging with people in their local community and so bringing to reality *Hope in the Main Street*.

While Rob was working towards his M.A. in Evangelism Studies at Cliff College, he took the opportunity to reflect on his experience at Arnold Methodist Church when two thousand five hundred people came into the church to sign books of condolence for Prince William and Prince Harry after the death of their mother, Lady Diana, and how that demonstrated the national experience of corporate grief. That experience encouraged Rob to develop his commitment to being a reflective practitioner and, in some sense, this book represents part of that process, giving Rob the opportunity to share his reflections with a wider audience.

Rob is a powerful storyteller, and in this book he shares honestly about his experience of the church's feelings of apparent failure after being attacked by arsonists in Preston, alongside the story of a second church which needed to be demolished to enable the building of a new purpose-built church and the launch of the community charity Intag, in an exciting phase of ministry. Rob then moved to Arnold in Nottingham where he and the church became the focus of the national media in caring for the family of murdered grandmother Marian Bates. Later, Rob took on the role as Bible Society's senior campaign manager before he returned to local church ministry at Knutsford Methodist Church in Cheshire. In each place where he has served, Rob has sought to reflect on the interaction between the Gospel and the particular context into which God has called him. The writing of this book is another phase of that reflective journey, and I know that Rob's intention is to encourage a conversation in local churches about how to bring 'hope in the main street' in each context and community.

My wife Joy and I were pleased to be present at the welcome service for Rob and Carol at Knutsford Methodist Church and we have had the privilege of being present in worship at that church a number of times in recent years. It has been exciting and encouraging to see Rob, as a reflective practitioner, working collaboratively and creatively in the community of Knutsford.

Hope in the Main Street is Rob's invitation to join in his latest campaign to inspire a local church (and others too) to bring hope into the communities of which they are a part and which they serve. In these pages Rob shares his journey with integrity and I commend this book to you knowing that you will be both challenged and encouraged by his reflective insights.

Chris Blake
Methodist Minister and Principal Cliff College (2008-2016)

Foreword by Steve Wild

I am deeply honoured to be invited to write a foreword for this book. I have known and admired Rob Cotton for almost thirty years. His sincerity and integrity as a man for faith and hope is outstanding and, like all things in his journey of life, this book is offered before the Cross that it may bring glory to God and no one else.

It is Rob's desire that the contents will bring hope into people's lives and into our local communities. In this book he is sharing stories of ministry and mission, from the murder of Marian Bates, to Biblefresh, Firefest, Hope 08 and future Hope campaigns.

Jesus spoke to people in stories. This story is the most powerful type of message, because it is God dealing with and working through a human being. I hope that it will empower others to share their stories.

These stories deserve a wider audience and can be used as a tool for mission. Perhaps there is a person you know who would value a copy to read? Every prison library should have one. It's great to see what the Holy Spirit can do with a life open to serve God. I pray you will be blessed and inspired reading it.

Steven Wild
President of the Methodist Conference (2015-2016)

Hope in the Main Street

Introduction

Thank you for taking the time to read *Hope in the Main Street*. It is a culmination of many years of writing a few words and then deciding that other things are more important, or it not being the priority of the moment. The fact that you are now reading this means that getting the book finished has become a personal priority that could not be ignored amidst the pressures of a busy local growing church in Knutsford, Cheshire. It is partly because of the people in that setting and their encouragement that I am determined to get my ramblings published, so that we can study and reflect upon each other's journeys together.

During a wonderful sabbatical I managed to get a few chapters written whilst drinking too many free coffee refills at King Street's Victoriana Vintage Tea Room, Knutsford. It was after a few months that during a revisit, when the manageress, Debbie Townsend, asked if my book had been published yet as she wanted to buy a copy, I knew it was about time to deliver!

I am writing as a grandad to two grandchildren (at the moment); the delightful Marin Faith and the beautiful Cassidy May Walker, with another about to be born to our son Steven and his beautiful wife Jenny. Their births have been surprisingly significant experiences in my life, when my perspective of the world in which we live and my hopes for their future begin to shape my own hopes for local communities and the Church's contribution to modern-day society.

At Marin's second birthday party, I was being the dutiful grandad, putting up balloons and banners, whilst also talking to my daughter Sarah's best friends, 'The Pink Ladies' Hannah Walker (North) and Laura Redding (Simpson), about our time together in Arnold, Nottingham. In the course of the conversation, I mentioned that I had been trying to write a book about this time and said, "It's probably only going to be of any significance to me," to which Laura replied, "I'd like to read it. That's our story as well; it's important to me!"

So even if people were only being polite, I am now determined to share my story of work and ministry in a number of different contexts as a way of sharing other people's stories and the way in which we have journeyed together in trying to bring hope to others in local communities. I would like to therefore thank all of those who have journeyed with me, worked alongside me, some giving many hours of voluntary support to the cause, others as colleagues who have encouraged me, supported me and used their gifts to complement any gifting I may have and sense of call that I have tried to live out with them. My apologies to those who may remember events differently, or who may have preferred some different emphases, but as I tell 'our story', I trust that you will be able to reflect honestly on 'your story' too.

My invitation is to journey with me through the pages *of Hope in the Main Street,* to explore the contribution of faith in the public square of life today. My aim will be to tell the stories and reflect upon them, hopefully in a way which enables everyone to do the same.

Some of you might ask how on earth in the context of the noisy neighbours secularism, atheism, materialism, new-age and multi-faith can the church of today even claim to have a unique place in, or contribution to, society? My claim will be that not only does she have this, but society still needs her to have this!

To the Church, my invitation is to consider how to bring hope in word and action to the villages, towns and cities of our nation. It was a privilege during my role as senior campaign manager at Bible Society to serve as part of the leadership team for Hope 08 with some of the most inspirational leaders the Church in Britain has today. The emphasis is on bringing transformation through sensitive engagement in local communities, where the Church's faith is actually put into action and loving concern for people is tangibly seen in practice.

So many clear examples of this emphasis can now be seen bringing 'hope in the main street' through Foodbanks such as Hampers of Hope, street pastors caring for vulnerable young people on the streets late at night, lunch clubs, youth work, children's work and even fostering of vulnerable young people through charities such as Home for Good and other agencies. In fact, I would dare to suggest that our nation could never afford to lose the contributions made by people of faith and the Church that they are part of.

I would love to feel that the reading of this book could not only enable people to reflect together about their life's journey, their faith, but also mobilise people to consider how they personally, or as part of a church, could respond to need in their own local community. The aim, therefore, in writing this book is to enable 'hope in the main street'.

18

1

Sarah's Spiritual Indigestion

Our daughter Sarah was on the telephone to Carol and me, some time ago now, when she said, "I've heard so many sermons, I can't take any more in, and I just want to do something!" It was a surprising comment from someone in a church which is known to engage in ministry to the poor and to emphasise the importance of living out your faith in community. Sarah has always been something of an activist in nature, rather like her parents, but she also wanted to know what God was calling her to do at that time.

I was reminded of the conversation I had when I met with Phil Bland to discuss the charity that he and a few church members had launched in an area of South Africa. The charity is called Hope Through Action and uses sport as a vehicle to work with literally hundreds of African young people each week, providing health education, sports exercise, literacy classes, empowerment and a safe space. Having worked as part of the leadership team of Hope 08, I had thought that this campaign might have been why they had chosen to use 'Hope' in the title. But when I asked Phil why the charity had this name, he said, "It was born out of frustration. I was tired of sitting listening to sermons and thinking, 'So what?'" This was not the response I had expected! Rather than just sitting listening to sermons about taking good news to the poor, Phil wanted to get on and do it. The charity had actually been earlier founded by Philip and Judy Green, with Phil Bland and other KMC (Knutsford Methodist Church) members giving it some structure and governance to enable the work to develop.

I find it really exciting that people such as Phil can be instrumental in bringing hope to literally hundreds of people, thousands of miles away. He can be taken well out of his comfort zones in the process, but then that is a very healthy thing and has certainly been a very positive experience for those individuals in KMC who have been taken on the journey with him. From a feeling of frustration after a sermon, hope has been experienced by young people in another part of the world and in the faith journeys of many others in Knutsford and beyond. Phil has been joined by Stu Crawford, Peter Thompson and Steve Wilkinson as fellow trustees.

I have the hunch that a lot of people in churches and in local communities encounter the same frustration of feeling that they have more to offer in the Church and in the world. In fact, in a recent interactive contemporary service I asked people to consider the Church as a football stadium, possibly even Wembley Stadium. I then asked them to think of where they felt they were in relation to the stadium: outside, watching in the stands, sitting in the stands, or actually playing on the pitch as part of the team. One fairly new lady in the church had the courage to say that she felt as if she was still watching in the stands, even if she now felt that she was on the front row of the stands. Needless to say, since this honest reflection I have visited her at home, had a coffee and a chat, and she has since taken on a new significant role in ministry. She is now an important part of the team playing on the pitch.

I asked my daughter Sarah to reflect upon her personal experience of spiritual indigestion and I will leave her to explain her own feelings:

> When I am taught and discipled about the life that Jesus and His disciples lived, it seems so far from my reality. Then I am reminded that this can be my reality too. When I receive this truth and His love and His Holy Spirit, my heart feels alive and I quickly want to get out there and do something!

> Sometimes I think it's good to stay a little longer and enjoy Him and rest, but not for too long! I remember becoming aware that if I just kept receiving all of this teaching but didn't put the theory into practice, I would be at risk of becoming lazy, frustrated, bored, apathetic or spiritually fat!

> I think a lot of people (myself included) get fired up and want to do something but then the task at hand feels too large and too daunting, we are faced with our own inadequacies and quickly feel overwhelmed and incapable. It can be easy to start craving the next conference or Sunday service to get back on a spiritual high again.

I am slowly learning to take a step back when I feel fired up by a teaching or conference I've been to and ask myself a few questions like:

- *What are the opportunities and gifts God has given me?*

- *Who are the people that I can bless?*

- *Where can I take another step of faith?*

- *Who is going to encourage me and hold me accountable so that I keep moving forwards?*

I am not where I want to be but I'm taking steps in the right direction. A few friends and I sent out prayer request cards to the neighbours on our street (it was amazing what we found out about people's lives and we have now seen some of our prayers answered), we made our neighbours little gifts at Christmas and decorated the street with flowers on Easter Sunday. When a friend of mine who is not a Christian had a baby, I asked if I could pray a blessing for her baby when my husband and I went to visit (blushing whilst I did it!) These are a couple of examples of how I try and live out my faith. Sometimes I lose my courage and don't offer to pray for someone despite the Holy Spirit's prompting, sometimes I get discouraged.

I still love going to conferences and worshipping in church, but I often encounter Jesus and feel His joy and His compassion when I'm out and about living my day to day life which I think is just as precious.

Sarah loves bringing the hope of Jesus into the lives of others and she is passionate about bringing that hope to people in the main street, in the marketplace, in the ordinary places of our existence. Phil is passionate about bringing hope to young people in Africa, and my son Timothy and his wife, Alexandra, have recently spent some time working with Hope Through Action in setting up a project with young people who have physical or mental health difficulties, and another for youngsters in a craft group in Mbekwini.

In recent years, our son Steven has loved bringing hope into young people's lives working on the Spear project which was launched by the registered charity, Resurgo Trust. St. Paul's Church in Hammersmith formed these charities with the vision to pioneer, develop and run socially transformative projects in the community as expressions of the life and faith of the church. It now hosts a number of projects, including Spear. Spear runs a six-week highly interactive programme aimed at supporting young people aged between sixteen and twenty-four who are not in education, employment or training (NEET). They have an impressive success rate of getting young people into full-time work or education, giving them real hope for the future.

Steven has now launched a new charity named GROW, based in Sheffield. GROW's vision is, 'Inspiring hope and unlocking potential in young people who have experienced care.' They believe that every young person has great potential to positively impact and contribute to society. They work to unlock that potential through delivering an employment coaching programme for ten weeks and by developing a supportive community.

I trust that a good number of us can explore how we can respond to the needs around us, particularly during Hope in 2018, to bring hope in the main street, in our villages, towns and cities; and all places, at all times and by all possible means to all people (see 1 Corinthians 9:22). No doubt there will be a few sermons, talks, stories, jokes, Bible studies, presentations and books encouraging us to do just that. When we have heard and read all that we need to, rather than just *speaking* about good news, we can *be* good news to and for other people, and in our doing and being 'good news people' we will bring hope when and wherever we can, and see 'hope in the main street'.

One Sunday morning a few years ago, someone passing by outside KMC asked a church steward standing at the door, "What time does the service start?" – meaning the worship service. But the steward promptly replied, "When the worship finishes!" It is as we are sent out into the world that we become effective as the salt of the earth and the light of the world; it is then that our service begins.

During my appointment as a Methodist minister in Preston, Carol and I met each week for a soup lunch and time of prayer with my colleague David Griffiths and his wife, Sylvia. I was always impressed by the work of The Emmaus Community in the Fox Street basement of Central Methodist Church, Lune Street, and David kindly reflects here on how the work began:

"This can't go on another year, David Griffiths!" said Gillian with great feeling as we stood around chatting in the snow on Fox Street after a group of us had seen everyone off the premises following the Saturday night Soup Kitchen. "Something's got to be done!" It was Terry, one of our regulars, who had kicked things off. We sometimes found him on the landing upstairs on a Sunday morning, where he had kipped down for the night. We watched that bitterly cold December evening as his shambolic figure wandered down the road to find a reasonably dry spot in one of the 'caves' in Avenham Park. Gillian was right. Something had to be done. The time had come for the Soup Kitchen, a well-established activity at Central, to prepare for a much more far-reaching ministry that would bring hope to many people far beyond the city centre.

And so, a year later, in the winter of 1989, The Emmaus Community, as we then called it, was up and running. Although we had planned for it to be open four nights a week from 8.00pm in the evening until 9.00am the following morning, within the first two weeks it became the 24/7 venture that it remains today. Everything was undergirded by prayer – conversations with the congregation about its impact upon the life of Central Methodist Church; the appointment of a management committee; advice from The Methodist Church Property Division in Manchester; health and safety; discussions with Preston Borough Council, the police, the fire service, and many more organisations and individuals. Overnight sleeping accommodation was provided in the hall beneath our church that led out onto Fox Street – the centre for so many years of folk who formed, and still do form, some of Preston's 'alternative community', as our Jesuit colleague and friend, Father Dennis Blackledge, described them when he took the funeral of one of its most notorious, and probably well-loved, members a few years later. A warden and volunteers were recruited. The years that followed were to be packed with joys and sorrows, successes and failures, anxiety and peace, anger and calm, brokenness and healing, division and unity. And a deep awareness that this was the road along which Jesus was leading us.

This project, like so many others, started when Christians had a sort of spiritual indigestion, frustration or a 'Popeye moment'[1] when they just knew that something had to be done to bring hope into what seemed like a fairly hopeless situation. And experience suggests that we can actually bring hope into people's lives.

There is a story of a young boy who threw a stone at the church's stained-glass window of the Incarnation. Stained-glass windows are one of the earliest forms of art that were used to depict something of the truth about God. The boy's stone nicked out the letter 'E' in the word 'HIGHEST' in the text 'GLORY TO GOD IN THE HIGHEST'. Therefore, until it was unfortunately repaired, it read, 'GLORY TO GOD IN THE HIGH ST'.

The Word of God cannot be dissociated from the action of God. As the blood flows through the body, so the spiritual life is kept healthy when the church interacts with its local community bringing hope in the 'HIGH ST' or, in the context of this book, in the main street. When the Church proactively brings 'hope in the main street' of our villages, towns and cities of our nation, it is only then that we are also bringing 'GLORY TO GOD IN THE HIGH ST'.

In James 2:14-17 we read, 'My brothers [and sisters], what good is it for someone to say that he has faith if his actions do not prove it? Can that faith save him? Suppose there are brothers or sisters who need clothes and don't have enough to eat. What good is there in your saying to them, "God bless you! Keep warm and eat well!" – if you don't give them the necessities of life? So it is with faith: if it is alone and includes no actions, then it is dead.'

---

[1] See the chapter *Unchosen – A Popeye Moment?* on page 165 for further explanation.

2

The Real Cranford – Knutsford

During my time of campaigning to prepare for Biblefresh (which enabled people to creatively engage with scripture during the Celebration of the four hundredth anniversary of the King James Bible) in 2011, I was visiting many Methodist churches who had really backed the campaign. I loved visiting Methodist churches around the country and began to feel that the primary calling upon my life, besides being a son, husband and father at the time, was to be a local church minister. And so, after initially exploring the possibility of doing a part-time appointment alongside a reduced role at Bible Society, it became obvious that I was being called to offer myself full time in the next round of the stationing of ministers process, where Chairs of District meet to send you to some unsuspecting circuit, church and community!

So, as the Stationing Committee met in the autumn of 2011, I received the telephone call from the Chair of the Notts and Derby Methodist District, Rev. Lorraine Mellor (President of the Methodist Conference 2017-18), to tell me that I had been stationed to Knutsford in Cheshire. As I had read the profile of the Knutsford Methodist Church, Circuit and Community, I had expressed an interest in the appointment as my first preference and, surprisingly, they had also made me their first choice.

I had visited the church a few years earlier as part of a Sons of Korah tour which I was hosting and remembered just how professional the staging, lighting and production of the event had been, so probably I hoped that this was an indication of what the church was capable of. In this chapter I would like to explore with you the current context of my ministry and mission before proceeding further.

The perception of the town of Knutsford is that it is made up of very wealthy people, many of whom are well known to the celebrity magazines and tabloids. However, this is very far from the truth; there is much more to be said about Knutsford and certainly not everyone is either well known or wealthy! Prior to our welcome service, one of our Nottingham friends, Pastor Roger Robb, asked, "Rob, what are you doing in a place like this? There's a McLaren showroom at the end of the street!" I didn't have the heart to tell him about the Mercedes, Range Rover, Tesla and various other nearby showrooms. You may see Harry Styles at the wine bar, and my wife Carol has seen both John Bishop and Les Dennis walking down the street, but I would like you to get to know the real Knutsford as you read this book, rather than the imaginary Cranford.

Knutsford is a historic and rather picturesque town just fifteen miles southwest of Manchester on the doorstep of one of the UK's most complete historic estates, Tatton Park. The town is steeped in heritage and has a thriving independent town centre which attracts many visitors to the rather charming Cheshire countryside. In fact, our son-in-law Fintan described Knutsford on his first visit as quintessentially English and all of our children have loved visiting us, as well as the coffee shops and bars, since our move.

The Victorian novelist Elizabeth Gaskell based her fictional town of Cranford upon Knutsford, and one of the other church leaders participating with us in the Lead Academy Learning Community from Headingly in Leeds recently found an article on Knutsford in *The Week,* a summary magazine of the week's news. It read as follows:

> *The people of Knutsford in Cheshire are to be set free – from centuries of walking single file. In 1794, Lady Jane Stanley, a lifelong spinster, agreed to pay for new paved footpaths in the town, but only on condition they were made too narrow for lovers to walk down arm in arm. Now, council bosses have decided to overturn her decree, and pedestrianise the high street. The inspiration for Lady Ludlow in Elizabeth Gaskell's Cranford, Stanley (Lady Stanley) wanted her epitaph to read: "A maid I lived and a maid I died; I never was asked and never denied."*

Now, our friend from Leeds, Pastor David, does not know Knutsford but he knows a few of us from KMC who shared with him in the Lead Academy training programme, so he thought it was fascinating to read about our town's history. But actually, he doesn't know that the article is referring to Bottom Street (King Street) rather than Top Street (Princess

Street) and that whilst we know that the council are having a discussion about King Street being pedestrianised, it's unlikely to happen for a good time to come! For him in Leeds, it sounds all very quaint in our quintessentially English town, but for us as residents trying to walk or push a pram up the pavement, it can feel inconvenient or even dangerous! So there are mixed feelings about Lady Jane Stanley's contribution of £400 to pay for new pavements and her dislike of people showing affection for each other in her hometown many years ago. There have been complaints from shoppers that the pavements are awkward, but they certainly add to the character of the town.

During World War II Knutsford was home to General Patton and it is also home to the most famous of all May Day events still celebrated in the UK for over one hundred and fifty years, Knutsford's Royal May Day. The procession each year comes complete with a Rose Queen retinue, a penny farthing display from our museum at the Penny Farthing Café, bands and many of our community groups.

Our official town guide tells you that tradition links Knutsford with King Canute who, legend has it, forded the River Lily in 1016 giving Knutsford its name, an event we commemorated in 2016 as many of us forded (or stepped over) the Lily. Knutsford is actually mentioned in the Domesday Book of 1085 as Canutesford and the town's first charter was granted to William de Tabley by Edward I in 1292 followed by the establishment of a court, fair and market in 1294.

Knutsford has historically been an important Cheshire town and quarter sessions had been held there since 1575, originally in the Market Place and later in a new building where the RBS bank now stands. In 1819 the Sessions House was built and whilst no longer in use, it still stands as quite a landmark in the town centre and has recently been converted into The Courthouse Hotel.

Behind the courthouse was Knutsford Jail. Work began on the new prison due to overcrowding at Chester and it was enlarged in 1853. By 1914, it was no longer taking prisoners and the building was demolished in 1934. The site is now occupied by Booths supermarket, which has been an important meeting place for the community in recent years.

Princess Victoria stayed at the Royal George Hotel just five years before becoming Queen and in the early twentieth century the architect Richard Harding Watt changed the landscape of the town with many Italian-styled buildings such as the Ruskin Rooms, Drury Lane, Legh Road, the Kings Coffee House and Gaskell Memorial Tower. Sir Henry

Royce lived in Knutsford and met Charles Stewart Rolls, beginning the world-famous Rolls-Royce partnership during this time. Plus, of course, John Wesley (founder of the Methodist Church) came to Knutsford to preach from the steps of a house near the Royal George Hotel (now Regent Street) on Monday, 20th March 1738. Wesley wrote in his journal, 'At Knutsford all we spake to thankfully received the word of exhortation.' It reads a little differently to the entries in my journal. These steps have now been relocated outside KMC on Princess Street.

Knutsford is a great place to visit, with its Heritage Centre, Museum in the Street, wonderful parks, independent shops, garden centres, coffee shops, restaurants, spa hotels, Royal May Day, promenades, RHS Flower Show, Literature Festival, surrounding countryside and beautiful vibrant churches. It is also a great place to live and it's a privilege to serve as a minister in the town. We even have some people who have found KMC to be their desired spiritual home and have moved to the area to fulfil that ambition. Even after listening to my sermons online and in person, David and Jackie Tomkins decided to move to the town to join KMC and have become an important part of the church.

The cost of living is certainly much higher than Calverton village in Nottingham (where we had been living previously) and I miss the size of portions at Pete's Fish Bar, the chip shop in the square, but there is a quality of life that is something to aspire to. The neighbours are friendly and even go away on holiday together; they all find it a great place to bring up their children, with excellent local schools, and say, "Why would we want to live anywhere else?" Knutsford is a town where there is still a real sense of community and shared values. It is great to walk our dog, Tammy, and to have people chatting with you, making new friends such as Alan Boot asking his latest theological question! It has also been good to serve as the Mayor's Chaplain for three terms so far.

When we first arrived in Knutsford and were becoming tired of unpacking the boxes, my wife Carol went for a short lie down on the bed, only to feel the whole house tremble. She thought it was a minor earthquake, but actually it was the rubble train rumbling past on the rail track at the bottom of the garden! During the first few weeks, we had a faulty bedroom window which could not be closed properly and so I was very much aware of the aircraft pilot heading for nearby Manchester Airport who seemed to be trying to land in our back garden! Well, that was what it sounded like every few minutes. But we have now adjusted to life in the idyllic Knutsford from the quiet Nottinghamshire village of Calverton.

There are expensive properties on Millionaires Row with gated drives of successful business or entertainment personalities and there are many other ordinary, lovely, hard-working people. People will watch the Real Cheshire Wives with footballers' wives and former models for their entertainment, but actually, the reality for the majority is certainly something very different, which is grounded in the fact that people are highly capable, well-educated and career-minded professionals. Some of us will never truly be part of the Cheshire set, but we will be getting on with life in beautiful surroundings, in a town that we can be rightly proud of and serve the local community.

It is true to say that our last local MP was George Osborne, former Chancellor of the Exchequer, but I have only recently had the opportunity to meet briefly with him, unlike my Nottingham experience of the past of being able to build a very positive working relationship with the Gedling MP Vernon Coaker. I would certainly value the opportunity to have the sort of relationship where you are able to discuss the needs of the ordinary local person, but then I was advised that he would be unlikely to profile the launch of our new Foodbank Hampers of Hope in his own constituency. At the time, it would have been a red-hot potato of a political issue, which the media would have loved, and the political mileage that some of the opposition would rightly make on this subject probably made it just too hot to handle!

George Osborne was certainly very supportive of The Welcome Charity on the Longridge Estate and has been instrumental in helping them to get a Big Society Award, alongside some of our Welcome Charity volunteers being invited to Buckingham Palace to receive the Queen's Award for Volunteering for their work in responding to need in the area. But I'm afraid that George was unable to participate in any of the work and worship of any of the local churches regularly due to the demands upon him.

I tend to feel that in a context where people are deemed to be successful, or wealthy even, that it is probably even harder for those who live with real needs and do struggle with the downward spiral of the poverty trap. The truth is that the need for churches to work alongside and to collaborate with other agencies and the local authority is greater than ever. Whilst the town is a great place to visit and to live in, that does not change the challenge to respond to the many needs which present themselves to us in modern-day society. And if this is true for the community and the churches of Knutsford, it is certainly true for the villages, towns and cities of our entire nation at this time.

Soon after our arrival in the town, the *Knutsford Guardian* interviewed me and asked, "Why did you come to Knutsford, did you know the town?" I responded, "There is a great team of people who are very welcoming, who are passionate about their town, who care very much about their local community and I am really looking forward to working with them." However, it has certainly been challenging to feel that I have finally been able to transition into my role as minister of Knutsford Methodist Church from a very different role at Bible Society. The church is larger in membership than anything I have tackled before and I found it to be a medium-sized church with, in my opinion, a large church vision and a small church structure. After fourteen years of fruitful ministry with Paul Wilson, who was an excellent preacher, teacher, pastor and administrator, they now had to contend with someone who had a very different Myers-Briggs[2] profile and approach, namely me! Paul is a friend whom I have great respect for and I now have the challenge of building upon the legacy of his ministry and transitioning the church 'from good to great'.

---

[2] The Myers-Briggs Type Indicator is an introspective self-report question-naire with the purpose of indicating different psychological preferences in how people perceive the world and make decisions.

3

Fifty Shades of Blue

I am not sure if it is my age, whether I am having something of a mid-life crisis, or whether, actually, other people can really identify with what I am feeling at the present time. In fact, I would suggest that it is not just me that is having a mid-life crisis, but it is also the Church and society as a whole that is having one!

I love the Church and am obviously deeply committed to it, and yet I also have a love-hate relationship with it. I love what the Church stands for and still believe that in some sense it is still the most effective channel to bring hope to our nation. And yet, I also believe that as the institutional Church faces the challenges of decline, it struggles to transition itself into being a 'discipleship movement shaped for mission', the catchphrase which has certainly captivated the Methodist Church in recent years. It makes me feel fifty shades of blue that many within the Church are just unable, or unwilling, to wrestle with the challenges.

If the Church is going to bring 'hope in the main street' and into the communities of the UK, then we have to prepare ourselves and understand the context to which we seek to speak into. Rather like the season of Advent, when we prepare our hearts and minds for the coming of Jesus at Christmas, so we also have to reflect carefully and prayerfully if we are to be adequately prepared for the challenges of mission and ministry in the future. I sense that many of us feel fifty shades of blue about the current state of play.

It was a lovely, relaxing Saturday afternoon. Carol and I were watching something on TV. We were not expecting anyone to visit, so there were a few papers on the table, envelopes from the morning's post were screwed up on the floor (after the stamps had been removed for the Leprosy Mission, of course), coffee mugs were on the floor, plates from lunch were still on the table and, as I was feeling a bit weary, I think I was probably about to have a little catnap. But then the doorbell rang and suddenly we jumped into action! The mugs and plates were being grabbed, the envelopes were being gathered, the cushions were being buffed whilst I went to answer the door.

My sister Cath and her family have taken to surprising us and just dropping in! Her most recent visit was when Carol and I were both out, so Chris (our brother-in-law) took a picture of Cath looking sad at our door when she was unable to get in! Then she posted it on Facebook with some relevant sarcastic comment such as "You're never in!" What she didn't know was that we were hiding behind the sofa! No, not really. I am only joking – we were both out, and so we were not prepared or ready for a visit.

On this occasion, however, we were able to tidy up very quickly; we could blag it, I suppose, putting the kettle on and getting our visitors to feel welcome and hopefully think that we were fully prepared and obviously pleased to receive them. You can do that with visitors at the door maybe (depending on the state of your home), but you cannot easily tidy up the church or your life at short notice. By the time the ring of the doorbell comes (so to speak), it's too late. This is what the season of Advent is all about in the calendar of the Church – preparing our hearts and minds for the coming of Jesus, though actually this is just as relevant for Christians at any time of the year. But how prepared are we today for the visits of the poor and needy? Certainly in recent times one of the things that has left me feeling fifty shades of blue is that we have felt quite unprepared for the demands of rather desperate, stressed, aggressive and yet vulnerable people who have unexpectedly arrived at our door.

So how prepared are we to meet the challenges which will face us, and respond to them? As a nation, I think that many of us are asking, "Where are we at, right now?" Are we all feeling fifty shades of blue about society as a whole with differing opinions on Brexit and a government struggling to find a majority, disillusioned by politicians, statutory bodies and institutions? Because I don't want us to just think of our personal lives or the Church; let's begin to think of seeing the hopeful signs of God's Kingdom in local communities and in our society as a whole as we tackle the things that make us all feel fifty shades of blue.

If we do pray, "Your kingdom come, your will be done, on earth as it is in heaven," then we are praying for the rule and reign (the influence) of God to be present in our lives, in our families, in our homes, our community, our town, our nation. Let's just for a moment be realistic about the state of play in our nation; not to be all 'doom and gloom' but to consider what makes us feel fifty shades of blue and then to understand the challenge that is ahead of us, to open our eyes, to understand the context in which we do mission and respond to the needs of our neighbours. And that begins right where we are as the Church, as we care for each other and model something of God's love for His world. We are His hands and feet; He has no other hands but *ours!*

So today this is our watch and we need to open our eyes to see the finger of God pointing things out to us. Look at our world and the need in Syria, Afghanistan, Pakistan, South Africa, The Sudan and North Korea – there is much to feel blue about!

Look at our society, families, ourselves, our Church, and we see a sick society in real need. In recent years we have had the phone hacking invasion of people's lives at tragic times; the MPs' expenses scandal; the banks – billions exchanged on the basis of lies; the Jimmy Saville case and the historic abuse of children by sports coaches recently highlighted; the Co-op Bank humiliated (of all banks with an ethical heritage); and therefore we have to acknowledge something is fundamentally wrong. Is it any wonder that we feel fifty shades of blue?

Christian biblical teaching has inspired people over the years; it is part of our nation's heritage and has been at the heart of our society. Our Judeo-Christian faith has been the basis of society, freedom and democracy, the legal system, charities, schooling, hospitals, and in the past the very ethos of our land has been Christian. We would have said that this was a Christian country. Think of the major initiatives against slavery and injustice. As church people and as Christians there has been an emphasis on personal holiness and social righteousness. We have been prepared to respond in appropriate ways.

Pope John Paul II has been quoted saying, "A culture that no longer has a point of reference in God loses its soul and loses its way, becoming a culture of death."[3]

There has been a terrible cultural shift towards secular humanism which has taken our nation in a very different direction, and it is away from God in Christ, which certainly makes me feel blue!

---

[3] *Dialogue Between Cultures for a Civilisation of Love and Peace;* a 24-page document sent to world leaders at the end of the year 2000.

You see this in education. If you are a teacher, I want to affirm you and to assure you of the prayers of the Church. One friend, Anne Keighery, in Nottingham, was asked to teach a class of six- and seven-year-olds recently about Advent and taught them the Christmas story. Not one child in the whole class knew the story. How shocking is that! And probably very few of their parents would know the story either!

That's why the work of Open the Book is so important, sharing the stories of Jesus with 700 children a week in the schools of Knutsford, to give them an awareness of our Christian heritage. Our team from KMC and other local churches have recently been filmed and there is a DVD available from Bible Society's website to find out more about this work.[4] How important this mission is in our local area, with Jill Lee, Peter Freeman, Liz Howden, David James leading their teams. And how important it is for Christians to be taking school assemblies these days, to develop relationships in the community. We need to make the most of these opportunities.

Writing as a grandfather, I feel that we need to be concerned with what is happening to our nation's children, particularly when you see that there are more children having children. There are children even being made infertile through sexual diseases. There are children having abortions without their parents even knowing, which seems scandalous! Fifty percent of children are born out of wedlock, but then, this is hardly surprising when in one government debate a few years ago it was stated that children don't need fathers! Marriage-based family life used to be (and still is, in my view) foundational to the fabric of our society. And, of course, if we had more time there is so much that we could say about the sanctity of marriage, fidelity and right relationships, but this is not the time to pursue these topics any further.

So, this is the context in which we live out our faith and seek to further God's kingdom; it's why many of us feel fifty shades of blue and why we need to speak into the needs of today's society. Some suggest that it is almost a post-Christian society, but I think that it can still change for the good. I think the word 'hope' is key. As people become more and more disillusioned with the state of our nation and our world, looking for some form of hope for the future, I think that there could well be a turning back to God. And I wonder how prepared for that we would be as churches? For us at Knutsford, even getting a good number on an

---

[4] See *www.biblesociety.org.uk*

Alpha course can feel like a challenge. Are we prepared to bring hope into the villages, towns and cities of the UK?

I am suggesting to everyone who reads this book, and particularly those who are feeling fifty shades of blue about the state of our nation, that we need to be prepared as individuals, as families and as a Church to bring hope back into people's lives. We need to pray and we need to serve.

Mother Teresa said, "If you pray without serving, your prayers will be in vain; if you serve without praying, your service will be in vain."[5] (This needs to be read again.)

But if we consider John the Baptist the forerunner, preparing a way for the coming of Jesus, I would like us to consider how we can prepare ourselves to be the people God called us to be and to do the things God called us to do. John the Baptist spoke into the darkness of his situation, telling people to repent (to change direction by seeking forgiveness for the wrong things in their lives and to turn back to God), to prepare a way for the coming of the Lord, to prepare for the kingdom – the rule and reign of God. He spoke passionately. He spoke about the kingdom. How we wish that the Church in Britain today could have that prophetic voice, speaking into the situation of our nation, weeping with those who weep, comforting those who need a shoulder to cry on and lifting people out of the gutter of their need. Because if *we* don't speak out with that prophetic voice, whose voice will people hear?

Pope Benedict XVI said, "We are living in alienation, in the salt waters of suffering and death; in a sea of darkness without light. The net of the gospel pulls us out of the waters of death and brings us into the splendour of God's light, into true life."[6]

It's like we need to jump into the mire of our world, knowing that Christ is with us, bringing the light of Christ into all the darkness of people's need. How sad it is that in Britain today many families are dependent upon foodbanks (such as Hampers of Hope or from the Trussell Trust) simply to survive. How much do we need the Church in Britain to respond and to rediscover her voice and to speak right into the darkness of injustice in today's society?

---

[5] See *www.maranathacommunity.org.uk/pdf/Maranatha-About-Prayer-sample.pdf*

[6] See *w2.vatican.va/content/benedict-xvi/en/homilies/2005/ documents/hf_ben-xvi_hom_20050424_inizio-pontificato.html*

Rick Alvey writes the following about Robert Louis Stevenson:

Robert Louis Stevenson, the author of classic books like Treasure Island, spent his childhood in Edinburgh, Scotland, in the nineteenth century. As a boy, Robert was intrigued by the work of the old lamplighters who went about with a ladder and a torch, setting the street lights ablaze for the night.

One evening, as young Robert stood watching with fascination, his parents asked him, "Robert, what in the world are you looking at out there?" With great excitement he exclaimed, "Look at that man! He's punching holes in the darkness!"[7]

When we invite Jesus into our hearts and lives, we are giving ourselves to further God's purposes, we are punching holes in the darkness! What an amazing image that is!

When we take seriously the Covenant Service[8] prayer, 'Put me to doing,' whether it is suitable to our own natural inclinations or not, and we sacrifice our comfort and resources to help others in need, we are punching holes in the darkness!

When we begin to tackle the many issues that make many of us feel fifty shades of blue, we are punching holes in the darkness!

When we take time to listen, really listen, we are punching holes in the darkness!

When we speak out kind words to lonely people, we are punching holes in the darkness!

Here's another way to put it: You're here to be light, bringing out the God-colours in the world. [We need to speak into the darkness.] God is not a secret to be kept. We're going public with this, as public as a city on a hill. If I make you light-bearers, you don't think I'm going to hide you under a bucket, do you? I'm putting you on a light stand. Now that I've put

---

[7] *ilifejourney.wordpress.com/2012/06/13/7176*

[8] From the earliest days of the Methodist societies, John Wesley invited the Methodist people to renew their covenant relationship with God. Wesley drew much of his material for the service from seventeenth century Puritans and subsequently made changes to it. The Wesleyan Conference revised it twice during the nineteenth century and other branches of Methodism had versions of it.

you there on a hilltop, on a light stand – shine! Keep open
house; be generous with your lives. By opening up to others,
you'll prompt people to open up with God, this generous
Father in heaven.

Matthew 5:14-16 (MSG)

And that's the challenge I want to bring to you today: to punch holes into the darkness of real need in our nation, to prepare a way for the coming of Jesus' kingdom. If you long for a better future in our homes, our families, our schools, our hospitals, our communities – then each one of us has to play our part in working for God's kingdom, speaking out the things that God has put on our hearts and minds. Have you got a dream – then how about that dream becoming a reality? Have you had a vision – then how about realising that vision?

You might even feel foolish, asking yourself, 'Who am I?' But with God's help and strength we can make a difference and even change the world – if only a little bit.

And as we consider the things that do make us feel fifty shades of blue, the context of the society in which we live and all of the pressures, not just upon us but upon our children and our children's children, I think that our Christian discipleship and heritage becomes all the more important. Our Christian faith and the faith of our families is a priority. So being in church – receiving the teaching, the fellowship, the sacraments – is an essential part of who we are, our family life and our church community. I know there are so many other things on offer for us and for our children/grandchildren, but we need to encourage them to be part of a church and to attend a Christian conference (making their faith a priority).

As a grandfather, I would urge you not to regret at some point in the future that your children do not bring up your grandchildren with Christian values. We may be busy, under pressure, stressed, but be prepared to invest in your spiritual health, your children's and your family's. Let's live in that place of readiness as we face the challenges of our society today.

All of these challenges come in the wider context of the gospel of God's love and grace, which Jesus embodies and offers freely to all, to everyone. And at times we will fail, we will get things wrong, we are not perfect people; the Bible teaches us that we have fallen short.[9] But part of being a follower of Jesus is not that we always get everything right, but that, like the disciple Peter[10] among many others, we quickly discover where we are going wrong and take steps to put it right. We confess our failings to God, we repent (as John the Baptist urged people) and turn around to go Christ's way and to follow His way, watching and waiting for Him.

Are we prepared for the mission ahead of us? Are we ready to speak into the darkness? Let's not just feel fifty shades of blue about our society today, but, like John the Baptist, let's prepare a way for the coming of Jesus into our lives and into our world.

---

[9] See Romans 3:23.
[10] See Matthew 14:29; 16:23; John 18:15-27; John 21:1-17.

4

Does Our Nation Need a Prophetic Voice?

There have been so many challenges in society recently with a global financial crisis having wreaked its havoc upon people's lives and Government having to make some very tough decisions during a time of ongoing austerity, though it can always be debated as to what their priorities should be. Certainly, it is true to say that the poor seem to get forever poorer; the needy become ever needier, whilst the rich inevitably seem to become even richer.

I had the privilege of hosting the *Justice Now* book tour for Jim Wallis during my appointment as senior campaign manager at Bible Society. Jim is a bestselling author, renowned speaker and preacher, public theologian, and international commentator on life, faith and politics. He founded the organisation Sojourners, in the US, and makes regular TV and radio appearances.

The tour was sponsored by Bible Society, Chapel Street Charity, Hodder Faith Publishing, Hope, Spring Harvest and Tearfund. And whilst there were a few challenges in pulling the tour together, it was a very successful high-profile opportunity to engage with some of the most important issues of the day.

Jim is a very dynamic, charismatic and driven character who is highly motivated about the work that he does in engaging the public square from a faith perspective. He is quite inspiring to work and travel with because he has the expertise to masterfully handle the media to communicate what he needs to, and to get the most out of every situation. But he is also a great speaker in a church context, so he is able to mobilise a partner audience to enable him to operate in the public arena with credibility and prayerful support.

To host and be the travelling companion of someone who has the calling and gifting to speak on behalf of the Church with a prophetic voice is an interesting and inspiring experience. It is true to say that the writing of Jim Wallis has inspired a generation of Christian leaders and therefore that prophetic voice has certainly been heard.

During the launch of Jim's recent book, *Rediscovering Values; In the City, Our Towns and Your Community,* he spoke of how the general public wants to get back to normal after a recent period of austerity, but in actual fact, our 'normal' is what got us into a time of financial crisis on the world markets in the first place. Things need to change. Bad decisions do have disastrous consequences. But it tends to be the poor and needy that end up suffering the most, rather than those who have thrived in the boom period. Jim was challenging people to consider what a truly godly economy might look like, and he set out some interesting principles to think about and act upon.

It was interesting to hear him referring to Gandhi's *Seven Deadly Sins* and how he shared them with the world's business leaders at the World Economic Forum in Davos, Switzerland, during a plenary panel titled *The Values Behind Market Capitalism.* Jim used them because he felt that they were an accurate diagnostic for the causes of the current crisis. They are as follows:

1. Politics without principle.
2. Wealth without work.
3. Commerce without morality.
4. Pleasure without conscience.
5. Education without character.
6. Science without humanity.
7. Worship without sacrifice.

Jim operates on a national and even an international stage but has the ability to speak into situations at this level in a way that most of us do not. There were sound bites that he repeated at each of our leaders' meetings and in the interviews, so that after a few days I felt that I could almost recite them, but I was hearing someone who could speak with a prophetic voice that which God had put upon his heart.

To hear statements such as, "We need to uncover some forgotten lessons that have served us well in the past and make sure the baby of our better choices doesn't get thrown out with the bathwater of our mistakes," is certainly challenging, but nevertheless true. Christian faith has informed, and the church has made valuable contributions to society in responding to times of crisis and need. And whilst we can be pleased about our historical contributions and the spiritual heritage of our nation, it is also true that once again we have to wake up to the current situation and our responsibility to respond. What is the responsibility of the Church and people of faith at this time? This is the sort of question that Jim would urge us to consider!

We do need to speak into the lives of people with a love which demonstrates genuine care and concern. But there is also a place to turn over the tables when we see that there is an unjust market. So for example, the Archbishop of Canterbury, Justin Welby, had no alternative but to challenge the methods of moneylenders such as Wonga who are making excessive profits out of vulnerable and desperate people, particularly when it came to light that there could be investment from the Church in a finance company which had been investing in such businesses. It was important that the Archbishop spoke clearly into this situation. Could his be a prophetic voice needed in our nation at this time?

But alongside those who can speak with a prophetic voice at an international and national level, it is also important that the Church and its leaders rediscover their voice in the local community as they share with local authorities, businesses, schools and other organisations. As a young leader, it was good to work alongside Rev. David W. Watson who was instrumental in starting a nursery school in both Cheadle and Tean in Staffordshire, launching a conference centre and numerous building projects, whilst also launching the Live at Home project at Cheadle under the leadership of Helen Wainwright, which has served a number of the rural communities with lunch clubs and day centres. David had a high profile in the whole Cheadle area, with regular coverage of his latest activities in the *Cheadle and Tean Times* (known locally as 'The Stunner'). Everyone in the area knew what the Methodist churches were doing and what they were about.

Previous ministers had each made their own contribution to the community, the church and to my own life. Certainly, it was exciting as a young boy to have younger ministers such as Jack Bates come to our little rural chapel in Whiston who could get us jumping over the pews, racing enthusiastically against each other. No risk assessments were needed in those days! But Eric Challoner, though older, certainly provided the right context in the Circuit Youth Fellowship which enabled me to be nurtured spiritually and discipled effectively to the point where I could take on the leadership of the youth group and begin speaking at the local chapels. Eric's prayerful and pastoral care of our family continued, thankfully, even in the twilight years of his life, until only months before his death.

Another person who greatly influenced me as a young minister was Rob Frost who encouraged so many of us to be the very best ministers and servants that we could be. Rob had a prophetic way of anticipating the future direction of the church spiritually and was the most entrepreneurial, creative and inspirational person I have ever had the privilege of knowing. In particular, Rob's leadership of Easter People and Share Jesus missions which reached out into local areas, and Seed Teams of mainly young people who would give at least a year of their lives to pioneer new projects in a local community, were visionary and effective.

But it was during Hope 08, when I served on the national leadership of the campaign, that I began to understand more fully how the Church can speak with a prophetic voice to the leaders of the nation. Hope had begun after good friends Roy Crowne, Andy Hawthorne and Mike Pilavachi had decided over a cup of coffee to challenge the whole Church to run a whole year of word and action mission. They pulled together a leadership team of representatives from the mainstream churches and key organisations such as Bible Society to help lead the campaign, which is how I personally was invited to participate.

Originally, the idea was to concentrate on the Christian festivals in the year as a focus for activity to engage local communities in the villages, towns and cities in the UK. There was a target set of five hundred of these settings in which partner churches would mobilise their members to organise community festivals, offer random acts of kindness and share their faith in very practical ways such as clearing up litter and painting in public spaces where required. The aim was to offer one million hours in acts of random kindness in local communities. There was a real emphasis on unity between churches working together, but in partnership with other agencies. As the profile of Hope 08 grew, so the number of villages, towns and cities involved grew to one thousand five hundred!

It was partly because of the media attention achieved that an invitation to meet with Prince Charles for tea at Clarence House was received. This was an amazing opportunity to meet with a senior royal and to talk with him about the many community projects that churches around the nation were involved in. I took Roger and Kerrie Robb, plus two members from the Family Church in Hyson Green, Nottingham, as guests because of the community allotment that they had run so successfully.

Prince Charles spoke to us with great enthusiasm about the project and seemed amazed by how many young people were actively involved in the different church-sponsored activities. He addressed the whole group in very positive terms, affirming the church for our contribution to society. But he also asked his personal secretary to contact Roger a couple of days later, advising of a couple of trusts that he should get in touch with and suggesting that he mention Prince Charles had asked him to speak to them. He did not need to do that, but obviously he had been impressed by what he had heard and wanted to offer his personal support.

During the visit, I stood next to the then Archbishop of Canterbury, Rowan Williams, who was very affirming of our work at Bible Society and of Hope 08.

In an attempt to engage him in conversation, I asked, "Do you come here on a regular basis?" with the assumption that he would visit such places frequently.

The Archbishop was very gracious and said, "Well, no actually, this is the first time that I have been here."

Hope 08 had given an opportunity for the likes of Roy Crowne, Andy Hawthorne and the Archbishop to meet privately with Prince Charles to speak of current issues and of how the Church was responding to need. But it was also at this point that the Archbishop began to wonder if this could be the time that Christmas could be re-established as a Christian celebration for the nation. And so a letter was despatched to No.10 Downing Street to see if we could be granted an audience with the then Prime Minister, Gordon Brown, to celebrate Christmas and to have a conversation with him.

When the invitation arrived and I shared this with church leaders and friends in Nottingham, the initial responses were something like, "When you meet Gordon Brown, you tell him..." And yet, after praying about the visit and for the Prime Minister, it felt right to pray God's blessing upon him.

When the day came, upon arrival we were greeted by a young member of staff who said that this was a very significant event because there had never before been an act of worship in No.10! The Salvation Army Band led the singing of some carols, who in their introduction commented that whilst they were from the local Westminster area, they had never before been through the door of No.10. The Bishop of London was in attendance, rather than the Archbishop of Canterbury, on this occasion, along with Nicky Gumbel, a fellow Methodist in Anthony Clowes (whom I was photographed with later), a few Christian dignitaries, representatives of Hope campaigns around the country and members of the Hope leadership team.

Gordon Brown had been away all weekend and had met with another Prime Minister early that Monday morning, but when he arrived his young son ran to wrap his arms around his father's legs. The Prime Minister was engaging and very amusing. He spoke of the importance of faith in shaping his early years as a child of the manse (a minister's son). His father would never like to make political comment to his congergation, he said, but the Sunday after an election his selection of the first hymn expressed his view. If he felt the right party had been elected he chose *Praise God from whom all blessings come,* but if he was less pleased with the result he chose *Dear Lord and Father of mankind, forgive our foolish ways.* If he was unsure of the outcome he chose *O God our help in ages past, our hope for years to come.*

Gordon Brown had everyone laughing almost immediately that day and then proceeded to emphasise the importance of faith in the public square, how faith had helped to shape his own values and passion for politics, before thanking us and congratulating the Hope leadership team for all that had been achieved during the Hope 08 Campaign. When it came to the time for the Prime Minister to leave, a few of us were selected to briefly speak and shake his hand. As he came to me, I was able to say, "God bless you, sir," and then, as his son stood next to him, I put my hand briefly on his head and said, "God Bless!" There were other conversations that day which may have appeared more important or significant, but to pray God's blessing upon Gordon Brown and his son was probably the most significant thing that I personally could offer on behalf of church leaders in Nottingham on that day.

I can now see on reflection why Jim Wallis was a personal friend of his and why during Jim's visit the former Prime Minister requested to meet with him. It was amusing that a girl in the office of Jim's publisher suggested that they meet in a local Costa Coffee. I'm not sure that even former Prime Ministers get to just walk into their local coffee shop to meet with a friend!

We cannot claim that the nature of Christmas as a Christian celebration for our nation changed as a result of our visit to No.10, but certainly it was a memorable occasion and added credibility to all that the Hope 08 campaign stood for. We later posed for photographs on the doorstep of No.10 and left with our lasting memories of a day of real blessing in every sense.

2014 was once again a year to mobilise churches around the country as part of Hope Together. The black majority and ethnic (BME) churches were very much on board and helped to launch the campaign at an all-night prayer event at the Excel arena with over forty thousand people present. When black majority churches pray, they certainly mean business and when they praise, the joy is just captivating. It is almost like experiencing an explosion of prayer, which the wider Church should learn from. I had not experienced anything quite like it since my visit to see the revival growth in South Korea with friend Colin Smith during our Wesley College days.

This year also saw the one hundredth anniversary of the First World War and also the centenary anniversary of when German and British troops declared an armistice in three different areas in their trenches. The troops sang together *Stille Nacht* or *Silent Night* across the barbed wire, but they also played football together. Probably the English team lost on penalties!

In Knutsford, after discussing the idea of a live link with Steve Benson to a German Methodist Church in acknowledgement of this auspicious anniversary, he suggested that Kathleen and Chris Loughlin would be best placed to make this happen, as they were good friends with Susanne, the Minister of Bremen Methodist Church in Germany. Kathleen and Chris visited the Bremen church and filmed information about their town, whilst Steve did a similar thing in Knutsford. It became a whole cultural exchange and the vision began to form of the two congregations singing together *Silent Night / Stille Nacht.* But Kathleen also challenged me to say a blessing in German to the Bremen church! After much rehearsal I nervously shared the blessing to camera and was relieved to complete it successfully. However, the congregation behind me were looking far too worried and anxious, so we had to film it all over again! I am assured by Kathleen that the very fact I was prepared to attempt to speak a blessing in German was very important and special to the German congregation. They certainly seemed to appreciate my faltering words, which apparently sounded quite authentic!

On Christmas Eve, we managed to link live during our Watchnight Communion Service after a rehearsal on the previous evening. It is hard to put into words just how meaningful this act of worship was. But having Susanne, a German pastor, sharing the peace with us and speaking to us live was certainly very significant and moving. In fact, the congregation were moved to spontaneously applaud her first response, it was so significant.

In sharing about the live link with a group of German Christians who were on a Celtic retreat in 2015, I noticed how moved some of them were to hear of our shared service. One of them named Simone said, "If only more people in Germany could have shared in such an event!" The hope at the time was to keep an ongoing relationship with the Bremen church, with a number of them wanting to come and visit Knutsford in the foreseeable future. We look forward to an exchange at some point.

There was also a Hope project to host Silent Night Carol Services in major football stadiums around the country as part of Hope's contribution to the centenary commemorations, with celebrity footballers sharing their faith with the gathered audiences. Alongside this, Alfie Boe recorded 'Silent Night' in collaboration with Decca Records to engage an even wider audience.

Hope Together has enabled churches to speak in unity with that prophetic voice alongside prophetic actions which demonstrate God's love for all people. But in the years to come, the challenge is to profile the Church's work in local communities and for it to be in the public eye, so that many will see the outworking of 'hope in the main street', in the villages, towns and cities of our nation. In a later chapter on Hope Together,[11] I will explore how we can dream dreams and see visions together of bringing hope to our local communities.

---

[11] See the chapter *Hope 2018 in Knutsford and Beyond* on page 251.

5

A Spiritual Heritage

During my appointment as Minister at Arnold Methodist Church, I had the privilege of taking a number of funerals within the local community. Many of the families that I was asked to visit to prepare for the celebration of their loved one's life had no obvious current church connections, but they felt it was important to have a service led by a minister, either in the church or just at the crematorium.

I really enjoyed meeting people and always felt that it was special to share with them at one of the most important points in their family life. What a privilege to give the tribute to someone's life and to support families through their grief; to give thanks for happy memories and to seek God's comfort at their time of loss.

I found that people wanted to talk about faith issues, because it was in God that they could see some hope. Death was not the end and the feeling of hope that they could possibly one day see their loved one again in heaven brought great comfort to them. There was also a sense that people wanted to justify themselves a little by dredging up some past association with the Church.

However, the last contact that many of them had was when they had joined a Whit Walk[12] many years earlier. Nevertheless, it was an important part of their story. They had possibly walked in a procession, or ridden on a coal wagon wearing fancy dress, or possibly they had just stood on the street clapping the procession. But participating in the Whit Walk was the last meaningful contact with the Church many people

---

[12] Whit Friday is the name given to the first Friday after Pentecost or Whitsun (White Sunday). The day has a cultural significance in the North of England as the date on which the annual Whit Walks are traditionally held. The Whit Walk was of Sunday school scholars (dating back to 19 July 1821 in Manchester) when a procession commemorated the coronation of George IV.

could remember and it was certainly always a very positive recollection of fun, childhood, family life and a real feel-good factor in the town with everyone joining in.

After repeatedly having conversations with families about 'the good old days', I decided to do some research about the Whit Walks, as they had stopped many years earlier. In fact, this event had not been held for around thirty years. If the experience of so many people was so positive, then why had the Whit Walks been stopped? Was it just a change in the local culture?

As I spoke to older people in the local churches who could remember the Whit Walks from their childhood, stories began to emerge of dressing up lorries from local businesses as colourful floats, the church banners and the number of people walking; how people 'came out of the woodwork' just so that their children, or they, could participate.

But then there were also the comments about the competitive spirits between the different churches who each wanted to have the best float. I was told of presentations of cups or shields being presented to the church with the best float and the debate as to whether there was a certain bias in the judging to some church over another! In fact, I was told that the ill feelings and the competition between the churches became so fierce that it caused a lack of unity and it was decided to stop the Whit Walks because of this. They could not work together and so the decision was made to finish the annual parade.

Years later in 1999, when I was part of the Local Area Forum and we were having a day conference to explore how best to bring together the whole town of Arnold, how to rediscover a feel-good factor and a real sense of community within the town, I made a few suggestions. I was pleased to even be on the Local Area Forum after there had been some debate as to whether having another clergyperson attend was going to be beneficial. But after Councillor Rod Kempster had spoken of the youth work that I and our church were doing in the town, it was felt that I had something to offer and the youth work seemed to give me some credibility. The major idea I suggested was to relaunch the Whit Walks, but in the form of a modern-day carnival, alongside the possibility of running other themed days in our town.

The idea was well received by the local councillors and community leaders present, particularly the thought of doing a significant event to celebrate the Millennium. So I was given the task of mobilising all of the churches in Arnold and to serve on a steering group with a few other council officers and interested councillors. There were a good number of different denominational and free churches in Arnold at the time, but there was also a good relationship between the leaders as a result of working together on the prayer project (Police and Arnold Churches Together) to reduce juvenile crime locally, and regularly meeting together to support each other.

Proposing that we work together on launching a carnival needed to be done in a sensitive way that brought all of the churches together in unity and enabled all to participate. This I did at the Churches Together Meeting, having already discussed the concept with the key church leaders, and all the churches were keen to be involved. The key was having someone take the lead in bringing together a representative from each church to plan a procession for the carnival, with a good friend, Sue Hall, serving as the secretary. The comment was, "If you will lead it, Rob, we are right behind you!"

And so our work began, with all the churches wanting to contribute a float or to share in hosting a float, with large groups of people wanting to walk on the procession, and both the Scout band plus the Boys' and Girls' Brigade Band marching at the front and part way through the procession. The floats were not named as being from any particular church; they were all from the Arnold Churches Together. If anyone asked which their church's float was, they were to be told that "all of the floats are from your church". Eventually, we were Arnold *Church* Together, all one in Jesus, as an expression of our unity together. A key verse for the planning group to reflect upon and to share with their church on Sundays was Psalm 133:1-3: 'How wonderful it is, how pleasant, for God's people to live in harmony! That is where the Lord has promised his blessing – life that never ends.' Part of the legacy of this is that each week now, a group of Christians are praying in the Methodist Church and then praying for people as part of Healing on the Streets. Where there is unity... the Lord commands a blessing.

There are a number of challenges to face and to overcome when planning such a major event in a local community, and the procession was just one aspect of the carnival weekend. The lorries had to be obtained for the procession, the correct insurance and risk assessments needed to be in place. But the expertise of Gedling Borough Council Officers meant that all of this was put in place, and a wonderful selection of activities on a stage in Arnot Hill Park and in the park itself were made available. There have been dance troupes, rock bands, craft fairs, dog shows, vintage cars, fun fairs, charity stalls and a flyover of vintage planes such as any town would be proud of. In fact, there have also been many thousands of visitors to the Arnold Carnival over the recent years.

The theme for our very first carnival procession was *The Promises of God;* we were rainbow people with brightly coloured costumes, with each float depicting a very positive message. Samba Wamba, a theatre arts group, helped to motivate people with workshops to make the costumes and to ensure the procession made the biggest visual impact possible. Synergy of colour throughout the procession, with all of the marchers wearing tabards and funny hats, certainly added a lot to the stunning appearance of the parade.

There was also an all-age act of worship at the end of the procession on the Saturday afternoon, followed by a *Songs of Praise* service on the Sunday evening, with all of the churches taking part. *Songs of Praise* had to draw together the traditional and more contemporary styles of worship to accommodate the different churchmanship of those participating. In the later years, the Salvation Army Band led the singing of traditional hymns, a worship band did more modern music, with Freddie Kofi making guest appearances to give things a contemporary mainstream feel for the non-church people attending, and we even had the Chariots of Joy Gospel Choir on one occasion. But our worship in the first year was enhanced by my friends from the rock 'n' roll band Revival helping to lead worship, which they later followed by a rock concert in the park.

I had appeared on stage with them at a number of charity events in the past, but to return to the stage as the Rocking Rev with a couple of thousand people waving their hands above their heads in Arnot Hill Park singing *Hi, Ho, Silver Lining* lives on as one of those classic moments that I will never forget.

I had the privilege of preaching at a number of the *Songs of Praise* events, but after speaking on the first occasion, someone came up to me afterwards and having asked if I had been the preacher, he said, "I heard every word that you said as I cut my hedge in the back garden!" There was no way of knowing how many people you were communicating with on these occasions in addition to the thousand plus who attended in the park. The Council financed much of what happened in the park and it was always the highlight of the calendar in the town. Certainly, much was achieved through the profiling of community projects on the stage and also in the charity marquee that was made available for every group functioning locally. How you quantify all that was achieved is hard to analyse, but certainly the relationships that developed and the partnerships that were enabled through meeting together at the forum were invaluable.

Each year there was a different theme for the procession which was decided prayerfully in advance, such as *The Fruits of the Spirit* and *Hope*. The message was always very positive and the public profile of the Church was certainly enhanced with literally thousands of people lining the streets to watch the procession walk past. There were good conversations with people and opportunities to engage people in different ways each year, with an Arnold Church Together tent or stall to meet with people. I met a couple, Terry and Sue, on one occasion and later married them at Arnold Methodist. Terry went on to be a church steward and to play guitar in the worship band, whilst Sue sang.

Arnold Carnival was a very positive example of the Church working in unity and in collaboration with the police, Gedling Borough Council, the Local Area Forum and Nottingham City Council to deliver a weekend for the whole community which brought people together in a way that had previously not been possible for many years. The Church could not have produced such an event in isolation from other bodies and it was certainly a good example of public square engagement of the highest possible calibre. Having the procession walk all around the town gave both the carnival and the Church a high profile and it proved an amazing way to launch the carnival as it arrived at Arnot Hill Park.

The logistics of the carnival could be quite challenging, with so many different aspects to the planning process. But with a timeline in place to give us effective targets to reach, and regular planning meetings and good communication with all of the groups and parties involved, it proved to be a concept which became a 'must have' component within the life of the town and the programme of Gedling Borough Council. The relationships formed enabled us to respond effectively when we were later faced by the crisis of a murder in our town which became national news, but this will be explored later in the chapter *The People's Princess and the Queen of Hearts*.[13]

Alongside the opportunity of sharing the gospel with the whole community in an engaging, credible way, and working in partnership with so many people, was the opportunity of rediscovering something of

---

[13] See page 140.

the spiritual heritage of the town and repositioning the experience (or lack of it) that people had of the Church and faith organisations. We were retelling the faith story of our town in a way which redeemed something of our past failings and demonstrated that the whole Church could work together in unity and in collaboration with others. The Church had come from behind its closed doors and it was evident to the whole community that it was very much alive and well, ready to serve them and to share God's love with them in a way which was wholly appropriate and really helpful to the town. This profile within the town and the relationships which were formed became strategically very important as we worked together to meet the needs of local people.

When I began ministry a number of years later in Knutsford, it was good to meet with town councillors who were discussing the possibility of a heritage weekend in the town. The concept was that local groups and schools would be invited to do their own presentation of the history of the town and the key events and characters, promenading along King Street (Bottom Street) every ten to fifteen minutes to their next performance area. The Heritage Centre in Knutsford was obviously a key driver to making the Knutsford Promenades happen.

The bidding process for funding delayed the early promotion of the Knutsford Promenades, but schools, groups and local businesses were quickly mobilised by the project director Robert Meadows and Sarah Flannery (in later years). There was some hard work and creative effort, but certainly it was successful in bringing people into the town, educating people and celebrating the heritage.

So KMC had the ideal opportunity to celebrate our spiritual heritage, in particular the visit of John Wesley to the town just over two hundred and fifty years earlier. Chris Sloan was invited to participate on behalf of KMC and he asked Liz Howden to write a short script about Wesley's visit which would be both amusing and engaging to people watching the Promenades. Liz then set about creating a short theatrical production, having previously written scripts for the Open The Book team who were taking assemblies in local primary schools, but this was a very different challenge.

Liz decided to connect the visit of Wesley, and his preaching from a set of steps outside a local public house, to the current day work of KMC, outside which the steps are now on display. A small cast of church members was formed and then, after a few rehearsals, Chris borrowed a clerical shirt and preaching gown from me to present the visit of Wesley to Knutsford in a contemporary form.

Whilst most of the cast were dressed in period costumes, the humour seemed to bring the sketch right into the current day, with Mike Tolchard playing an irreverent drunk giving Wesley some competition. A number of the public joined in with the banter, not realising that it had all been scripted, but that just seemed to add to the fun and authenticity of the piece. So a large number of people heard Wesley speaking about salvation and wondering where his steps had disappeared to during the seven performances on each of the two afternoons. It was an opportunity to tell something of the faith story of our town, and by enabling others to overhear a conversation about the faith of Knutsford in a bygone age, it drew others into that story.

Visitors included the then Tatton MP George Osborne (Chancellor of the Exchequer) and former MP Martin Bell in his iconic creased white suit. Mr. Osborne congratulated everyone involved in the *Knutsford Guardian*:

> *My daughter and I started at Brook Street Chapel to see the short history of Knutsford and the re-enactment of Cranford [the book written by Elizabeth Gaskill based upon Knutsford]. Then we made our way along Bottom Street, taking in bands, choirs, a John Wesley lookalike and Mrs. Highwayman Higgins. It was a great advert for the town – well done.*

Sally Lindsay from Coronation Street was the storyteller who retold the story of Mrs. Highwayman Higgins, local historian Tony Davies educated the crowd on the First World War in military gear, architect Andrew Green played Richard Harding-Watt (complete with a man-sized pencil) who designed much of Knutsford, and others dressed as King Canute and Elizabeth Gaskill. It was interesting to note that because our KMC cast performed an entertaining piece, John Wesley made the front cover of the *Knutsford Guardian's* coverage and attracted a good audience for each presentation.

The Knutsford Promenades continues to be a great community event each year, and on this occasion it was an opportunity to celebrate something of our spiritual heritage in the public square whilst making a clear link with our current work within the community by referencing KMC and Methodism being 'alive and well' in Knutsford. Whilst celebrating our past, we were very clearly anticipating something of our future mission and ministry in collaborating thoughtfully and credibly in the life of our community appropriately. Faith does have its place in the public square and can therefore always bring 'hope in the main street' (and on Bottom Street) of Knutsford.

In 2016, we commemorated the one thousandth anniversary of King Canute (Canutesford being the original name of Knutsford) with an attempt to have one thousand people fording the River Lily – from a Danish Ambassador to local school children. It was again an opportunity to profile John Wesley's visits to Knutsford as an important part of our spiritual heritage with our resident Wesley lookalike (Chris Sloan) and his assistant (Liz Howden) joining me in fording the River Lily in our bare feet! It is nowadays quite a small river which can literally be stepped over, but it felt fitting to join in the spirit of the occasion by removing our shoes and socks. This event was the climax to the Heritage Open Days (HODS) in our town as part of the national and international HODS, when many of our public buildings were open to the general public free of any charge for four days. We were certainly pleased to have the opportunity to receive a good number of visitors to KMC who wanted to find out more about the spiritual heritage of the church and our town.

I think that it is really important for local churches to understand their own spiritual heritage and to see how that fits with their local community's history. Many churches could simply get out their marriage registers and other historical artefacts to display during a Heritage Open Day. This has proven to be of great interest to people during our campaigns to culture at Bible Society, as it is important that we understand our roots. Certainly, the growth of ancestry sites where people can explore their family history is a very interesting trend. Our personal and spiritual heritage can be key to understanding our sense of identity.

6

Country Matters

"You can take the lad out of the country, but you can't take the country out of the lad."

When I was a lad... Please excuse me for a moment whilst I enjoy a little nostalgia and reminisce with you about my childhood, where I was brought up in the village of Whiston, Staffordshire, on my parents' dairy farm, at the local school and in Whiston Chapel. It was an idyllic, happy childhood with my siblings David, Andrew and Catherine.

My father, Charlie, was the Sunday school superintendent at the chapel, ably assisted by Dorothy Fowles, and a large number of the village children attended. We were 'chapel folk'. Carol lived in the neighbouring village of Alton (famous for Alton Towers) with her parents, Charlie and Elsie Clowes. Carol ran Alton Sunday School and loved the young people that she cared for. Methodist chapels were, and in some areas still are, an important part of village and rural life, but many sadly face the threat of closure in our current context.

The Harvest Festivals were packed out with all of the local farmers and village folks, with the Monday evening Harvest auction (and sometimes supper) a high point in the village annual calendar. Everybody seemed to come, even if they did not attend church at other times. I remember well the determination as a young lad of trying to bid for a bunch of grapes against some of my friends and family. It was all good fun and an important part of my childhood.

Sunday School Anniversary was a spectacular presentation after weeks of preparation, with everyone wearing their new 'Sunday best' outfits and sitting on a stage platform fitted at the front of the chapel. These days there would be risk assessments with health and safety checks, but the stage never collapsed in all of the years that it was carefully erected. In some ways it saddens me to think that the platform will never be needed again and the wood will have been used for other purposes.

There would be a special guest preacher for the anniversary and possibly for the Harvest. I particularly remember two young farmers – the Lowe brothers, Maurice and John – coming to lead our worship with guitars and singing modern songs. They were excellent at engaging both the young people and the adults, so everyone would want to hear them. But I also remember the storytelling of Vernon Egerton, an elderly farmer, who would have people in fits of laughter as he preached the gospel to them. My Uncle Ab would also sing a solo with his wonderful tenor voice on a regular basis; he would later support me in my ministry by bringing a few friends (The Sounds of Music) to sing concerts in Preston, Arnold and also at Knutsford. As a young lad, these village occasions were special and very credible as opportunities to bring together a large percentage of the village.

These events were also great family occasions, with my uncles, aunties and cousins all coming back to the farm for tea and supper with a few friends and the visiting preacher. It was good to be able to chat with the preacher more informally at these times, but they also brought the family closer together. Carol and I, a few years ago, went to hear our good friend Bill Parkinson preach in a remote Derbyshire village chapel called 'Cross o' th' hands'. Bill travelled many miles preaching in rural chapels; he was probably the most travelled local preacher in Methodism at one point. But when the hosts realised that we were friends of Bill, without hesitation they invited us back to their home for supper. We instantly felt at home as country folk from village Methodism.

For some people reading about this bygone age, you might feel that it is totally irrelevant to you personally, but I think that we do have to understand the different contexts within Britain, the cultural changes that have taken place, and to be open to learn from the positive things of our heritage. If we are serious about our vision to bring hope to our nation, then that cannot simply be focussed upon large, successful, known churches with big reputations in the cities and suburbs. So therefore, Hope Together would aim to bring hope to our villages, towns and cities.

When I was a lad... I will unashamedly continue! We had an annual Sunday school Christmas party with old-fashioned party games which were great fun. The young boys all looked forward to Postman's Knock (ask your parents what that is), but I was never sure that the girls did! There were village pantomimes such as Cinderella in which I got to play the part of Prince Charming opposite Wendy Prince, and there was a village youth club started during a Cliff College mission which ran for a few years – the only club of its kind in the village. Cliff students including Keith Garner (now Superintendent Minister at Wesley Chapel in Melbourne, Australia) would stay with local people such as my family. I will never forget Dad getting various students to ride one of his bulls in his field! Plus, there were circuit Junior Missionary Association barbecue rallies on our farm, called Sausage Sizzle.

There were two village shops, one which included the post office and offered weekly home deliveries. There was a garage which also had a store, two village pubs, St. Mildred's primary school, which I attended, a village hall built after many village fund-raising bonfires, and in more recent years a golf course and club opened. Alongside this there was St. Mildred's Church of England Parish Church and Whiston Chapel.

The shops have closed, as did the garage and school. One pub went many years ago and the other – The Sneyd Arms – has recently closed. One estate agent estimated that if the village pub closes, every property in the village will devalue by around £10,000! The Village Hall is in less demand since wedding licences have been granted to hotels, St. Mildred's shares a vicar with four other village churches and the future of the chapel is now under review. Long term organist Annie Bull describes the situation as "living on a knife edge".

Village life has changed. Local young people struggle to stay in the village because of the cost of property. The chapel Sunday school was lost when the village school closed because children from neighbouring villages no longer attended. The focus of friendships amongst children and their parents at the school gates moved away from the village. Culturally things have moved on with internet shopping and large supermarkets in nearby Cheadle and Leek commanding people's trade.

Does this all therefore mean that the village chapel (and possibly church) is very much a thing of the past and that it is almost inevitable for many of these to close? The honest answer is that some will close because of property matters and ageing congregations. But I still believe that there is hope and that there is a very real contribution to village life for these small causes to make. They offer a good community resource as an available space for meetings and an opportunity to bring people together to actually experience community.

In Nottingham, I loved being the minister in the village of Lambley alongside the larger church in Arnold. I found that I could escape and just be loved by the villagers, who seemed to relate to me as a farmer's son. In fact, as I write I have also recently become the minister of Plumley Methodist Chapel where I have been made very welcome and I am certainly enjoying ministry in a rural village once again.

When we had a village funeral at the little Lambley chapel, we packed everyone into the tiny chapel, even using the balcony up a strange spiral staircase. Linda Worgan, the organist, worked in the village store so everyone in the village knew when we had something special happening. The relationship with the Parish Church was also very positive and the regular United Services were well attended. The parish magazine was delivered to virtually every home and my monthly article was a good opportunity to develop a relationship with people.

I think the relationship with the Parish Church certainly enhanced worship for Lambley Chapel, enabling us to secure a much wider support base, alongside which the visits by the youth band Agape from Arnold were always appreciated. The young people loved chatting to the members and they were a breath of fresh air to the older folk. Plus, their parents and a few Arnold church members were encouraged to attend Lambley on an occasional basis to offer some support numerically and practically. And the few members at Lambley always hosted well using their cupboard of a kitchen to serve tea afterwards. 'Muriel the Masher' was in her element, whilst Linda and Maureen (the younger members) waited on everyone with assistance from some of the youth band.

Sadly, a number of the stalwarts died. There were building problems beginning to emerge and the few members left felt unable to continue sustaining the worship life of the chapel and it had to close. This, however, will not always be the inevitable scenario.

Rev. Nigel Collinson spoke to the Methodist Conference during his year as president about having a pastor in every church, where a local person appointed by the circuit would take responsibility for some pastoral care of the members and community alongside the Methodist minister. This chimes well with the idea of the Methodist Church being a lay-led movement, with an emphasis on the priesthood of all believers and the releasing of lay or local preachers to lead worship. I feel strongly that this needs to be explored more seriously and that alongside this we should think about being a discipleship movement shaped for mission in our smaller rural settings, before we assume that it is time to turn out the lights and close the doors on the Christian presence in our villages. I often refer to KMC being a church of over three hundred ministers, but what does that look like when you have ten or a dozen members? I certainly relish the opportunity to explore this concept with the members of Plumley Methodist, where there is great potential to bring hope into the life of the village through our monthly coffee mornings, where the whole community comes together on the first Saturday of each month, and through our mission and ministry.

As a young man, our youth fellowship were formed into a mission band under the leadership and care of my uncle Dennis, who later became my mentor and supervisor as a local preacher learning his trade (or 'on trial' is the technical term). We took services in the different chapels of our circuit, with someone nervously giving a word of testimony or leading prayers and a group of us leading a couple of contemporary songs or presenting a drama, which would have been the only time that they got to experience 'modern worship'. To have young people leading the worship really encouraged the village chapels, but it also encouraged us to develop our gifts and to even consider becoming preachers ourselves. It was in this context that I took my turn to give a short talk and then to tentatively preach for the very first time. And a number of us did go on to become Methodist ministers or lay preachers in our own right.

Alongside some Local Arrangement services in smaller churches, I feel that some form of mission band should be considered, using adults as well as any young people who are prepared to participate. The use of testimony as part of the worship would enable more people to relate to the worship experienced and to apply what they hear to their everyday lives and discipleship.

We have recently developed this idea in the Alderley Edge and Knutsford circuit in the form of a circuit worship team, consisting of adult members who take a monthly service in one of our circuit churches. These services are always well received and are a great encouragement, particularly to the smaller rural churches. It is my hope that some of the members will eventually go on to feel a sense of call to become local preachers, despite the demands of the latest training scheme!

In some settings, such as Snelson in Cheshire, it seemed totally appropriate to do things differently. And so, part way through their service, there is a break for tea and coffee as a 'fellowship time' when local news is shared, people catch up with each other, they sing *Happy Birthday* when appropriate, and during one recent visit we sang for Rev. Eric Challoner (shortly before his death), who was originally from the chapel, on his ninety-seventh birthday, despite the fact that he was not even present! This seemed totally appropriate in this context in a way that it would not work in a larger church. As a result there is a depth of fellowship and relationship because of the reality of sharing together. It reminded me very much of the short break at Trent Vineyard before the sermon, but in this context the supply of coffee and doughnuts is prior to the worship because the logistics of serving so many people during a short break would be impossible.

Reimagining the role of a small church or chapel in the community could be quite a challenge as members become older, tired and frail. But with the right input there is still hope for many of these because of the commitment of a few faithful souls. Maintaining many rural churches is less demanding, so long as the property is sound. Much of the regular maintenance is done by the membership, whereas in a larger church contractors, cleaners or caretakers tend to be employed.

With the sense of community being lost from many of our villages, I think there could still be a place for the small church or chapel to host a barn rally, concert or barn dance with a short faith comment by a guest speaker. Rather than giving up on some of the old ideas of the past, perhaps we should revisit them to see what we could learn from them.

The Agricultural Chaplaincy team in Cheshire are in demand as farmers are increasingly struggling with the stresses of modern-day farming and in particular the current threat of TB that farmers feel is caused through the infestation of badgers. The faith community has a very real pastoral contribution to make through the care of chaplains such as Sharon Mayer who also worked for KMC as our pastoral worker until quite recently.

I have been pleased to speak at the Chelford Market Harvest Festival and Cheshire Farmers recently, plus I have also shared at the Cheshire Show service in the church at the show tent. Faith is still on the agenda for many people working in agriculture and who have a very real appreciation of God's partnership with us in creation. In an increasingly secular society, opportunities to engage appropriately with people in rural contexts should be seized with both hands, whether that is quite literally in the market ring of Chelford, the agricultural show, the ploughing matches of Southwell or Cheshire, or the village fete or gala. Larger churches and dioceses should invest in these as wonderful opportunities to share the good news with the widest possible audience.

The Lowe brothers used to host a renewal weekend on their farm each year. People would travel a long way to attend and it was considered a spiritual highlight of the year. There must be farmers who could offer a field for a few caravans, a barn or cowshed for a rally, and even some sponsorship to ensure that a new generation of village people experience a sense of community and maybe even the hope which a living faith in Christ can bring.

In fact, my father and I were discussing the possibility of launching a Firefest conference/camp event at his small holding in Whiston not long before his sudden death, inviting people to bring caravans and tents to stay in whilst enjoying a faith adventure in the summer of 2017. But for local people it could have been their best opportunity to experience a Christian conference of this nature, and hopefully it would be a significant opportunity for the local churches to also experience a sense of renewal, reaching people who would not normally attend.

Putting sentiment to one side for a moment and understanding that we do not want all of people's energy spent on maintaining tired buildings, let's also understand that suburban churches will not reach out effectively to rural communities. They will encourage people to travel in from the villages to attend their larger churches, but that may not mean that there will be significant outreach to the outlying areas.

If faith has been an important part of shaping the values of our rural communities in the past, how will that happen in the future when our Christian presence is diminished or lost? For those people who reflect back fondly upon childhood memories of their faith experience in the village chapel or church, perhaps it would be worth considering how to reconnect with that part of their lives and how to ensure that future generations have the benefit of being nurtured spiritually too.

7

Young People These Days!

"Young people are not the church of tomorrow; they are the church of today."

When I was a young lad attending a small Methodist chapel in Whiston, there were two new ministers appointed to serve in the Cheadle circuit: Eric Challoner and Ralph Dale.

Mr. Challoner (as we all knew him at the time) started a Circuit Youth Fellowship (CYF) which met each Sunday evening at 8pm, with Bob Richards initially leading the group. A young couple, Kelvin and Francis Allwood, who were from a Baptist background, moved into Cheadle and took over the leadership. Kelvin was a long-haired young guy who could play rock guitar and he seemed really cool and very credible to all of the young people from around the circuit.

Kelvin formed a rock band, Solid State, from the more mature members of the youth group, with John Atkinson on bass guitar, Peter Challoner on rhythm guitar, Linda Atkinson and Ruth Mear on vocals, John Holmes on drums and later Andy Cope would replace Peter on guitar. We even performed a couple of rock operas, one of which was called *Resurrection*. I well remember stoning the biblical character Stephen with rolled-up tights which bounced around the church hall, and nailing Stephen Fowles onto a cross during his depiction of Jesus. These were great experiences for me as a teenager which helped to both form my faith and my personality.

It was great to go with both this band and Kelvin's later band, Thin Ice, to events for other youth groups who were hosting a coffee bar or an outreach concert at venues such as the Jesus Centre in Birmingham. I would later host a few discos during my days as a DJ, with Thin Ice as the guest band at Cheadle High School and at The Railway public house in Froghall.

It was at this youth group that I got to know my long-term friend Bernard Ward who is now the pastor of Norris Green Baptist Church in Liverpool. Bernard and I actually met at the farm of my school friend Andrew Carp (known as 'Fish') in Winkhill whilst chopping logs for elderly people at Christmas. Our friendship which formed at this formative time in our lives has certainly stood the test of time and we have shared in many key moments in both our lives. It was through being asked to give a young girl from Alton a lift to CYF (with friends matchmaking) that I was later to meet my wife to be – Carol Ann Clowes!

It is true to say that I took Carol on our first date to a Young Life Campaign Bible Study on a Friday evening at the home of Alan and Liz Steele. I am obviously a hopeless romantic at heart and know how to treat a girl!

There were CYF Christmas parties to attend at friends' houses, good speakers each week at the Fellowship with lots of fun and pranks played on each other. But during these days, I also heard people telling their testimony and speaking of their faith in such a way that I could not. As people told of being in a personal relationship with Jesus and knowing Jesus as a personal friend, I realised that I could not speak in such terms and had not experienced the "new birth" that they spoke of. At the age of fifteen, I quietly knelt by my bed and admitted that I had done things wrong, believed that Jesus died for my sin, and committed my life to serving Him as a follower and disciple. Little did I know what God had in store for me, or where I would end up travelling!

The weekends away at Consall Scout Camp were literally just up the road, but it seemed a great adventure at the time to sleep rough on a couch overnight and to share a wonderful residential weekend of music, games, walking, worship and teaching. We travelled over to Conway on an old gospel bus on one occasion to a conference centre in Prestatyn and on another occasion we even had a CYF holiday in Dolgellau in Wales at the home of a relative of one of my close friends, Jonathan Smith.

It was during this holiday that Bernard, Jonathan and I sneaked Gordon Charlesworth's keys out of his pocket so that we could hide his car in the middle of a field – much to his disgust. It was not quite so funny later though when Gordon's large Morris Oxford car broke down on the way home from the holiday. I offered to tow it back with him on the following Monday with my father's Land Rover. That particular journey home became more and more difficult as the tow rope continually broke and was eventually much shorter. It was quite stressful seeing the towed car becoming ever closer to my bumper, but we got home safe and sound, much to everyone's relief. It was all part of the experience of being friends together.

At the age of twenty-one, Mr. Challoner asked me to lead the CYF with the support of my then girlfriend, Carol. My granddad (Frederick Harold Cotton) came to my informal commissioning during the very first CYF I led at Waterhouses (his home church) to support me in what I was taking on.

There were guest speakers each week to find, and transport to arrange for the young people from different villages. I travelled many miles some Sunday evenings in my battered Ford Capri to get the young people home before eventually dropping Carol back to her parents' home in Alton. There was one occasion when the snow on the road was such that Vicky Dale (now Turner) and Carol had to climb onto the car bonnet to help it get traction to climb the hill. No modern-day youth worker could (or should) be so reckless. Can you imagine the risk assessments, health and safety and safeguarding issues that would present? Times have changed.

There was a weekly Bible study in our home at 192 Tean Road, Cheadle, when Carol and I married. There were outreach events, trips out to concerts or films; in particular, there was a good relationship with the youth group at Leek Baptist Church, who often shared a meeting with us, and we enjoyed attending Young Life Meetings in Hanley on a Saturday evening led by Alan Steele and Ray Lancaster. The YL outreach events were very creative with a theme determining the games, activities and sketches used. *Pirates' Paradise,* and the costumes worn, particularly sticks in my memory. One of our CYF leaders, Alan Howell, was a good friend to us at this time and he was always prepared to transport young people to events. However, his driving was not the best, so I always joked that I put the not-yet-Christians in Alan's car so that if the evangelist didn't put the fear of God into the young people, Alan's driving certainly would!

Carol and I were supported at this time by a small team of other leaders, but in particular my brother Andrew and his wife-to-be, Teresa Elliot, along with Mike Turner, Vicky Dale (Turner), Ray Turner, and siblings Clare and John Titterton (who later married my cousin Amanda, but sadly died prematurely). My cousins Alison and Carol Cotton were also regular attendees, plus my sister Cath in the later years. Various worship leaders led our singing with Tony Elliot, Dave Clarke and Steve Lowndes all featuring at different times.

We took CYF to a beach mission house in Llandudno for a weekend away and gave them a fairly intensive time of teaching and fun. However, as I look back with Carol's help on the experience now, I do know that we were far too strict at that time and didn't always see the funny side of their pranks!

During this period, Carol and I had strong opinions on how the church should operate and we decided to give Mr. Challoner the benefit of our wisdom. I told him that I felt it was wrong that he seemed to be making young people church members whether or not they had been converted to faith. No doubt he had a greater awareness than I of their spiritual state. And at a point when we were seriously wondering if we should join a more evangelical church, Eric Challoner very graciously said, "I'm really pleased that you have such strong views on church membership; I want you to take the next series of membership classes!" At a time when I was struggling with the Methodist Church, Carol and I ended up preparing young people for membership within it. How did that happen?

So we prayed for those young people in a way that we had never prayed for them before. A number of people spoke on the course which met in our home on a Sunday afternoon or mid-week. And with the help of leaders such as Ruth Mear and Alan Howell, we prepared for the final residential weekend, after which we would return to Cheadle Methodist for an evening service led by a team from Littleover Methodist which included Howard (a work colleague of Carol's from JCB) and his wife Dit McCullum.

During our residential weekend at Dovedale House, we focussed upon the life of Peter. I remember Eric speaking at the morning communion service of how William Booth had drawn a chalk circle and stepped inside it with the prayer, "All within this circle I dedicate to you." He then invited the young people to do the same. Eric was a pastoral evangelist at heart as well as being a great man of prayer.

I prayed that God would speak to those young people and in the evening service He certainly seemed to do so as around a dozen of them responded to the call to faith. What I had not banked upon was that God would also speak to me! I had an overwhelming sense of my unworthiness, but I also felt that God was calling me to serve him in ministry. This was not part of the deal! It was a very moving experience and I felt overcome by emotions as I also responded to the gospel call kneeling alongside the young people.

Carol and I discussed what had been experienced, but we decided to tell no one so that there would be no pressure to respond immediately. It was certainly a case of, "Yes, but not yet!" A few days later there was a knock on our door and it was Eric Challoner, whom we were surprised to see as we were not expecting him. Eric said almost immediately as he entered the house, "I'm sorry to come unannounced, but as I was in prayer this morning I felt that God prompted me to ask you if you've ever thought about becoming a Methodist minister?" *Oh goodness,* I thought, *God is even speaking to Eric Challoner about me now!*

I am not sure if I would have the grace to hear a young couple tell me all that I was doing wrong in the church, or to trust them with a leadership role if they did. Would I see the potential in either of them, to recognise God's call upon their lives, I wonder? Or would I just see an arrogant young man and his wife who thought they had all the answers?

Youth work has changed and I have always enjoyed the privilege of working with young people and alongside other leaders, especially those youth workers who have worked with me such as Amanda Digman (now a vicar in Carlton, Nottingham), Nick Thorley (now working for Christian Aid), Ben Williams (Trinity Methodist Church, Leighton Buzzard), Pete Davis and currently Dan Harris.

Later in the book I will be mentioning ALFIES, the multimedia event we launched in Arnold, and Chips 'n' Chat, a relational games and conversational evening at our home. But youth work can be both a joy and a frustration with lots of heartache as you journey with young people through their crises and angst. We have had the joy of working with Girls' Brigade, Boys' Brigade, Scouts, Guides and all sorts of uniformed organisations enriching the lives of young people and the Church. When a mature young man gets in touch to thank you for your support in difficult days, or to tell you that after leaving the church he is now a worship leader in some student church, it is a real joy. Youth and children's work is a massive investment of volunteers' time and energy into people's lives. But it is an investment that I believe the Church of the present and the future should be committed to.

8

Why Should the Devil Have
All the Good Music?

I have always enjoyed music, attending piano lessons with an elderly lady called Mrs. Shaw from a young age. The wide variety of music which I can appreciate has meant that I have been able to enjoy many different concerts throughout my lifetime and during ministry, from U2 to Tom Jones (my wife is a fan), Status Quo to The Allen Johnson Singers, Slade to the Carlton Male Voice Choir, James Morrison to Vanessa May, The Clash to Cliff Richard, Queen (with Paul Rodgers) to Tommy Cannon or Bobby Ball singing a solo, Thin Lizzy to The Maletones Welsh Male Voice Choir, Elton John to Simeon Wood (multi-instrumentalist), One Republic to Roy Wood, ELO2 to The Ramones, Siouxie and the Banshees to The Bay City Rollers and Take That – all have been enjoyable and memorable experiences.

As a young seventeen-year-old I was keen to encourage other teenagers from our Staffordshire village of Whiston to attend a youth club at the Methodist chapel. I was advised that if I wanted all of the young people to come then I should hire a disco. But we did not have any budget to hire a disco, so my school friend Andrew Carp (Fish) and I went to borrow equipment from my uncle David and auntie Beryl Stew who ran D & B Electrics and provided audio equipment to numerous shows, festivals and events.

Andrew and I hosted a few disco events at Whiston School for the youth club prior to him going off to study at Cardiff University, leaving me to fend for myself. One day, as I was working as a commercial apprentice at Creda (part of the Tube Investments group), the social secretary of the Sports and Social Club came to see me in the office.

"I believe you run a disco," he said. "I wonder if you could come to do a disco at the Sports and Social Club?"

"I don't really do that sort of disco," I replied.

"We'll pay you," he added.

"I'll come!" I heard myself saying.

So the disco that I began to run as a means of attracting other young people into the chapel youth club now took me into a residency at the Sports and Social Club, alongside cabaret acts which did three half-hour sets of varying styles. Another friend, John Walker, came to help me run the disco as we enjoyed going out to discos together and we began to share a singles record collection. I also bought a disco console from Squirrel Disco and therefore adopted the name and acquired his record collection. This meant that the selection of tracks available to play was one of the best at the time. I had a few disco jingles recorded, one of which was, "You're listening to the best sounds around, here on Squirrel Disco," followed by a closing jingle which mentioned John's name, which he was quite embarrassed about!

When John was unable to help, Bernard Ward and Jonathan Smith came on the odd occasion and my brother David also became a roadie when required. After a few years David Clarke became the regular roadie, loving music and putting on a show with the impressive lighting rig that we had available for our gigs. From a residency at Creda Sports and Social, I was then doing weddings, twenty-first birthday parties, corporate events and then a few nightclubs. These were great events to share; the atmosphere at some of them was electric, with people celebrating their special events, singing along with the records and responding well to the fun and games. A whole crowd of friends with their hands in the air singing *Hi, Ho, Silver Lining* or shouting, "Get off o' my cloud," at the top of their voices was a very positive experience to share. A room full of people doing a *Saturday Night Fever* style dance all pretending they were John Travolta was a sight to behold. Closing the night with a couple of Jimmy Ruffin classics including *Farewell is a Lonely Sound* and a jingle, "Well that's all folks from Rob Cotton and John Walke-e-e-e-er!" may now sound rather corny, but at the time it all seemed very credible.

There were opportunities to host a few events with Christian rock band Thin Ice, with lead guitarist Kelvin Allwood, my youth leader at Cheadle Youth Fellowship at the time, as I mentioned earlier. These were, however, the exceptional experiences, alongside many other events in mainstream venues.

The punk rock era was also significant, and in some ways exciting with a room full of mainly young men bouncing around doing the pogo! However, it was exciting for more negative reasons when overly inebriated youngsters started to bounce into each other and then into the lighting stacks, breaking lighting gear and starting a fight with each other. I guess the breaking point came when a young teen came to me to ask for a record, but he was obviously far too drunk as an underage drinker. When he became aggressive, I had to restrain him, but I also realised that whilst it was a charity event, I was responsible in some sense for putting him in a vulnerable state.

There had been other occasions that had raised questions for me, such as when it was suggested that a young man was about to pull a knife out because I did not have the Michael Jackson record released that week, which was unusual for us as we were importing tracks from the States ahead of other discos. A large bouncer grabbed him and literally threw him down the stairs of the nightclub. It was the first time I had seen someone fly unassisted, other than by a not-so-friendly bouncer! On another occasion John was jumped on by a group of lads in Leek at the Southbank Hotel as he made his way to the toilets. His brand-new velvet jacket was ruined and left as a remnant in the club somewhere.

However, seeing a young man totally drunk felt like the final straw and from that point I started to feel that it was time to call it a day. Letting go of the singles collection of one thousand seven hundred, plus a large number of LPs, felt like quite a hard decision and took me a little time to make. But then, being married to Carol and needing a new car, other priorities enabled me to make the sacrifice. Still, there are times when I hear a track on the radio that I do wish I still had that record collection!

At the time, I think that my love of music and the experience of hosting the discos had become too important to me. I did not have the maturity to cope with the experience. But years later, when during ministry in Arnold I wanted to launch a multimedia event for young people, the experience of hosting a disco was in some sense redeemed. I invited my cousin Alan Stew and a friend, James Ideson, to help me run the first ALFIES (Acceptance Love Forgiveness In Everyday Society) event, which was an open, inclusive evening with disco music, live bands, dance presentations, lasers, flashing lights and video clips. The evenings were themed and the clips, music and dance all illustrated the topic chosen.

My daughter Sarah and her friend Laura formed a dance group called Elevate (Elleiv8) and did presentations using a contemporary Christian or mainstream song such as *Shackles,* sung by Mary Mary (who recently appeared at Big Church Day Out). I had also met Freddie Kofi and his wife Sharon at a day conference named Touchdown which I had helped to organize with ministers Rob Hawkins and Pat Aldred in Castle Donington. Freddie became a regular guest at ALFIES and certainly helped to build the credibility and attendance of the event. We had up to one hundred young people attending each month and two discos were launched – Fat Sounds and Take 2 – which alternated in helping to run the evening. I was even known to join the DJs in a dance presentation cover of the song *Five Get Down* by the band Five. The music scene had changed since my days with Squirrel Disco, with youngsters singing along to *YMCA* instead of *Hi, Ho, Silver Lining* but earlier experiences had at least prepared me for hosting ALFIES.

ALFIES was a credible event to invite young people to and formed a good introduction for teenagers to the life of the Church. Chips 'n' Chat in our home was a more relational evening with silly games, Carol's chocolate cakes, chips and good conversation. But our youth workers, Amanda Digman and then Nick Thorley, developed the discipleship programme of the teenagers alongside these monthly events. Music creates such opportunities and I have had the privilege of sharing the music which has inspired me with a much wider audience. I have hosted many different music and media events in recent years from storytelling alongside Freddie Kofi, a Millennium Christian Pop Festival at Wollaton Park hosted by Cameron Dante (World Wide Message Tribe and Radio 1 DJ), to a mini tour with Paul Field and three full-blown tours with the Australian band Sons of Korah, who set the Psalms to music in the most creative of ways.

After meeting with their manager, Stuart Duncan, I had the opportunity to launch Sons of Korah in the UK as part of our Bible campaigning work at Bible Society. The band was formed in 1993 by lead singer Matt Jacoby whilst he was in theological college. Matt strongly feels that the psalms are song lyrics and believes that not only do they have a role to play in our daily lives, but they perform their role best as songs; they also teach us about God and show us how to relate to God.

I had the privilege of becoming a friend to the band, hosting the concerts, driving the tour bus and managing the tour logistics, ably assisted by Beth Lane (now Openshawe) as Assistant Campaigns Manager and on some occasions Mary Corfield (now Acland) who stepped in to provide additional cover, with Elaine Young and Jackie Hendra also offering administrative and practical support. The tours included visits to major Christian festivals ECG, Pentecost, Christian Resources Exhibition and Roots (Salvation Army), alongside media interviews and concerts at church venues. These venues included Christ Church Clifton (Bristol); Methodist Central Hall Westminster (MCHW), Swan Bank (Burslem), Bath City Church, Leyland Road (Southport), Arnold (Nottingham), Guildford Baptist, Holy Trinity (Boston), Bolton Mission, Greenhill Methodist (Sheffield, hosted by my cousin Alan Stew), Central Methodist and St. Peter's Ruddington (Nottingham), St. Thomas' (Trowbridge), Liverpool Hope University, Clifton Moor (York), Burniston (Scarborough) and St. Peter's Free Church (Dundee). Freddie Kofi was the support act on two of these tours.

Some of these concerts attracted large audiences of around a thousand people, whereas others had much smaller attendances. However, as a piece of Bible advocacy, these were probably amongst some of the best things I was ever involved in at Bible Society.

It has also been creatively rewarding to dabble in helping to produce an album with Paul Field during Biblefresh[14] and a couple of albums with Freddie Kofi too.

The story of a Methodist minister who had been a DJ was intriguing to the *Nottingham Evening Post* a number of years ago and so a story about the Rocking Rev with my top ten pop songs of all time, alongside a picture of me playing a guitar and jumping into the air like Pete Townsend, made a credible feature and led to more opportunities. A fundraiser rock 'n' roll night with the band Revival who performed songs from the 50s and 60s enabled a different phase of outreach, when the late Rod Kempster asked me if I would sing with the band. People sponsored me to sing *Blue Suede Shoes*, but to enter into the spirit of the occasion I wore a large Elvis wig and a bright shocking pink teddy boy drape coat which looked amazing, even if I say so myself!

---

[14] The Year of the Bible, celebrating the four hundredth anniversary of the King James Bible.

Nottingham Evening Post again featured me as the Rocking Rev and the Radio Nottingham presenter Brian Tansley came to each event to introduce me and the band, alongside promoting what we were doing. But Brian, after a little persuasion, then wanted to sing a duet with me as Beatle Brian with the Rocking Rev. We sang one Beatles and one Cliff Richard song together on this occasion, but the friendship and working relationship continued for a few years. Revival did charity events with me in Arnold Town Centre and also helped to lead the *Songs of Praise* in Arnot Hill Park at Arnold Carnival, followed by a rock 'n' roll concert party on a warm summer evening. What a highlight that was!

People came to chat to me afterwards about getting married in church and about what I had preached in the *Songs of Praise* service, probably as a result of seeing me sing with Revival. Other people contacted the local funeral director to ask if the Rocking Rev could take a funeral for them. "Our daughter had a real sense of humour and we want someone to take the service who doesn't take himself too seriously!" It was a tragic situation of a young girl who had committed suicide, but because the family felt they could relate to me, I was able to minister to them and offer hope to the large number of friends who attended the funeral at a very difficult time in their lives.

With the media interest in the Rocking Rev, I was then contacted by Framework, a charity working with homeless people in providing hostels and accommodation and for those also moving into their first homes. They asked if I would participate in a fundraising initiative called 'Jail and Bail'. I accepted the invitation and was duly arrested by two community policemen as I finished our Friday morning shoppers service. I said the closing prayer, when a large policeman came into the hall and said, "Rev. Cotton we are arresting you for impersonating Elvis and for taking too much interest in the local community." The congregation had been forewarned and laughed as I was taken out in handcuffs for some photographs, much to the surprise of passing shoppers.

The church administrator, Maureen Carter, was then quickly explaining to people that it was a charity fundraiser, but when I was put into the police car, I asked the officers if they could put on the siren for a few moments, just to gain everyone's attention. They kindly obliged and then took me to my shop window prison at Nottingham Community Voluntary Services, where I was dressed in a convict outfit (with arrows on it) and given a telephone to ring all of my contacts for bail money to be donated to Framework. The only problem was that some friends wanted to donate money to keep me in the prison as long as possible. We raised around £1,500 in just a short time, during which I spoke to Brian Tansley live on air at Radio Nottingham and blamed him for getting me into trouble as my Beatle Brian partner-in-crime!

At Mapperley Sports and Social Club, during one of our Revival rock 'n' roll events, I met Lynne and her husband Nigel, who were the landlords of the Friar Tuck in Arnold at the time. I said that I would love to do an event at the pub and, could I come to talk to her? She had not really realised who I was when we met, as we had just had a casual conversation on an evening that I was not singing.

When I walked into the Friar Tuck, someone shouted, "Hey up, it's the Rocking Rev!"

Lynne looked surprised and said, "I wouldn't have talked to you had I known you were a vicar."

"Why not?" I asked.

She replied, "My family don't like the Church."

Lynne showed me the skittle alley at the back of the pub and said I could do an event there, but I wanted to be in the main area of the pub so that we could be more visible to the general public.

So I said, "Oh, I was hoping to use the pub itself for some folk music and storytelling – nothing too religious – and to bring a whole crowd of people for meals."

The pound signs seemed to flash within Lynne's eyes and she asked, "*How many* people?"

I replied, "Seventy to eighty people, I hope."

"You can come if you like, but you won't get me into that place, you know," she said in reference to the church.

In fact, there were ninety plus people who attended our first Folk 'n' Food event, and at the end of the night as we were clearing away, Lynne asked if I would like a drink.

Over a glass of apple juice, I asked Lynne, "So, why do you not like the church?"

"When my father died, the vicar was not very nice and would not allow us to bury Dad in the main graveyard," she responded.

"I guess you don't know that my mum died last week," I said to her, much to her surprise.

Lynne talked about her dad and I spoke of my mum. At the end of the evening, as I was about to leave, she asked, "Do you do christenings at that church?..."

A whole series of Folk 'n' Food events followed every few months, with a positive relationship developing with Lynne, Nigel, the staff and the regulars, who seemed quite bemused to find a load of Christians having such a good time in their pub. On some occasions there would be a short pub quiz, storytelling which started with funny stories and built towards something of more spiritual significance as the evening developed, and folk music by Blackthorn Down (consisting of church members). Lynne's grandchildren started to come to the Girls' Brigade and every time I organised an event in the community she gave a full box of crisps for the children and insisted on loaning me her pub's soup cauldrons for the catering. To be honest, whether or not I needed them, I always accepted, to give her some ownership of what was happening and to enable her to attend.

A barmaid then asked if I would marry her (to her fiancé, of course), and on the big day, as Lynne made her way into the church, I had prepared a large role of red carpet and rolled it out in front of her, much to her disgust and embarrassment. She tried to hit me because she remembered her comment about never getting her into church. She was a tough lady with tattooed arms and a hard image, but she also had a heart of gold, cared for people and enabled positive things to happen in her community. She became an unlikely ally to the work we were doing in Arnold.

Recently I was asked to sing in a rock band consisting of church members for a charity concert and dance presentation *Strictly Come to Knutsford* at the Curzon Cinema. The name of the band is Mid-Life Crisis. I have a funny feeling that some felt that I was having a mid-life crisis, singing in a rock band! After singing *Blue Suede Shoes* complete with my Elvis wig, I then joined in the final song which was, of course, *Hi, Ho, Silver Lining*. After all, why should the devil have all the good music?

I am of the opinion that we should never take ourselves too seriously, that if we are prepared to laugh at ourselves and to allow others to laugh with us, then we can find great opportunities to bring hope where there is sadness, help where there is need, partnership where there are possibilities and a lot of joy into people's lives.

I'll never be the greatest singer, musician or compère, and some of my music might not be that good, but I can still share my love of music with others.

9

The Woodhouse

A member of the Wedgwood family named Ms. Ann McKeig-Jones was trying to sell her family mansion, The Woodhouse, which was set in six acres, but was unable to attract a buyer. After a conversation with Rev. David Watson (Cheadle Circuit Superintendent Minister) she decided to offer the property to Cheadle Methodist Church for £50,000! She even gift-aided the remainder of the property value as a gift to the church.

I was then approached by David to consider taking on the role of warden and setting up a Christian conference and retreat centre with Carol. At this point I was working for Refuge Assurance in the Uttoxeter area, but I had already felt a sense of call upon my life a couple of years earlier. Carol and I strongly felt that it was right to accept this challenge and when I found out that a young apprentice named Anthony Afford (who was likely to get my post when I left) was going to leave for another post, I visited my Refuge line manager, Geoff Potter, at home to explain the situation and then offered my resignation. Anthony succeeded me at Refuge Assurance and I began work as Warden at The Woodhouse Christian Conference Centre in October 1985, with Carol six months pregnant with our son Steven.

David Watson then told me that he wanted me to have church member Ivan Wareham working with me in the gardens as he had been quite depressed and it would be good for him. Ivan came to help me tidy up the grounds and garden, though he did not communicate with me much as his medication seemed to keep him in a fairly subdued state. However, our daughter Sarah, who was just over two at the time, kept asking him questions: "What are you doing now, Ivan? What's that, Ivan? Did you hear me, Ivan? Are you alright, Ivan? Can you come here,

Ivan?" Whilst Ivan could gladly ignore me, he could never ignore a little child, and he became very fond of her.

When we opened The Woodhouse six months later, after a complete refurbishment, Ivan was giving guided tours of the property which included a talk about what would be done in each part of the house. Church members who had known him and his health issues for some years were amazed at how confident he seemed and the transformation that had taken place in his life. He was now a man with self-respect and a real sense of purpose, which was due in no small way to a rather persistent and talkative two-year-old who would not take no for an answer!

Souvenir plates, thimbles and mugs had been designed by a church member, Les Gilbert, for the opening, which were then sold to raise much needed funds. Bob Richards (former CYF leader) helped to design the marketing brochure and I began to market the centre to church groups at Synods and in Christian magazines. I also joined Christian Camping International who helped to market the centre in their publications and to groups overseas.

Our first group of young people from Tunstall Methodist Church, who had physical and mental health disabilities, were followed by Ilkestone Pentecostal Church, but we had groups from a whole range of churches, both adults and young people. Carol did much of the catering and some cleaning, with my mother helping in the kitchen and my sister Cath waiting on people in the dining room. Youth Church members Carly Eaglestone (now Clowes) and Melonie Phillips (now Bowyer) also assisted. We had various people working with us, with Gwen Johnson working in the office and Tracy assisting in the kitchen. There was a group of people from local churches who came for a soup lunch and to pray each week with Carol and me, just to support us, which was led by Gordon Etheridge. We also had a small prayer and praise evening each month which attracted a very supportive group of praying friends.

We hosted a number of special evening fundraiser events with a chicken dinner followed by a speaker such as Colin Stevenson (from Scripture Union) who did a number of conjuring tricks as he spoke. We supplied eggs to church members from the hens we kept, and tomatoes and lettuces from the garden to local shops and people. We kept a few sheep and young cattle on the land, all to make the project financially viable.

We met some wonderful people during our time at The Woodhouse and certainly it broadened our outlook and understanding of the church. We were able to share a Chinese Christmas dinner, care of the Coventry Chinese Christian Fellowship and to host a romantic candlelit dinner for the Christian Singles Fellowship. But we also had visitors from Germany, France, India, Australia and the USA. The German group shared in an act of reconciliation at Coventry Cathedral, whereas the Indian group treated us to a cultural experience of a curry evening followed by Indian dance and music, which was memorable.

There were individuals who came for a personal retreat to seek God's will for their lives. We were available to share with people when that was appropriate, or alternatively they could have time and space to enjoy the facilities, the grounds and the wonderful Staffordshire Moorlands countryside. There were also many groups who came for a conference or holiday.

Scripture Union hosted a Bible week for young people at the centre and the Band of Hope also ran a training week. Retreats and conferences were being repeatedly booked year on year; the reputation was growing.

But there were also challenges which took us out of our comfort zones; for example, the group of young people with physical and mental health disabilities from Tunstall Methodist Church. One young girl named Anna said how she wanted to become a nursery nurse, but commented, "Who would give me a job when I look like this?" Mum was particularly touched by the appreciation of the young people and repeatedly said, "We have so much to be thankful for!"

The Birmingham District of the Methodist Church brought a coach-load of young people who had been referred by Social Services for a holiday experience at The Woodhouse. I felt more like a bouncer during that week than I did a conference centre warden. I took them for a visit to my parents' farm where they were shocked to realise that a cow was not the same size as a dog! They had never seen farm animals in real life before.

A young fifteen-year-old boy named Nicholas seemed to be constantly in trouble, even throwing a glass at another boy when he had been rude about his sister. I took him out of the room and told him that he was going to get himself in trouble if he didn't change his ways. He told me that he had already been in trouble and it transpired that on one occasion he had set his sister's bed alight in an attempt to get attention.

On the final night of their stay I was talking to the leaders in the conference hallway and Nicholas shouted from one of the bedrooms, "Is that Rob?"

"Yes," I replied firmly, "get to sleep."

Suddenly the bedroom door flung open, the leader standing guard at the door was brushed aside and Nicholas bounded down the stairs to see me.

"I just wanted to say goodnight. I won't see you after tomorrow. Goodnight, Rob!"

He then went quietly back to bed.

We waved goodbye as the coach left, but when it arrived in Birmingham the young people would not get off as they did not want their experience of being cared for and loved by a group of very dedicated leaders to come to an end. A week later, the phone rang at The Woodhouse one evening, with the operator asking if I would receive a phone call (reverse charges) from someone in Birmingham named Nicholas. I accepted the call thinking that he might be in trouble, only to find that he wanted to say thank you and to see if we were alright!

I had always thought that it would be wonderful to work for the Church and to meet some wonderful Christian people, but I wonder if you have ever heard the expression, "There's nothing so queer as folk"? Or, in Staffordshire speak, "There's nowt ser funny as folk."

One morning as we were preparing for breakfast, a lady came into the kitchen with two bowls of cornflakes and asked, "Can we have these in the microwave, please? We like our children to have hot cornflakes for breakfast!" And I thought, "Hot, soggy cornflakes? How strange, how peculiar!"

On another occasion, a man came to me in the dining room as I was pouring cups of tea. "Could you pour my wife some tea?" he asked. But as I went to pour her a cup of tea, he said, "No, no, no, could you pour her some tea on this bowl of cornflakes, please?" And I poured the tea on the cornflakes, hoping that no one from the Management Committee would come in to see what I was doing and think just how peculiar this was.

But the very best example that I can offer is when a rather large man came up to me with a pillowcase one Friday evening after arriving. I wondered what could be wrong with the pillowcase; had the stitching come undone, or might there be a dirty mark left on in the wash? He then said, "Excuse me, but could you put my pillowcase in the fridge?"

I assumed that I had misheard him so I said, "Sorry?"

"Could you put my pillowcase in the fridge, please?" he repeated.

I thought that he must mean the washing machine or something, so I asked, "What did you say, I seem to be mishearing you?"

He persisted with my apparent deafness, "I suffer from insomnia and if I have a warm pillowcase then I can't get to sleep, so if you put it in the fridge, I will fetch it later and then be able to get to sleep, if that's okay!"

I put the pillowcase in the fridge thinking, "How strange! How peculiar!"

When I told the story to other group leaders they said, "We wish you had told us that last night; we'd have brought you thirty-six pillowcases as we couldn't get the youth group to sleep!"

In the King James Version (KJV) of the Bible, 1 Peter 2:9 reads, 'But ye are a chosen generation, a royal priesthood, an holy nation, a *peculiar people;* that ye should shew forth the praises of him who hath called you out of darkness into his marvellous light.'

When I reflect upon my experience at The Woodhouse, I would like to suggest that I have met a few peculiar people, but God's purpose for our lives is not to be peculiar in the sense of what we eat or how we prefer our pillowcase to be prepared, but to allow His transforming love in Jesus to make us different and in that sense peculiar!

Carol and I worked at The Woodhouse Conference Centre for three years. Sadly, after a few years, the Cheadle Church then felt that it was no longer a financially viable project. But the truth is that after selling the centre, it is today offering quality care for young people with learning difficulties through an independent trust.

It has been wisely said that when a person with vision meets a person with money, the person with money gets the vision and the person with vision gets the money! This was in some sense what happened in the story of The Woodhouse.

There are many examples around the country of projects which have been realised through the generosity of either a few key donors or a large number of faithful people who both owned and worked hard for a vision. Hope can be brought into people's lives when visions are realised, even when that is only for a particular season.

As I look back on this important formative stage of our Christian ministry, I do still have a vision for a similar form of retreat and healing centre. In fact, in 2004 Carol and I were preparing to leave local church ministry in Arnold to explore this possibility more seriously. Some friends would say to me at the time, "So Rob, you are giving up your ministry, but you don't have any job, income or home – that makes a lot of sense!" It was certainly a major step of faith for Carol and me to take.

But I shared this vision at the Easter People Conference, alongside the possibility of my having a wider ministry. A lady came up to me afterwards and said that her friend had a vision to do something very similar on her farm in Yorkshire.

When we met the friend concerned, she offered to donate her farm to a charity that we were in the process of setting up. This was seemingly an amazing answer to prayer and we were all set to move to Yorkshire, with a school for Tim already secured. Unfortunately, only a few weeks before our move, she was persuaded by some friends to withdraw her offer! This was a major shock for us as a family and for all of our friends. But thankfully, the very next week I was meeting with Bible Society to discuss the possibility of doing some consultancy work on their next campaign in Bristol. This quickly became an interview for a full-time post, which resulted in my becoming their church liaison officer and eventually their senior campaigns manager. All we then had to do was to find somewhere to live in the seven weeks before we had to be out of the circuit manse!

The vision for a place of prayer and healing was not realised at that time, but the vision of having a wider ministry was realised in a way that I could never have dreamed of through my work with Bible Society. God redeemed what could have been a disastrous failure in my life, to become a time of incredible favour. Such is the faithfulness and favour of God.

10

From Pub to Church

After almost three years working at The Woodhouse Christian Conference and Retreat Centre, I began to realise that whilst I had enjoyed ministry at the centre, it was time to test the sense of call to ordained ministry in the Methodist Church. However, when I shared this with David Watson, he suggested surprisingly soon that Carol and I leave The Woodhouse to take on a role as lay pastor in the circuit, helping him to care for Gorsty Hill United Church, and Dodsleigh and Alton Methodist churches.

During the year that I was going through the process of candidating for Presbyteral Methodist Ministry, Carol and I were to move to Tean for a very happy period of ministry with the support of some great people including Jess and Joan Hurst. The problem was that the Methodist Chapel there had been closed and had been sold for a road-widening scheme, whilst the United Reformed Church had been sold to be converted into flats. I was advised by one church leader, "You will have to wear a tin hat; you will be in trouble when you go to visit a number of people!"

Having sold both church worship areas, the churches joined together to form Gorsty Hill United Church and the congregation worshiped in the Methodist Church Sunday school. Next door to the Sunday school, the Gardeners Arms Public House was sited. For a Methodist church to be purchasing a public house was controversial at the time. But that's exactly what the church did! The function room of the pub was knocked down to allow space for a new worship area and the public house itself became 'Church House' with meeting rooms and a flat above, where my sister Catherine would later live for a time whilst also doing some caretaking duties.

My role as the lay pastor of the church was to lead worship on a regular basis, encourage fundraising, launch new initiatives and to offer some pastoral care to this and two other Methodist churches in Alton and Dodsleigh. Carol was able to work part time in the Gorsty Hill Nursery School throughout the week which was run by Ann Thorley, Sandra Dawson and their team (Nora Dawson in the kitchen).

We were able to launch a youth club with young people such as Nick Thorley (who years later joined a Seed Team, became a youth worker with me in Arnold and eventually worked as a regional manager for Christian Aid). We made joint youth trips out to the swimming baths with the young people from Gorsty Hill and Dodsleigh; we had male voice choir concerts; we started a Bible study in our home, alongside which church members raised significant amounts of money for the building of a new worship centre, with the ladies even doing a sponsored slim at the time. So we were literally in good shape, it was a very exciting time for all of us and a wonderful preparation for theological training at Wesley College, Bristol.

I will never forget the day when Rev. David Watson, George Dawson and I sat in the office of our architect Phillip Hulme of Hulme Upright, each opening an envelope with the quotations from prospective builders who were tendering for the contract. The problem was that each of us thought that the others would have a much lower quotation, only to find that they were all much higher than we expected. No one spoke at first, as we realised that this was going to be even more of a challenge than expected.

However, with a lot of hard work (especially in baking cakes for the most impressive of coffee mornings), fundraising events and sacrificial giving, the church rose to the challenge. The impetus both spiritually and with the building project began to grow. It was a privilege to attend the church dedication and to be photographed with all of the dignitaries at the official opening ceremony. The architect's design of the ceiling is particularly worthy of note, but the whole worship centre is a commendable achievement for the church members and friends there.

At one point we were trying to devise some new ideas to raise money for the building fund, so I suggested that we consider hosting a Family Fun Day at Heath House. Alongside the possibility of raising the money required, it was also an opportunity to engage different people from our local community because of the interest in Heath House. *The Hound of the Baskervilles,* a feature film about the adventures of Sherlock Holmes, had recently been filmed at the house, with entire areas of the property being redecorated especially for the film.

One of our key members, Anthony Mottram, had lived in a cottage on the Heath House Estate when his father had worked for the family and he was therefore personally known by Mrs. Phillips the owner. I asked Anthony to contact Mrs. Phillips to request an appointment and we then went to discuss the possibility of the event. Mrs. Phillips was very gracious and hospitable during our visit, giving us permission to proceed with our plans.

The day arrived and large numbers of people attended from Tean and the nearby villages. Everyone wanted to see around the estate. We had a whole range of activities which included various fun games, competitions, stalls and face-painting in gazebos on the lawn with the imposing backdrop of Heath House. The nursery school staff (including Carol) ran a teddy bears' picnic dressed in their furry costumes on the rather hot day. I think they were almost passing out with heat exhaustion by the end of the afternoon.

Mrs. Phillips allowed people to climb the tower staircase onto the roof to see the spectacular view of the beautiful local countryside. But when she saw the demand for this activity, having initially said that people would not be allowed into the house itself, she then offered the opportunity of a guided tour of the downstairs of the house by local historian George Short, on the basis that they donated £5 to the building fund. This opportunity was grasped by a good number of those attending, which swelled the funds considerably.

The glorious sunshine, the setting and the whole family feel of the event provided a wonderful opportunity to showcase the vision for the new worship centre and the life of the church. It certainly created a platform from which to develop further relationships for the future mission of the church in the local area and community.

The Heath House Family Fun Day gave me a real insight into what could be achieved with the right relationships in the community and how a large-scale fun event could enable a church to engage a much wider audience of people. This was my first experience of the local church engaging in the public square effectively. I would take this experience and the insights learnt into my future ministry. It was great to recently return to Heath House and to relive these memories when Carol and I attended the celebrations of Ann and Tony Thorley's wedding anniversary and the wedding receptions of our nieces Becky and Emma.

There was also a major emphasis upon the pastoral care of the three churches, and it was fairly early in this appointment that I was asked to visit a young girl named Katie Eagle and her family. Katie was known to a number of our church members as she had been in the nursery school and several people had babysat both for her and her brother. Katie had been diagnosed with cancer at a very young age and the church wanted to offer pastoral care and support in whatever way we could to her parents and the whole family.

I went to the door as a very inexperienced young pastoral worker, not really knowing what to expect. I was afraid of how I might react if the little girl had no hair because of the treatment, with my knees quite literally knocking, wondering what to say and do in a situation that I had never faced before.

Katie's grandmother was caring for her that day and they welcomed me into the home with Katie shyly hiding behind her gran's legs. Gran was trying to get Katie to speak to me, so she told me that Katie was saving up her pennies, which they had been counting before I had arrived. Disneyland was on the TV and so I asked if she was saving to go to Disney. Katie suddenly became quite animated as she said, "Yes, I get one pound every time I have an injection and five pounds every time I have some treatment!" I almost said how lucky she was but stopped myself. "Oh, that's good," I heard myself reply.

Somehow I managed to strike up a friendship with this lovable little girl and her family. The church members continued to babysit, send flowers and even at a later stage raised money for a proposed visit to Disney. The prayer life of the church suddenly came alive and became more significant, with the prayers of intercession for others of much greater relevance to people. Some church members surprised me as they just pushed some sweets through the family's door as a way of expressing love and support. How do you offer hope in these situations other than through coming alongside people and gently sharing something of God's love?

On one visit, I took a magic colouring book in my case, thinking that if all else failed, I could at least show Katie the one conjuring trick I knew. Her mother answered the door and I found that Katie was quite distressed and in pain after her latest treatment. She did not really feel like talking to me and hid behind her mother on this occasion. I said to her, "Oh, I'm sorry you don't feel very well; I was going to show you a little magic trick." The crying instantly stopped as Katie was totally intrigued. The phone rang and her mum asked if it was okay to leave Katie in my care.

I told Katie my funny story of how I went to buy my daughter Sarah a colouring book whilst visiting Llandudno. When I had purchased the book in Wales, it had certainly contained pictures (which I showed Katie as I told the story), but when I returned to Staffordshire the pages were all blank. (I opened the book again to reveal blank pages, much to Katie's delight.) I had complained to the shopkeeper in Wales the following week, to find that the pictures seemed to reappear in Wales, only to disappear on my arrival back in Staffordshire later. And then, amazingly, last thing at night before going to bed, the pictures all became coloured in! (As I revealed pictures full of colour, Katie was in raptures of delight.) I told her that Jesus had come that she might have life and have it to the full (John 10:10) – a life full of colour!

It was a simple trick, but Katie was gripped, and when her mother returned to the room, Katie was laughing. I had not realised that her grandfather used to show her tricks as a younger child. I could not help but to ask Katie if she would like her very own magic colouring book.

When I next visited, Katie saw me walking up the path and opened the door to me. I told her the gospel story again and showed her how to do the trick. She was thrilled and immediately after asking her parents' permission, went round each of her neighbours in turn, telling them my gospel story and showing them her new trick, whilst I chatted to Mum and Dad.

When Katie was taken into hospital for her next treatment, she took her magic colouring book with her. Each doctor, nurse or consultant who came to see her had to be told the story and see the trick before giving Katie her treatment. And if a child on the ward was upset, or worried, or missing their parents, young Katie would go over to them with her magic colouring book and tell them the story to cheer them up.

When talking to Katie's mum before leaving Tean, I told her that I had been frustrated with God and sometimes asked Him why Katie had suffered so, and where was He in this situation? The only answer I got was that He was at work through a silly magic colouring book and the love of His people. The truth is that in some very dark places and even in very dark times, God is always at work to bring hope and help in those situations. It might not make it easy, but God is there in the muck and mire (as Christ was in the stable) bringing hope even in a seemingly hopeless place.

After leaving for theological college and living in the caretaker's flat at St. Andrew's Methodist Church in Filton, Bristol, it was a joy one day to receive a postcard from Disneyworld with a very happy Katie pictured realising her dream. Katie had also raised money for the hospital ward which had cared for her with a sponsored swim during a time of remission.

There was a phone call one day to say that Katie had sadly died. Balloons were released at her funeral to celebrate a short life well lived. I thank God for her as I write this and for the privilege of knowing a young girl who amazingly brought so much joy and hope into the lives of other people, particularly cancer patients. If in her situation she was capable of bringing hope and God's light into dark places, then surely anyone reading this can do the same.

11

'Sharing Jesus' – Renewal in the Church

The pioneering work of one of my spiritual mentors, Rob Frost, has inspired churches and their leaders to engage people in the main streets of our world with the relevance of the Gospel today. I have been privileged to serve alongside Rob, Andy and others in hosting Easter People, Seed Teams and many other projects.

When Carol and I first attended Easter People it was at a time when I was nervously exploring God's call upon my life. During a celebration led by Rev. Paul Smith, he asked everyone to pray together in small groups and suggested that if anyone would like the others to pray about something then they should request prayer. So I turned to pray with a group of people I had never met, amongst the thousand or so attending and as no one else was speaking, I asked them to pray for me.

"I'd like you to pray for me as I'm candidating for the Methodist Ministry," I said nervously, at which point a young woman burst out laughing, which at first I thought was a little rude.

But then she asked, "Where are you going to meet the candidating committee?"

"Manchester," I replied.

"Which day are you going?" she then enquired.

"Tuesday," I answered.

"So am I!" she said

Of all the people that I could have been praying with that evening, I was to pray with Helen Reah and her friends, who laughed when we all realised what an amazing coincidence (or God incident) had just occurred. So Paul Smith left the platform when he saw the laughter and after a brief explanation, he prayed for both Helen and me using the words of Philippians 1:6: 'Being confident of this, that he who began a good work in you will bring it to completion, even more as you see the day approaching.' It seemed like a word of affirmation that we both probably needed at that time.

On the very first day of theological college after both Helen and I had successfully completed the candidating process, we were feeling nervous about all that faced us. And certainly I was wondering what I was doing amongst all of the academic and capable people present. But then the Principal Harry McKeating told us that we were accepted, and in leading the morning prayers he used the same verse from Philippians. Helen turned round to smile at me and I had the sense that God was about to prepare me for all that He had in store for me.

The Easter People conference became an important part of our family diary and pilgrimage, with each of our children having significant spiritual experiences there. We were later able to take large groups of young people and adults to the event from both Preston and Nottingham and it became very important to our churches in moving people forward spiritually. For many people, particularly in the Methodist Church, Easter People was instrumental in bringing them into renewal, if not into faith initially. A large number of people felt God's call upon their lives to ministry of various kinds and certainly the teaching and preaching was of a consistently high standard.

At Easter People delegates heard the latest worship songs and were able to purchase the songbooks at reduced prices at the close of the conference. The latest resources were made available and the latest initiatives were launched each year at the event. If a church leader wanted to move their churches forward, then they took a group to Easter People.

I had the privilege of serving at the event as a Line Manager which means that I was able to lead celebrations at a range of venues in Bournemouth, Torquay, Llandudno, Blackpool and Scarborough. I had the privilege of leading with Ann Richard's band B4U, Northern Light (from Burniston, Scarborough), Paul Douglas, Ingol's worship band, Agape (the youth band from Arnold), Freddie Kofi, Paul Field, and Simeon Wood with Liz Babbs. Alongside these bands there were various drama groups, dance groups, mime artistes and guest interviewees.

There were various friends who led the celebrations with me – too many to mention – but it was a particular joy to have my daughter Sarah leading worship at the Spa Complex Grand Hall in Scarborough, alongside Phil Gough. There were also the guest preachers and Bible study leaders. I will never forget the look on R. T. Kendall's face when he asked if he could borrow my Bible to lead a Bible study, as he had left his at the previous venue. I was horrified when a large handful of notes slid out of my Bible across the stage platform much to the amusement of the delegates. The way R. T. looked at me and my total embarrassment added further entertainment value to that morning's study.

After leading a celebration in Bournemouth in 1997, good friends Rob and Katie Hawkins said, "Wouldn't it be great if we could do an Easter People styled event in the Notts and Derby area?" Rob and I met with Pat Aldred and we managed to launch a 1997 event called 'Touchdown' in Castle Donington at the Methodist Church, Baptist Church and local school. We called it Touchdown due to the nearby East Midlands Airport and the need for a local grass-roots conference to resource and inspire local Christians. We were aiming to equip those Christians who could never go to Easter People because of family situations or finance.

There were prayer concerts with Jane Holloway (Evangelical Alliance and The National Prayer Centre) where people could leave their baggage, followed by our preparation for take-off in a Bible study, followed by the in-flight lunchtime catering, with first and second flight seminars, followed by evening celebrations and a late-night fringe. Paul Douglas's band led worship with me and friends from Easter People such as John Hibberts and Dave Martin; and Lyndon Bowring (founder of Care) came to preach and lead seminars. It was at Touchdown in 1999 that I met Freddie and Sharon Kofi, who became close friends and worked with me on many projects afterwards. Having some good friends in the area who worked with us such as Paul Dunstan and Pete Brown helped us to mobilise five hundred to six hundred people to attend the Day Conference which was very significant in moving individuals and churches forward in their experience of renewal. Easter People and Rob Frost had inspired a few of us to launch a credible conference in our own region, which we were able to run effectively for three consecutive years, after which I went on to launch Arnold Carnival with the local council in 2000. I still meet people whose lives were impacted and blessed through Touchdown.

Rob Frost was someone who just seemed to be in step with what God's Spirit was doing in the Church and in the culture. Rob had a great team of people around him such as Marian Izzard, Roland Bryan, Martin Brown, Malcolm and Jean Claridge, plus a whole group of dynamic young leaders alongside his son Andy. Rob invested in young leaders, which is why he became a spiritual mentor to so many of us who served alongside him, very often sleeping on church hall floors to make a project financially viable!

With Martin Brown's leadership he developed young people through the Seed Team programme. I had the privilege of hosting Seed Teams in both Preston and Arnold. The Seed Team was normally a group of young people who felt called to give at least a year of their lives to serve God through pioneering new work with the church in their local community. The team would get part-time jobs to support themselves and the church would provide them with accommodation.

The Seed Teamers gathered for a residential training week at the start of a Share Jesus Mission in different regions of the country each September. This tended to mean that a number of us would help with the training whilst sleeping overnight on a church hall floor. These were great times of fun – as uncomfortable as the floors might have been. At the close of the training we would station the young people to their teams and in the evening we would commission them for the mission ahead. Teams were sent as far as Poland, Estonia and France, all of which made a significant contribution and impact during their mission, which is still referred to with much appreciation today.

It was great to have a team of Joanne Fryer, David Fletcher and David (known as Matt) Branston in Preston. They were able to work alongside me with the young people whilst encouraging the church family and they were also able to produce some high-quality drama which was particularly effective in the local school.

In Arnold the Seed Team eventually only consisted of just David and Karen Wilkinson, after two members decided to leave. This Seed Team was jointly hosted with St. Mary's Parish Church, which helped to cement the relationships between people in the two churches. The Seed Team year also helped to develop the youth work in both churches. From the Seed Team year, the Methodist Church was then able to employ a part-time youth worker, Amanda Digman, before eventually recruiting a full-time youth worker in Nick Thorley. The Parish Church has also recruited several people, with Michael Bullett from our youth group being one of those leading that work in recent years.

I also supported a Seed Team in Harrogate for their year together and I had the privilege of visiting two Seed Teamers, Lesley and Janice, who were sharing God's love with new-age travellers on Cool Mountain in Cork, where they were caring for young children in a nursery school they had launched. This work was, at times, very challenging with the health issues of some of the travellers, the elements, plus a modern-day witch dancing around their caravan in an attempt to put a curse upon them on occasions. I found it a very moving visit with the barefooted children responding to the love of the team. I wanted to put shoes on their feet, or to wash their dirty little faces, but this would have been totally inappropriate in that setting. It was good to support Christians who were prepared to offer unconditional love, at no little cost and inconvenience, to people who had need and yet were not always responsive. Our own son Steven also joined a London-based Vision Team after school, assisting with the work in Raynes Park and even being mentored by Rob to collate his latest book, to which Steven then contributed a chapter.

Share Jesus Missions were a fairly intensive experience involving a team coming from different parts of the country to share with a local church who were trying to reach out into their community. Teams would visit local schools, individuals and community projects during the day, before leading an outreach event each evening. Towards the end of the week, there would be a larger celebration event at which Rob or a guest speaker would preach, with music, drama, comedy, illusions all used to present the Gospel in a credible way. I was able to help lead missions at Court Hey Methodist in Huyton, Liverpool; Swan Bank in Burslem, Stoke on Trent; and in Leeds as part of Carnival Leeds. These missions had a huge impact on local churches and upon many people's lives which should not be underestimated.

Rob toured extensively with numerous theatre and multimedia projects sharing a vision of the Church's mission and cultural engagement in credible ways. Artistes such as Paul Field wrote the musical scores for most of the productions, and Steven Deal wrote the drama scripts which were then performed by Polly Deal and other actors who formed the theatre companies he collaborated with. These tours were always accompanied by a book, with possibly a musical score and script made available so that local churches could present them for their community at a later date. I hosted and promoted a number of these tours and presentations, which were always a significant experience for our church members. In more recent years, I personally have been able to collaborate with Paul Field during my role at Bible Society on a couple of CD projects, but this only served to emphasize just how incredible Rob's achievement of presenting various projects to packed theatre audiences really was.

Amazingly, Rob knew when the time was right to draw Easter People to a close, which was a very difficult, and in some ways painful, decision for both him and many of us who had journeyed with him over the years. Some of the key leaders (Ashley Cooper, Steve Lindridge and Graham Horsley) did then launch a new event called ECG alongside partners such as my good friend Roy Crowne, which would certainly build upon the legacy of Easter People. However, it was certainly very sad that within months of the final Easter People in Blackpool, Rob died after only a very short illness.

But Rob and Andy had already shared the vision of Pentecost Festival in the country's capital which would provide another opportunity for me to work with both of them in the envisioning of various organisations who were to partner in hosting the festival. The vision was in some ways far too big for any one organisation, so the collaboration of major organisations and high-profile London churches was key to making the festival work. The birthday of the church was a good opportunity to showcase it at its very best; it was certainly a case of 'the Church has left the building'!

At Bible Society we participated in Pentecost Festival, when I was able to host Luv Esther at the Shawe Theatre, and later Bill Johnson with Freddie Kofi and Australian band Sons of Korah (as part of their tour) at MCHW[15]. We had also previously hosted a showcase concert for church leaders with Sons of Korah at MCHW to launch the Pentecost Festival programme.

Whilst I might still be personally saddened to think of Rob's premature death, I am pleased to know that Pentecost Festival and other initiatives since have continued to engage people in the amazing main streets of our capital and even throughout our nation in a way that Easter People and previous campaigns I have been involved in could not. At Pentecost the Spirit was at work not just in the Church, but in the marketplace and main streets of our world too. And, in a very modest way, I am now working with Knutsford churches to host a small Pentecost Picnic birthday party on The Moor each year. So I thank God for initiatives such as Pentecost Festival and for Rob Frost, from whom I learned so much and who taught me to dream big dreams.

At Pentecost, in Acts 2:17, Peter is referring to the book of Joel (Joel 2:28): 'In the last days, God says, I will pour out my Spirit on all people.

---

[15] Methodist Central Hall Westminster.

Your sons and daughters will prophesy, your young men will see visions, your old men will dream dreams.'

I am not sure if I am dreaming dreams or seeing visions these days, but certainly the Church today needs people who do both and our nation certainly needs this even more so if we are to experience greater hope for and in our local communities.

12

Preston is My Parish

John Wesley, the founder of Methodism, had a saying, "The world is my parish." I love the sense that ministry can be to the whole world and as a young Methodist minister about to leave theological college, I probably believed that I was going to change the world, that revival would break out once I got 'out there into the real world!'

The day arrived when we would finally find out where the Methodist Conference was going to send us for our first appointment as circuit ministers. The envelopes were to be put in our pigeonholes in the students' common room just after tea, which meant that Carol and I would travel in from Filton, where we lived in the caretaker's flat at St. Andrew's Methodist Church. We very much enjoyed being part of the church community at St. Andrew's for the years that I did my theological training at Wesley College, Bristol, but on this occasion having to travel just prolonged the wait.

We arrived at college and found the brown envelope in my pigeon-hole, which we hurriedly took to my study upstairs. I nervously opened the envelope to read the words 'Ingol and Eldon Street Methodist Churches, Preston'. We grabbed the map book to remind ourselves that Preston was in Lancashire and that it was just before Blackpool. How weird it was to know that after months of waiting, the writing of a profile and all of the preparation, that in a few months our family would be moving to Preston.

The following day, we received a phone call from one of the circuit stewards named Bill Parkinson, who along with his wife Mary became good friends to our family and surrogate grandparents to our children.

"We've got a little building project for you at Ingol," said Bill.

"Are we going to be extending the church?" I innocently replied.

"No, we want to build a new church!" said Bill enthusiastically.

We then went to visit Preston a week later as we were very keen to see the churches and to meet the people. So Bill arranged to meet us just off the M6 at junction 32 in the car park of Fulwood Free Methodist Church. I got out of the car looking at an amazing suite of building premises, to be told by Bill that, "This is not yours! Your church is down the road."

We followed Bill's car and as we travelled down Tag Lane, Bill indicated as if to warn us about some bumps in the road. When we arrived at 6 Mayfield Road, which was due to be our home for the next five years, he asked, "Did you see the church?" His indicating had been to tell us that we were passing the church, but both Carol and I had missed it because it had been partly hidden by the hedge in front of it.

Ingol Methodist Church had been built as a mission hut style church plant from Fulwood Methodist Church to last twenty-five years – about fifty-five years ago. It was a timber-framed building which had been clad on the outside, with a church hall built next to it on Whitby Avenue. This was the building project vision to which Bill had referred: replacing a mission hut with a purpose-built worship centre.

However, it would be fair to say that many of the church members had very fond memories of that little mission hut. They had baptised their children there, some had been married there and they had buried their loved ones there. When the day came for that mission hut to be knocked down, it was quite an emotional experience for the individuals who, whilst they shared the vision for a new worship centre, still struggled to see their 'church building' being destroyed.

But the exciting thing about Ingol was that there was a strong group of young leaders who would work hard with me. This was a very committed group of people who had a real sense of vision and hope for the future of the church and what it could achieve in the local community. It was good to have people whom you could easily relate to and even go with to watch the football of Preston North End at Deepdale. In footballing terms, to be able to say that you saw David Beckham's first league appearances and scoring his first goals (direct from a corner and a free kick, of course) is very special.

It was great to get to know and to become firm friends with such a good team who took on roles such as church steward, development chair and treasurer, and worship leader.[16]

Cliff Richard was once asked for the secret of his success and longevity as a pop star during an interview I heard. He replied, "I surround myself with exceptional people." I have always remembered the comment and have had the privilege of working with exceptional people during each of my appointments who have enabled me to punch above my weight at times. I have had some great colleagues, staff and friends to stand shoulder to shoulder with during my circuit ministry and work with Bible Society and Evangelical Alliance.

The *Methodist Recorder* did a feature on the North Lancashire District during my final year at Ingol, which included an interview with me about my appointment. It was a very exciting five years of ministry and the reporter made the comment, "Where Rob Cotton is the minister, positive things happen." It was a generous remark, but it would have been more accurate to comment, "Where there is a strong leadership team, positive things happen!"

For the leadership at Ingol the key thing, as we started to actually think about why we were building a new worship centre, was to work out who we were being called to be as a church and what we were being called to do. There are many ways to do this, but whichever method is chosen it has to be done. It is helpful to have conversations with the key gatekeepers in a community such as local councillors, teachers, health visitors, doctors, police, social workers and business people. It is important to understand the issues locally so that you are strategically able to respond to the needs of the local community as well as the worshipping church family.

In Arnold we partnered with Tearfund in a research programme called The Toolkit Process which later became Church, Community and Change, which enabled us to discover what the needs actually were in

---

[16] Some members of this team that I would like to acknowledge here were Steve Gregory (steward and preacher), Amanda Gregory (Sunday school superintendent), Julie Lowes (church secretary), David Lowes (steward), Jonathan Bonnick (steward), Eleri Bonnick (Sunday school teacher), Bob Stradling (worship leader and development treasurer), Helen Stradling (worship group and toddler group) and Zoe Ainsworth (steward). Alongside a very young team were of course people like Bill and Mary Parkinson, Ted Lowes (church treasurer), Janet Lowes (catering) and Lillian Topping (steward).

our community. It took almost three years to complete the process. And in Knutsford we participated in a Lead Academy learning community over a two-year period with other churches of a similar size to KMC, alongside an internal consultation with our church called 'From Good to Great'. We were and are a 'good church' and work together to become a 'great church', the church which we believe that God calls us to be.

At Ingol there was some serious fundraising to do, as there was only a small building fund. Much of the money would be given by individual church members who made great sacrifices to ensure that the necessary money could be made available. There were times when I had to stand before the church family and tell them that there was good news and bad news. The good news was that we had all the money that was needed; the bad news was that it was in their pockets! As the leader, it was my responsibility to advise the church members when there were deadlines looming, which meant that the finances had to be in place before we could proceed any further and secure the necessary grants from the Methodist Churches Property Division and The Rank Trust. The church members always responded positively to this venture of faith.

But I must make special mention of Des who collected items from church members and then got up very early in the morning to attend car boot sales to raise money for the church. He had also acquired a large quantity of green string from football nets which he then sold on spools to people needing string for gardening purposes. He became affectionately known as 'Green String Des' and I still think of him each time I am doing gardening which requires something to be secured with string.

Another significant step forward was when we took a group of people to see a new church which had been built at Higherford in Barrowford, North Lancashire. I had met the minister Rev. Derek North at a Synod and after chatting with him, he had agreed to meet with members of our development group to discuss how their building had been achieved. We were very impressed with the design and build work and when we heard that Stocks the Builders of Leeds had done the work, it seemed an obvious step forward to ask them for a quotation. Finding Stocks the Builders probably saved us twelve to eighteen months, because suddenly the development became achievable in the shorter term.

Another important aspect of this redevelopment was being able to think through what we wanted to communicate to the local community. We wanted to have the entrance on the main road, Tag Lane, and to express the fact that we wanted to be open and welcoming to the community. The design of the development therefore had to reflect this.

The theology of our buildings should be considered carefully before proceeding with the planning process. Many of our properties probably communicate things which we do not intend. For example, the worship centre entrance can be on the main road, whilst the community centre is on the side road or at the back. What we do on a Sunday is therefore seen to be of far more importance than anything we do to serve the community. This is also symptomatic of the attitude that what we do on the Sabbath is sacred and that our work throughout the week is simply secular. This is the great sacred/secular divide, which is a denial of much of what we believe about whole life discipleship. All that we do in our daily lives should be to serve God and therefore an act of worship to Him.

There were events organised to raise the finance we needed to begin building, but they became an important part of our outreach into the community. In particular, the Saturday coffee mornings were quite a highlight of inviting people to come and share with us as part of our extended church family. This enabled us to engage a much wider constituency of people and encourage them to join in the worship life of our church. This was certainly a period of growth numerically, with new groups and youth work developing. I had the privilege of welcoming sixty new members to Ingol Methodist Church in the five years I served there.

Former Archbishop of Canterbury George Carey writes in his book *The Church in the Marketplace* that the renewal of the church premises should never be in isolation of the spiritual renewal of the people. Some churches tend to focus on one or the other, feeling that they will concentrate on the redevelopment of their premises in the first instance as a priority because of that need, but the energy expended upon this is such that other things are kept on hold. Carey suggests that the one should be hand in hand with the other.

The situation at Ingol Methodist Church was an experience of renewal in worship, small groups, evangelism, outreach, children's and youth work, and the worship area. The opening ceremony was a proud day for the whole church and especially everyone involved in the redevelopment process. My parents came to share in the day as they were regular visitors to Preston, sometimes staying in their caravan at Bill and Mary's farm. It was a proud day for our whole family too.

The other factor which had proven very significant in making the redevelopment happen in a very short time period was that a young couple, David and Julie Lowes, who were very much involved in the life of the church, had planned their wedding to be the first marriage conducted in the new church building. Everyone wanted the church to be ready for them and everyone wanted theirs to be the first wedding. It would be such an important day for the whole church.

However, the registration of the building for marriages was a lengthy process and I could not guarantee that it would be completed in time for the wedding. So I had to visit David and Julie and tell them of my concern, at which point Julie burst into tears. I felt awful at the time, but in actual fact the registration came through the day before the wedding! The registrar still came to register the marriage and the wedding was an amazing celebration of Dave and Julie's love for each other and their desire to make God central in their relationship.

Building a new worship centre on the main road of Ingol, which clearly expressed our desire to welcome and be open to the community, brought hope as the church served them. It was an exciting time of ministry for me personally, but having such a good team to work with was what made everything possible – praise God! It was a good example of collaborative ministry as we worked together in partnership with others.

13

Charlie – Saint or Sinner

It was another day of catching up with admin, when the door bell ringing was in some ways a welcome distraction. But my heart dropped when I saw a scruffy-looking man whom I did not recognize standing at the door. There had been a number of people calling at the house begging as the address was on the noticeboard and various people would come to tell some story and then ask for money to purchase a train or bus ticket. This might sound cynical, but the requests were continual.

I opened the door to speak to Charlie, who said that he wanted to speak to me about some of the issues in our local community: "Do you know that there is someone giving crack to children at the school gate?" So he had my attention and I invited him in. "Have you heard that drug addicts leave their needles in the primary school playground and a small boy has found a needle and stuck it into a girl's bottom today? She has been taken to the hospital for an AIDS test!" Charlie continued.

I was still expecting a request for money and his accent did not help my impression of him. I was wary of what he might be hoping to get out of the situation. However, he surprised me when he said to me that he had been in prison and that some people might warn me about him. He then asked me to meet with him and a few other church leaders to discuss the problems in the local community to see if we could do anything to make a difference. It seemed an unlikely alliance, but the stories had gripped my imagination in such a way that I could not refuse to explore further.

Charlie managed to persuade an Anglican named Dorothy, a Catholic named Eric Hyland (coming on behalf of Father Peter Dolan) and I to meet with him to talk through the issues and to see what could possibly be done. We quickly mobilised a few other Christians and the head teacher of the primary school agreed to allow us to have a public meeting at the school.

I chaired the very first public meeting of INTAG (Ingol and Tanterton Action Group) with the local police inspector invited to respond to questions on crime, the North British Housing Association responding to housing issues and local politicians and press also invited. There were two hundred people who attended, much to the surprise of the local councillors who said that no one ever managed to get so many people attending public meetings. But Charlie had mobilised as many people as he possibly could from the estates with promises that things were going to change. He had an incredible ability to tell the stories of his estate and everyone seemed to know him. He had a reputation, which was not totally positive due to his personal history and some people were very wary of him because of this. One politician, when he met me in the centre of Preston, said, "I cannot afford to be as naïve as a Methodist minister in working with such people!" However, Charlie had the ability to be a catalyst for change on the estates and he certainly had a vision to see that change become a reality.

The very same politician who accused me of being naïve for trusting Charlie was later to invite me to become the mayor's chaplain when he was appointed as the Lord Mayor of Preston. It was his way of acknowledging the work that was being done in the local community by INTAG.

The housing association were embarrassed by the number of longstanding issues there were with their properties. Dealing with tenants one at a time was quite different to responding to the complaints of a gathered audience in front of local councillors and community leaders. The issues were dealt with much more efficiently, and after our approaches, the rent office which had been closed and used for storage was made available to us as The INTAG Centre. This centre was used as an advice centre for all manner of issues including debt, benefits and drugs counselling, with youth work in the evening and space for young mums during the day. The INTAG Centre was a symbol of hope for the estate.

One of the startling facts was that through the housing association, men who had come straight from a hostel were given a flat with no carpets, curtains or furniture. They would arrive at The INTAG Centre looking totally lost, having not eaten, without any benefits available to buy themselves toiletries or food. The transformation that took place in their lives by just giving them a listening ear, basic food and getting curtains put up for them was amazing. You could actually see the change in their faces and demeanour; it was very satisfying for our volunteers.

But I was not convinced that my church congregations truly understood the significance of this transformation in people's lives. So when I was offered a bed and a sofa for someone, I took a church steward from each of my churches, Jonathan Bonnick and Mark Goodinson, to help me lift the furniture up the flights of stairs to the flat that one man had literally just moved into. The look on their faces as they saw the conditions of the flat, and the abundance of appreciation they received from him changed their perception totally. Jonathan said to me later, "I would never have believed that someone could be living like that, only a matter of a few hundred yards from my home!" Having key leaders understand the situations of need in our community more clearly was important in securing the support of the church for INTAG. There would be no point in continuing this work without the support of the church behind me. INTAG had to be owned as part of the mission and ministry of our church if we were to move forward together.

A young child was killed by a speeding car on Tag Lane, with an elderly lady also being knocked down and seriously injured. Charlie invited me and another of our trustees to meet with the parents of the child, who were keen to do a protest march against speeding traffic. They were trying to make sense of what had happened. INTAG mobilised the community and arranged the march shortly afterwards complete with banners and a police escort. Carol and a number of young mums – Amanda Gregory, Helen Stradling and Zoe Ainsworth from our church – walked with their pushchairs, whilst I was leading the very dignified procession up the road.

We stopped at the point where the youngster had been killed and held a two-minute silence before I led a short prayer of thanksgiving for the child's life. This was well observed and there was a real dignity about the whole procession. It was very poignant and quite moving, a real privilege to be standing alongside the bereaved at such a tragic time in their lives and to see how they wanted at least some good to come out of their child's death. A protest march ensuring that this could not happen to another child was felt to be redemptive in some sense.

A few weeks later, there were no speed cameras, proposed zebra crossing or speed bumps, despite the media interest and the conversations with the council and police. The parents and their friends in the community were understandably impatient to make sure that no other children would be killed on the road. It seemed as if we were overtaken by a head of steam in people organising a second protest march. There was not enough time to mobilise people properly and the permissions from the police were hastily sought and granted to me at the last moment. But on the day of the second smaller march, the impatience brewed over into ill tempers and some people decided that a sit-down protest completely blocking the road would be more effective. Motorists were becoming increasingly annoyed and bad-tempered about the delay and the police asked me to get people moving. I vainly attempted to persuade people that this more direct action was not the best way forward as we would lose credibility for our cause. The police then advised me that as the person responsible for the protest march, I would have to be arrested if I did not get the sit-down protest removed!

I sometimes wonder how effective it would have been to allow myself to get arrested. Could I have written a commentary on the book of Romans from my prison cell? Or was the right way forward to persuade the majority of people to move, to avoid further confrontation with angry abusive motorists and to allow the odd character to get arrested? The latter option seemed to work at the time and I was still available for the meeting later that afternoon that I was due to chair! Years later speed cameras were erected and speed bumps installed.

One young man named Craig, who came to see us at the INTAG office, had a problem with alcohol. We offered him support and advice and he came off the drink, but a couple of days later he turned up at the church during an event, struggling in detox. He was shaking violently and he could not even hold the cup of tea given to him without spilling it on the floor. Zoe Ainsworth (an INTAG trustee and church member) and I took him to the hospital to get some support.

The attitude of hospital staff seemed to change considerably when they realised that he was in the company of a qualified social worker and a minister; he was taken more seriously and listened to. I suddenly realised that he had probably been to the hospital on a number of occasions before. No doubt the patience of staff could be severely tested by people struggling with their addictions. But to see Craig staffing the INTAG office, and offering support to other people within only weeks of this experience, was certainly very rewarding at the time.

Charlie rang me early one Sunday morning to ask me to visit a young woman who was experiencing domestic violence. I sped up the road to meet Charlie, who took me to the young woman's home. There was a policewoman in attendance as I sat chatting to the badly bruised mother. I had prepared myself to witness the young woman's injuries, but not to see her young son also beaten. I sat next to the young seven- or eight-year-old child whose lip was cut, nose bloodied and eyes bruised. He looked into my eyes and stuttered, "My Daddy did this to me!" I felt a surge of anger swell up within me that I had not felt for some time. The child was a similar age to my own children and I felt so annoyed at this violent father; no child should ever have to utter such words as, "My Daddy did this to me!"

I offered support and encouraged the young woman to press charges, but the policewoman said that she was unlikely to do so. She needed the financial support of her boyfriend and she would forgive him, even if this was likely to happen again. I left feeling that there was little we could do but be available to offer support and advice. The young woman was trapped by her poverty and, despite advice given, she took back the boyfriend even though the incident would likely be repeated. The only hope that she had in that situation was the thought that there was somewhere to go for the support and back-up that she needed, particularly when she knew that someone was going to have a little word in the boyfriend's ear. What the police were powerless to do, the estate had a way of responding to.

There were lively discussions on a number of topics, particularly drugs. The drugs counsellor made available to us was being particularly effective and a used syringe bin was erected outside the local surgery as a direct response to the story of the child being stabbed with a used needle. But the local drug dealers were not too pleased with us and there were graffiti attacks on the centre, plus I was told that I might be warned off. It is at these times that you become more vigilant about your children's safety, particularly after school. But the suggested threat never materialised into anything more than just that.

Young people were bored on the estates and so a football club was started named INTAG Colts. The team's shirts were sponsored by a local firm and the community policeman helped Charlie and his volunteers with some of the training. The police then sponsored a football competition complete with a trophy and medals for all the winners. How amazing it was for the young lads of the estate to achieve something for themselves and to win in life for a change. A second team soon started after younger boys were given something to aim for. However, I am not going to persuade you that this was always a success story. It was hard graft for volunteers and demoralizing at times when people did not turn up for games and especially when one of your most trusted volunteers did a disappearing act with all of the club's money! There is a cost involved in nurturing young dysfunctional lives and there has to be a real sense of vocation and vision about it, particularly on a cold, wet wintery weekend.

As previously mentioned, today there are speed bumps on Tag Lane where we held our protest against speeding traffic. Instead of a small centre, there is now The Intact Centre, a youth and community centre with full-time staff organising summer play schemes, detached youth work and environmental work in the area. There is a partnership with the Youth Service and local council to manage the facility. My one sadness is that the churches have taken more of a back seat in recent years, but the driving force to launch it was very definitely the local church seeking to bring hope to those in need and to respond to the issues of a struggling community.

INTAG was (and still is) a symbol of hope on an estate with major challenges at the time; it became a listening ear to the vulnerable and a voice for the voiceless. How amazing it would be if there were such places of hope for the whole community in every community, a listening ear to the vulnerable and a voice for the voiceless – but then, surely that's what the local church is called to be: a symbol of 'hope in the main street'.

It is good to note that the current CEO of INTACT (the name has now changed) was recently recognised in a New Year's honours list for services to the local community.[17] *No one* would ever have considered giving an unlikely community hero such as Charlie (who sadly died a couple of years ago) any such prestigious awards for envisioning the project in the first instance, but hopefully he would be pleased to know that his contribution is not forgotten.

---

[17] *www.lep.co.uk/news/community-heroes-among-honours-list-1-6344026*

14

For Such a Time as This

The lights flood the smoke-filled stage set, the rock music begins to play and the young dancing girls appear. This was the Bible, presented like you had never seen it before. It was a strange mix of Jesus Christ Superstar and the very best rock concert you had seen. This was the premiere performance of Luv Esther, the Christian rock opera written by Ray Goudie from NGM of Bristol (who has sadly recently died) and produced by Murray Watts, known for his work with Riding Lights and *The Miracle Maker* film.

It was one of the highlights of a Bible Society media campaign in Bristol during 2005 which I helped to run as part of my campaigning role. I had persuaded the campaign team to book the Colston Hall, a large capacity venue for the performance, because we were partnering with so many churches and organisations, alongside the promotional work that NGM were doing locally. There was a real synergy as churches invited their congregations, schools were mobilised to attend and our media campaign attracted plenty of media coverage.

The story of a young girl called Esther who managed to attract the attention of the king who fell in love with her is told throughout the musical in a very contemporary and engaging style. The professionalism of the cast and crew means that the evocative tale becomes enthralling to the viewer.

A sinister plot by Haman to have the Jews annihilated is brought to Esther's attention by her Uncle Mordecai, who asks her to speak to the king on their behalf. The problem is that Esther is not allowed to visit the king without his permission and anyone going into his presence could be killed. Esther is afraid and hesitant at first, but Mordecai, in urging her to help, says, "Who knows, but it might be that you are in your privileged position for such a time as this!" So Esther takes life into her own hands by going to see the king to seek his help. She is prepared to risk everything to save her people.

Why does God use the most unlikely of people to bring about transformation of people and places? Band Aid was launched by a scruffy Irish rock singer nearing the end of his career and a few unlikely pop stars. It seemed incredible to think that such a motley crew could be used to bring about any sort of transformation in our world, never mind to raise the finance to feed the starving millions of Africa. And yet they were able to mobilise people and to attract the media's attention in a way that no politician or church leader could at that time. Sir Bob Geldof was referred to as Saint Bob in the media and as surprising as that may still seem, it is a reminder that throughout scripture, God calls the most unlikely of people for a particular task at a particular time. 'For such a time as this' are words which spring to mind from the book of Esther.

How often has it been true that an individual is raised up for a particular purpose at a particular time? I have certainly always believed that I have been in the right place at the right time. That is part of my story and is also why I have always had a sense of calling for each place that I have had a ministry.

But I think it is also true that there are a few surprises along the way. I would suggest that God chooses the most unusual or unlikely of people to do His work at times! Why cannot God just use nice people, or people like me? Some people can be rude, obnoxious and unlikeable, yet God seems to use them for His purposes anyway. The most ambitious, arrogant, self-important, egotistical, power-mad people seem to have strategic places in the economy of God throughout scripture. The weak and hurting also get a look-in with God too. The Bible seems to suggest that God uses imperfect people (like you and me) to further the work of His kingdom – and that has to be good news!

When I reflect upon the work of INTAG in Preston, Charlie was either a hero or a villain, depending on whom you were speaking to. There were people on the estate who knew that if you wanted something done, or if you had a problem, you either went to the INTAG Centre or to Charlie. Charlie then probably took you to INTAG, or phoned the volunteers or me. However, there was some jealousy of Charlie because of his hero status and his dubious past. The local man who turned his life around, who had a strange sense of purpose and self-worth through his work with INTAG, was always the object of suspicion or disapproval. Some referred to him as Fagan because of the group of young lads who congregated at his house, treating it as their second home. There were allegations that he was training them to be his cronies!

Things came to a head one evening when Charlie was coming home on a Saturday evening from the local pub with his friends. Someone shouted abuse at a group of policemen who set about arresting the group. In the course of the arrest, Charlie was badly hurt and hospitalised, so he made a complaint against the police. Charges were brought against Charlie for affray and he was locked up. It was suggested to Charlie that if he dropped his complaint against the police for the assault on him, that the charges against him would also be dropped. He dropped the complaint, only to find that the charges against him proceeded and he was taken to court.

I wrote a personal letter to Charlie's solicitor which was read out in court. I spoke of Charlie's work on the estate and his contributions to the local community asking that these be taken into consideration. Charlie was released shortly afterwards and he thanked me for my support. The truth is that I will never know for sure what happened on that Saturday evening and who was to blame for what. I do know that Charlie had been seriously hurt and that as soon as he was well enough, his work on the estate continued. I guess that I was just a naïve Methodist minister who was trying to make a difference and to work with others to bring hope into some desperate situations and into people's lives. The one thing that I do know for sure is that without Charlie, the work of INTAG would never have begun.

One important lesson that I learnt through my experience of meeting Charlie was that I should not pre-judge people just because of their background, accent or appearance, despite my experience of other people whom they remind me of! It is always good to hear their story, to listen before making a judgement.

Always be an optimist. It is easy to assume the worst of people and situations, but we need to be prepared to appear naïve and to start from a position of childlike belief to see where that leads us.

Do not be risk-averse. Be prepared to fail, or to be let down by people or situations. Faith does not consist of playing it safe, sticking with what we know, not sticking our head above the parapet and never allowing our neck to be on the chopping block.

Alongside key people in a local community who have a heart to make a difference (some of whom will be the most unlikely of allies), you also need to win the trust of the gatekeepers and decision-makers, so that you can secure the relevant funding you need for projects and open the door to obtaining resources such as the building acquired for INTAG.

Esther was an unlikely hero to save her people from annihilation, rather like Charlie was a very unlikely hero in Preston, but then, he was used 'for such a time as that'! I would like to feel that each one of us can be the right person, in the right place, at the right time, for such a time as this.

15

From the Ashes of Disaster

The bad guy had James Bond (played by Daniel Craig) right where he wanted him; if you had no faith in 007, then you might be tempted to believe that he was about to come to an untimely end. It was one of those defining moments in one of the better Bond films, *Skyfall,* with Bond strapped to a chair and a very convincing baddie, Javier Bardem as Raoul Silva, prowling around his prey, speaking with his best bad guy menacing tone.

Then Bond says, "Everyone needs a hobby."

Silva asks, "So what's yours?"

Bond replies, "Resurrection," just prior to making his escape and turning the tables on Silva.

The Church is in the resurrection business too, but all too often it seems we need a few prompts and helpful reminders about whom it is that we serve. I have shared with some churches that have very definitely been through a resurrection experience either spiritually, or of their mission and their buildings.

It was 3am in the morning and I was disturbed by a ringing sound after a rather heavy weekend of celebrations at Eldon Street in the Plungington area of Preston. Yes, it was the telephone and I quickly managed to get out of bed to answer it. A couple of miles away, Bob Mayor had got up in the night and looked out of his bathroom window to see a 'red sky at night' which at first he thought looked like a lovely glow and then suddenly he realised it was just over Eldon Street Methodist Church and it was a fire. This particular red sky was no 'shepherd's delight' – it was a disaster. Bob phoned the fire brigade and then he rang me. "Rob, you had better come, there are three fire engines at the church!"

I hurriedly dressed and sped to the church. We had just celebrated our sixtieth anniversary weekend after recently refurbishing the worship area. It had looked its very best for almost thirty years after we had painted the ceiling and stripped and varnished the floorboards. I had loaned people's precious memorabilia, marriage certificates, wedding photos, baptismal certificates, Rose Queen souvenir doilies from years before with a daughter's name on them, artefacts that had been treasured by people for many years which I had faithfully promised to take care of and then left on display as part of our Anniversary Exhibition.

Thoughts were racing through my mind of the senior citizens who would be devastated if their treasured personal memorabilia were destroyed and I remembered how pleased everyone had been with the Anniversary Exhibition and the response of visitors, some new people and those returning for the weekend.

The car screeched to a halt outside Eldon Street Methodist and with my emotions running high, I ran straight into the burning church in an attempt to save some of the exhibition, but a rather large burly fireman complete with breathing apparatus quickly grabbed me.

"What are you doing?" he shouted at me. "You cannot go in there; it's too dangerous!"

"But I'm the minister. I have to save people's certificates and photos," I protested.

"It's too late, sir."

I was forced to stand outside coughing from the smoke fumes I had inhaled, feeling totally stupid and helpless.

The fire brigade were very thorough in their work, soaking everything to ensure that all of the embers of the fire were completely extinguished and that any risk of the fire restarting was totally eradicated. In fact, if the smoke damage had not destroyed the memorabilia, then the water certainly had.

There was a pile of charcoaled wood outside the church which had been soaked to extinguish the fire's grip, amongst which a scorched cross had survived despite the best efforts of the fire. The stained-glass windows were broken, or were bulging because of the heat, and the floor had been burnt through into the basement youth club below.

My heart sank as I walked inside the church building. The exhibition was all badly damaged by the fire and water. I looked vainly, trying to find any materials that seemed remotely salvageable, but without much success. Some of it I would later return to the owners damaged, but at that point I could not think how I was going to face them. The words written above the worship area, "This is a house of prayer," had been ruined. I knew that the man who had painted them years earlier was the father of three of our church members, Rhoda, Joyce and Jean Simmonds, who would be really upset to see the treasured memory of their late father destroyed. How was I going to tell them that the church could never be the same again?

On a lighter note, I rang the Chair of the North Lancashire District (the Methodist nearest equivalent to a bishop), Rev. Michael Wearing, who had been our anniversary preacher on the previous evening, to tell him about the fire. In explaining the extent of the damage, I said that the flames and fire damage had almost reached the church organ. Michael responded, "Have you got any diesel that you could put on the organ?" We both laughed and it seemed to lift my feelings of gloom as I realised that it was not the greatest of church organs and to have lost it would not have been the end of the world. It seemed to change my perspective a little, particularly as I realised that the rather uncomfortable bench pews which tended to kill the backs of those who sat on them were sadly fire damaged and it might mean that the church would have to replace them with comfortable chairs!

I also recalled that during a moment of faith-filled enthusiasm at the sixtieth anniversary celebrations on the previous evening, having seen the sizeable congregation sharing together, I had boldly announced, "This is the turning point in the life of our church!" It obviously was, but not exactly in the way that I had expected with an arson attack closing the worship area and a lengthy refurbishment process required.

Michael then drove to the church just to be with me and as he spoke to me about Methodist Insurance Company, I began to realise that this was not the end for Eldon Street Methodist Church; it was actually a new beginning. I rang some good friends called Tim and Janet Widdess later in the day, who were very sympathetic, and Tim said something quite profound: "From the ashes of disaster grow the roses of success." I thought he must be quoting a Psalm or Proverb, possibly a theologian, so I asked him which book of the Bible it was from, to which he replied, "Chitty Chitty Bang Bang!"

Tim will probably never let me forget that I thought his theatrical quote was in the Bible, but then, good friends do have a way of keeping you grounded and are great for your humility. Thank you to Tim and to my other friends who regard this as part of their mission in life.

The sorting out of the insurance claim was a long and painstakingly challenging affair in costing the different items of damaged goods. Our thrift shop, launched a year earlier with nearly new clothes and bric-a-brac for the local community, lost almost all stock with the smoke damage, my books were almost all smelling of smoke, as were all of the hymn books. The Sunday worship took place in the church hall.

But the local community rallied around us, because people were genuinely upset, angry and shocked that people would carry out an arson attack on a sacred place. People had married in the church, had their children baptised, buried their loved ones and met as a community over coffee there. Families had long associations with the church. Even the students studying at nearby Preston College were sad that their supply of second-hand clothing to make into fashion garments from The Thrift Shop had come to a temporary end.

The media coverage of *The Lancashire Post* and *Radio Preston* helped to generate the sympathy of the local community and churches began to offer their support, with a charity concert being held on behalf of our refurbishment. The resurrection process had begun.

After the initial shock and the terrible sense of loss that people experienced, the church began to fight back; the arsonists were not going to beat us. This brought us to the task of reimagining what the church could be like. After the refurbishment, we had been very pleased with the look of the worship area and we were unlikely to change it for the better again. However, the fire had forced our hands; now we had to reconsider what changes had to be made to best facilitate our worship and enable God's mission into the community.

Those who had mobility issues were unable to climb up the chancel steps to receive Communion and so we had made a portable Communion rail at floor level, so that we could all receive Communion together as a church family. The large chancel area had a screen put across it halfway down; this formed a lovely prayer room behind it for our smaller afternoon services. The outside stained-glass window, which had been badly damaged by the fire, was repositioned as a new window in the partition of the prayer room so that the front aspect of the worship was the same, but totally renewed as a 'resurrection window'. This also meant that the external window was safe from vandals throwing stones at it from the outside.

The uncomfortable pews were sold and replaced with new comfortable chairs. The whole church was redecorated and the floor once again stripped, though the contractors had to be continually monitored to ensure that the finish was of a very high standard, rather than anything substandard through cost-cutting on the time allowed for each aspect of the work.

The front of the building had always appeared unwelcoming and disabled toilets needed to be provided in the entrance area. Additionally, a further storage area was required and a better kitchen facility was needed if the work of The Thrift Shop was to be developed. Not all of this work would be completed in the first phase of this redevelopment, but the church now had the confidence and the support of the local community to raise the needed finance.

Social events to raise the funds required developed the outreach of the church and The Thrift Shop grew from strength to strength.

The church is always in the business of resurrection and seeing the opportunities that present themselves even in the midst of what can feel like a disaster. There were those ministers who asked me if I had the contact details of the arsonist as they would quite like them to visit their church! There have been churches with dry rot, woodworm infestation and leaking roofs who have taken the brave decision to seek God's new purpose for them and to reimagine what their mission to the community requires them to do. And a vision for resurrection has then been born.

At Eldon Street it was very definitely a case of "from the ashes of disaster grow the roses of success" in that particular season in the life of that community of God's people.

As I wrote in an earlier chapter, *From Pub to Church*,[18] years earlier at Tean in Staffordshire, there had been a time when two struggling churches had to make some difficult decisions. The struggling United Reformed Church had to seriously consider their future as the congregation was dwindling, whereas the Methodist Church discovered major problems with its roof. The two churches decided to unite.

The newly formed shared congregation initially met in the Methodist Sunday school; I was appointed to become the lay pastor of Gorsty Hill United Church and had one of the most exciting periods of ministry I have ever had. The church made the steps of faith required to press on and to eventually build a new church building. It was an exciting time as we saw the new worship centre gradually being built and what a proud day it was when it was finally opened! What could so easily have been a

---

[18] See page 81.

disaster for the church's mission in Tean was actually the catalyst for church unity and a whole new season of mission and ministry within the local community.

It is not just James Bond whose hobby is resurrection; the local church is in the resurrection business too, as part of the mission and ministry of Jesus. We are into the resurrection of people's lives through personal transformation and also of buildings and projects which aid this transformation in lives and local communities through bringing tangible hope.

Whilst this chapter is mostly about changes to church buildings, the buildings are a spiritual home for the church (the people of God) who host numerous activities which cater for the needs of all ages: from preschool playgroups, nurseries, toddler groups and mums' groups to luncheon clubs, coffee mornings, Bright Hour fellowship groups, Scouts, Guides, Boys' Brigade, Girls' Brigade, youth clubs, dance groups, keep fit groups, foodbanks, Alcoholics Anonymous and University of the Third Age. There is such a range of activity which takes place on church premises as a valuable resource for the whole community.

In fact, I have often found it a challenge to keep a track on all of the people who make the church building a temporary home to meet their personal, social, educational, cultural, as well as spiritual needs. So we make our premises as warm and welcoming as possible and we see this as part of our mission and ministry for the local community. The sense of well-being that results can certainly enhance your community and will enable some people to transition into the worshipping congregation too.

Amanda Vickers, our church administrator at KMC, is the person who deals with all of our bookings and is the welcoming face of KMC for many of our mid-week community groups; she is ably supported by Angela Simpson, Christine Templar, Ruth Peake, Sue Boler and our caretakers Sid and Pete. This is a key role within the church, if we are to be attractive to the community and to avoid the church becoming something of a disaster area. As well as having gifts in administration and logistics management, the patience of Job is also required!

16

Experiences of Redemption

Carol and I were living in the caretaker's flat at St. Andrews Methodist Church, Filton, Bristol, during my theological training at Wesley College 1989-91. Seven or eight of the students' wives were expecting babies at the end of our first year in college and we were pleased that Carol was expecting our third child.

During the summer holidays we went with Carol's parents, Charlie and Elsie Clowes, to stay in a log cabin in Prestatyn, North Wales. We were having a lovely holiday together, when Carol began to feel unwell and even had a small loss of blood. We went to see the campsite doctor, who advised us to go to the hospital as a precaution to have Carol and the baby checked out. At the hospital, the doctor initially thought that it was nothing to worry about and that the stomach pains could just be a bad case of constipation! We laughed about it, but the doctor felt that it would be wise if Carol stayed in overnight, so that she could have a scan to make sure everything was OK. I was told to telephone the ward at 10am so that I could arrange a time to collect her.

The following morning I duly telephoned the ward to enquire about Carol and if it was alright to come for her. The nurse who answered the phone said that she would go and find out. She returned to the phone to apologize and say that Carol would need to stay in the hospital and may need surgery.

I was a little shocked and naïvely asked why she would need surgery.

The nurse abruptly replied, "Well, you do know the baby's dead, don't you?"

I was totally stunned and just could not take in what I had just been told. "What do you mean the baby's dead?" I blurted out.

"Oh, I'm sorry, Mr. Cotton, I thought you knew that the baby had died. Mrs. Cotton will need surgery to have the baby removed!"

By this time my head was spinning, trying to take in all that I had just heard.

"Perhaps you had better come in, Mr. Cotton. I'm sure Mrs. Cotton would like to see you."

Even now, twenty-seven years later, as I reflect back upon this difficult part of our family journey, I still feel quite shocked at the way in which I was told that we had lost our baby.

One of the most helpful things that happened during Carol's stay in hospital was when Carol wanted to see our children Sarah and Steven before she had the surgery. I drilled it into the children that they were not to mention the baby to Carol as it may upset her.

However, as soon as they arrived on the ward, Steven's eyes were transfixed upon Carol's tummy where her baby bump was still clearly visible. Steven then just blurted out, "The baby's dead, isn't it, Mum?"

Sarah glared at Steven as if he had let the side down and said, "Steven!" in her most exasperated tone.

Carol just smiled and found the whole thing rather amusing and actually it broke the ice and allowed her to have a lovely 'grown-up' conversation with the children. The innocence of a child just accepting what had happened and wanting to talk things through was exactly what Carol and I both needed at that time. Obviously, there was still the operation to face, but Carol probably felt much more prepared for this after our family time together.

Over the summer I was doing my block student placement with Rev. John Hibberts at Swan Bank Mission in Burslem, Stoke on Trent. John, his wife Val, and all the Hibberts family, were very gracious with me during this time, allowing me to see the reality of church and family life with all of its demands and pressures. I was also able to help lead a Share Jesus Mission with Steve Wild (former president of the Methodist Conference) which was a great privilege and real fun. Trying to do a Radio Stoke interview with Steve pretending that he was talking to his puppet Clarence the Frog, when in fact he had left him at his accommodation and he was talking to an empty hand, was unforgettably hilarious. Not everyone tries to do ventriloquism on the radio!

I stayed overnight with Rev. Ralph and Kathleen Dale whom I knew from their days in the Cheadle circuit. Ralph Dale knew scripture and could quote it word for word like no one else I knew and when he asked me to speak at a Bright Hour meeting about my calling I could not refuse.

Not only did I share about this, but also about losing a baby and how angry I felt towards God at that time.

It was a very real time of sharing, and afterwards two elderly ladies in particular spoke to me privately. My own anger towards God had given them permission to share with me. The first had just found out that she had cancer and felt angry towards God. The second only spoke to me when others had left. She shared about having to give up a baby as a young single mother, marrying "a bad man" who abused her, before eventually marrying a lovely gentleman who had died a few years earlier. Her close friends knew of this gentleman, but not of her more difficult past, of her guilt for giving up her child or her feelings of loss. As we spoke privately, I believe that after many years, this lady experienced healing and knew afresh God's love for her.

Back in theological college after the summer holiday, friends and fellow students still had to find out about our loss and this was made no easier by the fact that seven other wives were due to either give birth or had recently given birth. On one occasion, Carol walked into the Spouses Bible Study Group to find herself facing several other mums nursing newly-born babies. At this point our friend Eunice Attwood jumped to her feet with her baby son Simon and just plonked him on Carol's knee saying, "Here you go, pet; you look after our Simon." It was an unusual approach to the whole situation, but exactly what Carol needed to feel any sense of being comfortable, or cope in that situation at a time of loss.

Some students struggled to know how to handle the situation, or to know what to say. It seemed to cause something of a crisis for some of the trainee ministers because they began to question themselves about how they would cope with such a pastoral crisis when they had to respond to similar situations in their own churches. One good friend who had never had to face anything like this before knew that he wanted to support us although he felt quite inadequate at the time. He walked the five miles from Wesley College to our Filton flat, rang the doorbell, and when we answered he just burst into tears and gave us a big hug. He didn't have to say anything because we knew exactly what he wanted to communicate to us and we will never forget that he came to visit that night. The fact that people cared seemed to bring some sort of hope to us at this time of loss.

Theological college is a strange place to experience such a loss because there are those who would want to help you to make sense of the situation, or who feel that they should be able to understand what is happening. But easy answers, even when they are supposed to be theologically or pastorally sensitive and helpful, can just sound fairly meaningless when you are hurting. There are no easy answers. My pastoral tutor at college who offered personal support was able to share how he and his wife had been unable to have children themselves, but he still seemed to understand our sense of loss despite the fact that we had two other perfectly healthy children.

However, the breakthrough moment in terms of the healing process was when Rev. Bill Denning, a part-time tutor who mainly focused upon enabling students to explore creativity, offered to meet with us. There were those in college who almost dismissed him as "Freaky Bill" because his creative way of reflecting theologically took many of us into new territory which was well out of our comfort zones. But when Carol and I met with him on his remote farm and saw the simple chapel that he had developed in a small cowshed, we were able to say exactly how we felt about losing our baby. Nothing was out of bounds – we could even be angry at God if that was how we really felt. Everything was permissible and seemed appropriate in the circumstances.

A week later we arranged to share a service of thanksgiving with Bill which would include a naming ceremony, a reading from Psalm 139 including verse 13 – "You created every part of me; you put me together in my mother's womb." – and an opportunity to read any reflections or meditations that we had written. We lit a candle and played appropriate music as we shared the simple ceremony together. It was a time of letting go, giving thanks and experiencing the beginning of a healing process together.

I would never say to anyone else at a time of loss that I know how they feel; in fact, I would actually say, "I can't possibly know how you are feeling, but when Carol and I lost our baby we found it helpful to tell God how we were feeling. If you are angry at God, then you should tell him, because God is big enough to take your anger; He wants you to be real with Him and that's the most real kind of prayer I know!"

There have been situations when other couples have tragically lost a child and I know that having had this experience, that I have been better able to empathize with them and that they have valued knowing that I have had a similar experience of loss. But it is also the case that any experience of loss actually better equips us to come alongside people. We became the wounded healers and part of working through our own experience of loss is to help others and to see God redeem that experience through the good that can be achieved in bringing support, hope and healing to others.

17

"Bad Things Should Not Happen to Good People!"

There was just something about the way that the nurse and midwife looked at each other that rang an alarm bell in my head, but then we were just so pleased to see the safe arrival of our latest child, Timothy Robert Charles Cotton, that we chose to be oblivious to any possible problem. He was, after all, our beautiful newborn baby. But then after a little while, there was the comment that the doctor would like a little word with us both. This was never going to be good news!

The doctor was very reassuring, but he said that there may be a problem with Timothy's forehead, and whilst in some sense we would have preferred to ignore the issue, it had become apparent that the shape of Tim's head at the front seemed a little different. This began a series of visits to various hospitals, from the Preston Royal Hospital where we met Dr. Clarke, who then referred us to Mr. Super, a geneticist of Manchester Children's Hospital. It was during this visit that a nurse suggested that there was something wrong with Tim's stomach, that he may have a tumour! We were exploring an issue with his forehead and suddenly we were rocked with another bombshell. Thankfully this was just a false alarm which was quickly corrected.

It was then that we were referred to Alder Hey Children's Hospital and to Mr. Paul May, a worldwide leader in the field of craniofacial surgery, who was very quickly able to give us the diagnosis of Cranio-synastosis. Our first impression of Mr. May was that he was surprisingly young to be a leader in his field, charming and yet quite distinguished with his red-spotted dicky-bow tie. Paul May had a wonderful bedside manner and was able to explain to us exactly what he and his team were intending to do during this major operation. We had every confidence in this team as a result of the explanations given, but it was still a daunting prospect to prepare for, so to know that our friends and church members at Ingol Methodist had called a day of prayer was certainly very important to us at the time.

I well remember when someone said to me, "This shouldn't happen to you or yours; you work for God!" There was certainly part of me that wanted to strongly agree with this sentiment, particularly as it felt like we were working hard in the service of God and had been for some years by this time. But the harsh reality was, and still is, that my family and I are not exempt from all of the normal experiences of life. Knowing God's blessing upon our lives (as we have) does not necessarily mean that we simply live in a state of constant blessing without any challenges in life. Part of my journey and experience is that whatever we go through, God has been with us every step of the way and I would have hated to go through these experiences without my faith and the support of Christian friends.

A Wesley College friend and contemporary, Martin Abrams, came to visit on his motorbike, wearing his leathers and clerical shirt, much to the amazement of the ward nurses. They had never seen a young trendy cleric before and it certainly challenged their stereotypes, much to our amusement at the time.

If you can imagine our young nine/ten-month-old son with a rather cute surgical cap, having had his head shaved and being taken into surgery after Carol had escorted him for the anaesthetic, perhaps you can understand just how difficult it was to let him go into the operating theatre, despite our confidence in the surgery team. We went to the café for coffee (and a breakfast), followed by a walk, but this was always going to be a long, long day.

When we were finally allowed to see our young child with a turban dressing completely covering his head, having had surgery from one ear across his head to the other, surrounded by wires and tubes (sixteen in all, I seem to recall), we felt totally helpless to do anything other than just hold his hand. Plus, the bruising was such that he looked like he had been in a fight with Carl Froch. His eyes were completely closed with the mass of bruising to his forehead and obviously as a nine-month-old child, he did not understand why he could not see! There had been no way to prepare him for this temporary blindness, or for the whole experience of surgery and various treatments. As a child, he just had to trust his parents, as we were trusting the surgical team. The hope was that as he was so young, he would simply forget!

On the fourth day, the Thursday, as we sat nursing Tim, slowly a peephole appeared in the corner of one eye and he was straining to look up at us as we held him. He suddenly realised that he would be able to see us again and a tear rolled down his cheek. And being honest, I know that Carol and I had a few tears in our eyes too at that moment. It was one of those defining moments that as a parent you have the privilege of sharing with a child. We held him closely; that's all we could do.

I cannot speak highly enough of Paul May, Mr. Richardson and their whole team. Certainly, there were a few minor blips along the way, but their care and professionalism, along with that of the whole staff of Alder Hey Children's Hospital, needs to be acknowledged with our family's grateful thanks. However, this was not to be the end of the story.

At eighteen months Tim somehow managed to bang his head and a large haematoma (gathering of blood in a lump) appeared on his forehead. So he had to have that released. At three years old, he then had to have a bone graft from the back of his head to the right-hand side of his forehead. Imagine having to keep a three-year-old on his bed in the hospital because of the instructions of the nurses. It was certainly challenging. But when Paul May came onto the ward, he took Tim off his bed and said, "Do you want to play football?" Tim's face lit up as he got his football, but the look of horror on the nurses' faces as a senior consultant played football up the ward with their young patient was a picture to behold!

There was also an awful operation for grommets in his ears, which was difficult, but at the age of almost eleven, when we had moved to Arnold in Nottingham, it became clear that his forehead was not developing normally on the right-hand side and therefore Mr. May and his associate Mr. Richardson offered us further major surgery. This time it was in consultation with Tim, as he could now have a say in what he wanted and ultimately, with our help, he had to make the decision.

The operation in some sense was for cosmetic reasons, in that this was not a life-threatening situation. But the ear-to-ear surgery would also involve bringing his eyes closer together, rebuilding the bridge of his nose and reshaping his forehead. As we went to watch our beloved Notts County with church members Peter Ryland and Ian Clarke, I remember them whispering to me, "We think Tim looks fine. Perhaps he doesn't need the surgery!" But Tim himself wanted to proceed and so we signed the relevant forms and began to prepare ourselves for another stay at Alder Hey, which felt quite daunting even with the advent of the newly-built Ronald McDonald House for parents to stay in!

A couple of weeks prior to the surgery, I was leading the main celebration at Easter People in the Grand Hall of the Spa Complex in Scarborough. I was challenging people to respond to God's love and to put their whole trust in Him. And yet I was feeling anxious about the prospect of Tim's surgery. I realised that I needed to personally put my whole trust in God and to place the people and things which were most precious to me into His care. So I felt it right to share with the large gathering of a couple of thousand people about Tim's operation and how I needed to trust God and to place Tim into God's care at that time. I then invited them to do the same with their own lives and the things, people and situations which were special to them. I was not asking anyone to do anything that I was not prepared to do myself personally. So I went down from the stage to kneel at the front in a moment of personal rededication and commitment of Tim and our family into God's hands. There was a large response that night. It was an overwhelmingly powerful experience.

I was then more prepared spiritually for the surgery and thankfully Tim had also got a lot out of Easter People too. It was always an important time for us as a family. But on the day of the operation, only one parent was to be allowed into the anaesthetic room and it was to be my turn to escort him.

The nurse had rubbed some gel onto Tim's wrist which was supposed to numb the pain, but as the needle entered the vein, it obviously caused discomfort and hurt him. But as a young eleven-year-old he was determined to be brave for his Dad, so he didn't make any fuss as a tear rolled down his cheek. I held his hand and said, "It'll be alright, Tim," after which he very quickly fell asleep under the anaesthetic.

My fatherly moment was then abruptly ended as the nurse uttered the cruellest of words, "You can go now, Mr. Cotton!"

I didn't want to go! But I knew that I had to leave and to trust them and to trust God. I left feeling quite shell-shocked and not really being able to speak. So when Carol saw my face, she was immediately concerned and rushed to me asking, "Is everything alright? Is Tim OK?" And for a moment she could not get much sense out of me because I did not know what to say. My mind was racing and thinking through all that had just happened.

I did eventually put her out of her misery as I managed to mutter, "He's fine!"

I knew in that moment that if I could have the surgery on his behalf, then I would have done that. I'd like to think that I became a better man that day. Certainly, I knew that I understood God's love for me in a much deeper way, in that Jesus did take my place in dying for sin and death upon a cross. It is hard to put into words just how profound an experience it was personally and some might not grasp the reality of this particular experience as part of my journey. However, it seems right to share as openly and honestly as I am able, if this is to have any integrity.

Tim would probably share this journey in a different way and I am merely offering my own personal perspective, but he amazed us with his bravery throughout this whole chapter of our lives. He even shared on camera how much he was looking forward to seeing all of his friends at church, thanking them for their prayers and support. No doubt at some point in the future, there will be a time to look back at some of this footage, but as I write these lines it seems very fresh in my memory.

The memories of Sarah and Steven playing with Tim on his bed in hospital, the support of family and friends, and the prayers of many Christians around the country will never be forgotten. Tim made an amazing recovery and developed normally from this point, being passionately involved in playing football for Gedling South Bank Blue in defence. I loved to watch him playing so competitively, particularly in the centre of defence and especially if I was entrusted to be the linesman. I took great pride in flagging the opposition forwards offside.

Whilst Tim has had his challenges, he has a very real faith of his own and worked hard at Sheffield Hallam University, qualifying as a mental health nurse. He met a lovely young lady at church named Alexandra Mills and they have a wonderful group of mutual friends. Tim had a sense of call to serve God in South Africa after a short mission visit to Mozambique with his great friend Jonny Sellman. And after conversations with Phil Bland (Chair of Hope Through Action and member of our Knutsford Methodist Church), he seemed all set to work at one of their centres, but this had to be delayed for almost two years because Tim suddenly contracted keratoconus.

Keratoconus is a degenerative disorder of the eye in which structural changes within the cornea cause it to thin and change to a more conical shape than the more normal gradual curve. Keratoconus can cause substantial distortion of vision, with multiple images, streaking and sensitivity to light all often reported by those affected. It is typically diagnosed in the person's adolescent years. If both eyes are significantly affected, the deterioration in vision can affect the person's ability to drive a car or read normal print. In Tim's case the deterioration in one eye was so rapid that we feared that he was going to lose his sight.

This condition, as far as we are aware, is in no way connected to the cranio-synostosis and it required Tim to have rather painful recently approved surgery on the eye worst affected, which basically involved the scrapping of that eye to flatten the conical shape and to enable regeneration. Thankfully the surgery was a success and the eye seems stable.

In 2015, Tim and Alexandra (then engaged to be married) decided to volunteer together with Hope Through Action at the Mbekweni Sports Centre. Alex would be running a craft and arts class, whereas Tim would be working with young people with mental health issues using sports activities as part of their rehabilitation. This was an exciting adventure for them after they had raised the relevant finance required. It was certainly challenging, particularly for Tim, as they lived with their different host families in the township.

The climax of their time in Mbekweni was organising a gospel concert in the sports centre for all of the local children and young people. Tim and Alex worked hard to make this a success and were thrilled to host an amazing event for over a thousand people. Everyone seemed to be so happy with the outcomes and it was great to hear the comments of local people as Tim introduced them to us during our Skype conversations. The children in particular were obviously very fond of both Tim and Alex as they spoke and it was lovely to see the beautiful young people who were clearly benefiting from their work and valuing the relationships they had.

Their time in Mbekweni was coming to a satisfactory conclusion, when on Easter Monday evening, as Carol and I prepared to go to ECG in Scarborough, we spotted on Facebook the shocking announcement that Tim's best friend Jonny had been killed in a car accident. We were not sure if it was a cruel hoax at first, but after a difficult telephone conversation with Nadine, the wife of one of Tim and Jonny's former housemates, Mike Simms, it became apparent that the sad news was in fact true.

The following day, I had the unenviable task of ringing Tim and Alex to break the news. I rang early the next morning so that Tim and Alex would be together on their way walking to work, rather than separate in their hosts' homes.

Tim answered, "Oh, hi, Dad." He was really pleased to hear from me first thing in the morning.

After just a few comments, I then had to say, "Tim, I have some bad news for you. It's not any of the family, but it is Jonny."

"What about Jonny?" Tim asked.

"I'm sorry, Tim, but Jonny's been involved in a car accident."

"How is he?" Tim questioned. "Is he alright?"

I suddenly realised that I had not actually told him the worst news of all! "I'm sorry, Tim, but Jonny's dead."

"Dead? But he can't be, he's only twenty-two!" said Tim in a state of disbelief. "Are you sure this is right?"

I felt awful having to break such news to Tim and Alex. They were both clearly shell-shocked and very upset by the news. Jonny was due to be a groomsman at their forthcoming wedding only a few months later. Having spoken to Phil Bland the previous evening, as the Hope Through Action Chair of Trustees, to forewarn him of what had happened, the preparations were already well under way to arrange for Tim and Alex to be flown home later the same day. This obviously meant that they were unable to say their proper farewells to the children they had worked with, or to other members of staff, but the priority was then to be home with friends and family.

Tim and Alex were met at the airport by Jonny's parents and their friends Ben and Grace. It was a time for Jonny's closest friends and family to be together and to prepare for the funeral thanksgiving. Tim took a lead in organising the service at St. Thomas' Church Philadelphia Campus and gave one of the tributes to Jonny. We were again very proud of our son, who at a time of great personal loss was able to support and to bring comfort to others in the way he spoke. It is probably true to say that because he has experienced so many difficulties and challenges in his own life, he is able to be empathetic with others and to speak from a place of experience.

The wedding day of Timothy Robert Charles Cotton and Alexandra Mills was just a wonderful day celebrating their love for each other and for God. A friend joked that Alex wanted to keep her maiden name as well as Cotton so that she could be Alexandra Cotton-Mills. But this was only a joke! It was a great wedding service, followed by a lovely reception at Lower Bradfield Village Hall, with the bowling team and the cricket team playing outside on the village greens as we enjoyed our canapes, ate ice cream from the traditional vendor complete with straw boater hat, and played outdoor garden games before the main meal. The day was all that we could have hoped for and more. It was such a special day. There was a tribute to Jonny in the order of service and Tim made a very moving reference to him in his speech. But it was a day filled with joy after which Tim and Alex travelled in our car for their honeymoon in Scotland.

However, if you are now anticipating the "and they all lived happily ever after" part of this particular story, whilst we certainly hope that this will be the case for Tim and Alex, there was to be still another chapter in the journey of surgery for Tim. Tim and Alex are very happy, but he had returned from South Africa with a small lump on his forehead which looked like a cyst, which then burst. He was able to conceal the lump, with his hair covering it for the wedding. But after a long-awaited doctor's appointment he was then referred to a consultant at Sheffield Hallamshire Hospital.

After all that we had been through with Tim, we found that he needed further major surgery, resulting in a new incision on his forehead to remove an infection which seemed to be in the plate and bone put into his head during earlier surgery. We are still not sure at this point how this happened, but we then found that a further, much bigger operation would be required and that he would again be referred to Alder Hey Hospital and to Mr. Richardson!

Once again, we were waiting for appointments and a date for surgery. This was certainly not the start to married life that we wanted for Tim and Alex! And once again, I have had the privilege of sharing our family journey with various people who have been prayerfully supporting us as a family, whilst challenging local church congregations to trust God with all that they are and have, all that is precious to them. But I could only do that in the context of having to trust God personally, dedicating all that I am, all that I have and all that is precious to me, including Timothy!

The day of the second major operation, which actually took place during Mr. Richardson's clinic at Aintree Hospital in Fazakerley, Liverpool, was certainly a long and hard one, particularly for Alex, waiting for her husband to return from surgery. And then seeing Tim with an impressive scar right across his head, which again looked rather like a zip with all of the staples, was not an easy experience for a young wife, nor for Carol and me, as we relived the experiences of Tim's childhood.

Thankfully the surgery was a success; all of the infection was cleared and the healing process went well. Timothy may still be offered some cosmetic surgery on his forehead in the future, but he and Alex are unlikely to accept the offer after all that they have been through! But once again, the surgical rollercoaster journey of the past few months seems to have been survived and has been yet another testimony to the faithfulness of God to Tim and to our family.

I think that explanations and reasons for these things can be overrated. In fact, I will often say to people at a time of bereavement or pastoral difficulty that I do not have all the answers, but that I am always ready to listen. Even theological statements can get us into hot water, or deeper water than we expect, particularly if we are sharing with people who are hurting or going through a time of suffering. One thing I have found helpful is the comment by the German theologian Dietrich Bonhoeffer who said, "Only the suffering God can help." A God who, in Jesus, understands suffering and has experienced it can be empathetic, help us, bring comfort and be alongside us. God has been faithful to us as a family and whilst we continue to place Tim and all of our family into God's hands, we do have a real sense of hope and trust in Him.

Bad things do seem to happen to good people and we are not excluded from that, but we do know, in the words of John Wesley, "The best of all is, God is with us."

18

Alpha: A New Approach –
From Good to Great

'The enemy of Great is Good,' writes John Collins in his book *From Good to Great,* a statement which I found to be so very true and a real inspiration.

I have been a minister in a number of good churches, with good people working hard to serve their church, local communities and God. And yet there is always that sense that with God's help they could be great churches. There have been some struggling causes that I have had the pleasure of visiting as a guest preacher and encouraged people to the best of my ability. But wherever I have visited, I have always seen the great potential of churches to make an impact in their community. The local church really can bring 'hope into their main street'. However, to move from being a 'good church' to being a 'great church', serving their local community, can be a challenge.

When I moved to become the minister of KMC, at first I was not sure quite what my role would be. What did I have to offer such a good church? The challenge was to help make a 'good church' into a 'great church'.

This was explored in an afternoon workshop called *From Good to Great* in which I shared something of what I had heard from the church throughout a listening phase in the first few months of the appointment. Carol and I had invited every house group in the church around for a Cake and Coffee event in our home. It was during these events that I had asked people to share something of their story in just three minutes using an egg timer, followed by two group exercises of describing KMC to me in a pen portrait of a few words, followed by a sharing of their hopes and dreams. The workshop was an important review of how people understood who we were as a church and who God was calling us to be.

As part of the afternoon workshop, I wanted to encourage the church to consider seriously how we could become 'great for God'. There have been a number of good Alpha courses in Knutsford over the years; sometimes there were six or seven people attending and on other occasions there were fifteen or sixteen people attending. As the new minister at KMC, I wanted us to build upon the work of the past, all that has been good, and to transition the church 'from good to great'.

I began to share with the church a vision to launch the Alpha course with a guest speaker who would grab people's interest and whom people would have enough confidence in to invite their friends, family, work colleagues and neighbours. And so, I invited Darrell Tunningley to come to speak at our Alpha launch dinner. Darrell had been a friend of mine on Facebook for some years, but when Martyn and Rosemary Johnson mentioned his book *Unreachable,* which tells the amazing story of his life being turned around as a result of attending Alpha, it seemed that he would be the ideal speaker for a launch meal. His story is the subject of the next chapter. I believe that my predecessor Paul Wilson had traditionally spoken himself, so to invite a guest was quite a departure from usual practice.

The proposed visit of Darrell was then promoted at all of our Christmas services and events, with a short promo DVD taken from YouTube. This seemed to intrigue people and also to give them confidence to invite their friends. One couple who later attended the course told me proudly that they were regular in church, in that they attended every Christmas Day service! Only the wife was able to attend the launch with Darrell, but when she heard of the difference Alpha had made in his life, she booked them both onto the course.

Darrell Tunningley began his criminal career at the age of eleven by stealing badges off expensive cars. By the age of sixteen he was selling heroin and cocaine and funding a £300-a-day heroin habit before being jailed for five-and-a-half years for being the driver in an armed robbery.

Darrell joined the Hope Corner Community Church in August 2000 and after a few years of friendship with Pastor Finch's social worker daughter Rebekah, twenty-six, they began dating. The couple married in 2005 and have two children, Benjamin and Lydia-Grace. Darrell is now a senior pastor at the church, alongside his father-in-law.

He also helped found Hope Corner Academy – a church-run special educational needs school. Darrell's comment about himself in *Unreachable* is, "If God can reach me, He can reach anyone!"

The other concept to envision was the thought of doing Alpha as they would do it at HTB[19]. To actually host Alpha in the church worship area and then to even have a candlelit dinner in the church for the launch event did seem to grab people's enthusiasm. I was well aware that Steve and Jane Gibbons who prepared our meals were professional caterers who were well capable of delivering quality food to wedding receptions and certainly to an Alpha Launch event.

Having run the Alpha course for many years, some of the key organisers had been on training courses at HTB and others had attended worship conferences. So to replicate what they had experienced and loved as an important experience in their own spiritual journey was exciting. However, there was the small challenge of moving all of our heavy church chairs to enable this to happen. Previously this had only happened on a very occasional basis. Thankfully these chairs have recently been replaced!

Places were booked for the launch dinner and it was made clear that those bringing friends to explore the possibility of attending the Alpha course were entitled to attend the dinner, whilst everyone else who just wanted to hear Darrell speak could sit in the balcony. This meant that whilst seventy-five enjoyed the dinner, a further ninety-five came to hear him speak.

Darrell spoke very openly and honestly about his life; he was inspirational in what he said and how he shared it. After allowing him to share his story, I then interviewed him before allowing a Q&A session which people very much appreciated. Darrell was funny and entertaining whilst also bringing a challenge to attend the next Alpha course and to follow Jesus. His book *Unreachable* was in huge demand at the end, but the exciting thing was that fifty-five people signed up to do the course. The Alpha team's experience of handling all the logistics came into play and they hosted the course efficiently and effectively. Still others joined in the first few weeks, so that the overall attendance was sixty-one people, although not everyone attended every week.

The numbers attending Alpha created an impetus within the church, with a whole group of people offering to move the chairs after morning

---

[19] Holy Trinity Brompton church in London.

worship and to put them back after the presentation each week. This also changed the nature of evening worship, making it café-style and therefore more informal and interactive in its nature.

The food during the course was excellent, as I expected, and the sessions were mainly presented using the Alpha DVDs, although I had to present a couple of sessions myself due to a fault on one of the DVDs. The four discussion groups went well and there was certainly honesty and sensitivity to where people were in their journey.

The Holy Spirit Day was held at the church and there were a number of opportunities to respond including the possibility of receiving prayer, which a few people requested. Some people began to attend church as a result of coming on the Alpha course and certainly a good number joined a new house group. Others felt the need to attend the next course which was launched with another Alpha dinner, at which Linvoy Primus, a former professional footballer, was the speaker. I had been determined to offer a credible invitation to everyone who attended our Real Lives festival a few weeks earlier and Linvoy seemed the ideal speaker to invite shortly after the festival, as a large number of football-mad non-church contacts were due to hear Dan Walker, the host of BBC's *Football Focus* and *BBC Breakfast*.

Linvoy has been the favourite player of many fans at Portsmouth Football Club in recent years. After starting his career in 1990 at Charlton Athletic, he has had an eighteen-year career as a player at Charlton, Barnet, Reading and finally at Portsmouth, where his career came to an end through injury in December 2009. The Milton Stand at Fratton Park, Portsmouth, was renamed The Linvoy Primus Community Stand in honour of his outstanding services to the club.

Linvoy released his autobiography in 2007 entitled *Transformed* and, as well as being joint founder, is actively involved with the Christian charity Faith and Football.

Linvoy was a lovely character whom people warmed to immediately. He was very relaxed as he shared his inspirational story of life in football and how, through his amazing conversion to Christianity, he triumphantly overcame disillusionment, lack of self-belief and numerous rejections, leading to a life and career which was totally transformed. Linvoy shared his story after our Alpha meal in a warm, non-threatening style, after which I then interviewed him before we opened it up for others to ask their own questions. It was great to hear of some of our footballing heroes and of Linvoy's experience with managers such as Tony Pulis (then at Stoke City and now at West Bromwich Albion), Alan Curbishley (then at Crystal Palace) and Harry Redknapp (amongst others).

As Linvoy told of his Christian journey we trusted that his story and life experiences encouraged, challenged and inspired others to have a relationship, like he has found, with Jesus Christ. His life story and experience demonstrate that there is always hope of personal trans-formation, but that this also brings hope and transformation into other people's lives, even other professional footballers! Linvoy has appeared in a recent Alpha promotional DVD which was shown in church for a number of weeks before the launch dinner. With Linvoy's help we launched our next Alpha course as part of our ongoing mission and ministry.

The following year we invited Billy Ainscough, a lovable and amusing scouser who told his very moving story of how he survived the Hillsborough disaster, where ninety-six people were killed from over-crowding within Hillsborough football stadium in 1989. Billy's main priorities in life were Liverpool Football Club and alcohol. But after clearly hearing God speaking to him in the midst of the crush of Hillsborough, when he felt that he had little time to live, he called out to God for help, only to be miraculously saved from certain death. This totally transformed his life and his priorities, so his personal experience really had an impact upon all who heard him, and encouraged a good number to attend the Alpha course.

We then invited Simon Pinchbeck who had been a policeman, but seemingly changed his career to become a criminal, and then had a real life-change and became a Christian. After twenty-three years in the Metropolitan Police, Simon left after receiving a not guilty verdict on an assault charge. He became obsessed by money and material things and entered into a life of crime. After being ripped off for a large sum of money by his new-found colleagues, he was left at the lowest point of his life, facing prison or maybe even death. That was when God threw him a lifeline in the shape of a friend named Bryan Robertson. Seeing the change that faith had brought to Bryan, Simon made a choice to turn his own life around and so began exploring the meaning of life through the Alpha course.

Simon shared his inspirational story of transformation using his cockney humour and an easy-going storytelling style. He told of being a policeman at Arsenal football ground (where he was nicknamed "The

Walrus"), clashing violently on the terraces with football hooligans, and of how his life has also changed from crime to following Christ.

The theme of the evening was *From Copper to Crime to Christian* and his amusing approach certainly caught the imagination of the people attending, as did the story of total change that took place in his life when he became a Christian. He had definitely seen life and experienced some very dark situations and characters, but God had miraculously brought him through to a point where he is able to speak of God's love for him and for other people.

Right Reverend Mike Hill (Bishop of Bristol) was our speaker in 2016. We had become friends during the Bristol campaign whilst developing Bible Society's Media Campaign. Bishop Mike grew up as a Knutsford lad; a local boy who made good. He had been a young scally locally and had attended Knutsford Methodist Church Youth Club because it was the place where all the attractive young girls attended. That was his only reason for attending anything at a church as someone from an unchurched background.

Local people remember his mother's gown shop on King Street, with Mike a young football-mad boy who attended the Glebelands Pre-paratory School. Some even attended school with him to witness his spectacular downfall from the top stream right to the bottom, because of his bad attitude at Wilmslow Grammar School in the 1960s. People were able to relate to his story as a local boy who came to faith and surprised all of his teachers by becoming a bishop and taking up his place in the House of Lords. But more importantly we were pleased that some of them then took part in the Alpha course. It is also good that the working relationship with Bishop Mike means that he returned again as the keynote speaker at Firefest in 2017, when he also took a number of classes at Wilmslow Grammar. There will, no doubt, be other significant points in the future when he will be invited to return.

In 2017, our Alpha launch speaker was comedian Bobby Ball, who was certainly hilariously funny, but also inspirational as he shared his own testimony of personal transformation when he became a Christian in 1986. Bobby Ball, with Tommy Cannon, has been part of one of Great Britain's funniest and most successful comedy double acts. Bobby is currently appearing on TV as Lee Mack's father, Frank, in the hit show *Not Going Out*.

Bobby himself says:

I want to show people that being a Christian is not boring. In fact, it's the opposite. It's great! God wants us to have fun, laugh and enjoy this wonderful life he has given us, because He has given us eternal life through His son Jesus. I want people to see that God does care and He can fill any gaps in our lives through His Son Jesus Christ.[20]

Launching an Alpha course has been a different approach for KMC, but it has certainly been fruitful in the numbers attending to date and it also expresses something of our intention to transition the church 'from good to great'. It has not been without challenges and the logistics have stretched us at times, with the need for a much larger band of volunteers and leaders, but the experience has been very positive, even if it has been a challenge for the core team.

I would suggest that HTB with Alpha International have enabled many churches to transition themselves through the nurture of new Christians and the building of a real sense of community in hosting meals and discussion groups as part of their Alpha courses. When Rob Frost invited me to host the Methodist National Alpha Conference some years ago, I was asked to attend a conference leaders' planning event and was sent a very detailed briefing document to explain their requirements. The ethos that they would like for the venue of the conference was detailed, even to describe that it was advisable to put a bowl of rose petals in the ladies' toilets and to scatter a few on the surfaces. There was also a request for bowls of peppermints for the prayer ministry team to suck on prior to praying for anyone, to avoid having bad breath when praying over them.

My volunteers were amazed by such requests and in some sense felt a little patronised by the level of detail. "These Londoners coming up north to tell us what to do…" commented one helper. However, at the start of the conference, for around three hundred delegates, there were bowls of peppermints ready and toilets adorned decoratively with rose petals in a 'we'll show them' attempt to demonstrate how well we could host a conference in the East Midlands city of Nottingham.

The point I would like to make is that immediately after the Alpha conference, there were rose petals in our Arnold Methodist Church toilets

---

[20] Taken from Bobby Ball's briefing notes for hosts of his events.

and prayer ministry was enhanced by bowls of peppermints. I am not going to suggest that these things are still in place or practised in that particular church today, but I would certainly dare to suggest that by modelling how to host and to do things most effectively, many churches have begun to think more seriously about their own welcoming and hosting of people. It raises the bar for all of us when we experience excellence and it creates a desire within us to transition much of what we do 'from good to great'. Alpha has been strategically important in this and I trust that many churches will seek to model excellence in what they do, to bring hope to their local communities.

Perhaps you could ask yourself and your church this question: "Is 'good' good enough for God in your church and community?" If you are keen to offer the very best to God and to the community that you are seeking to bring some hope into, then a serious examination of the life of your church is called for. There are a number of review processes to consider, but at the present time we are finding that Lead Academy exercises are proving very helpful in our journey 'from good to great'.

I had received an invitation letter which invited a number of Methodist churches to become part of a two-year learning community, under the rather catchy heading of *Turning the tide – death or glory*. The letter grabbed my attention because it seemed to address the issue of church decline, which, whilst I did not feel that KMC was declining, it was still a concern to me. 'The statistics tell us that if church attendance continues to decline unabated over the coming years then the lights will get turned out for some denominations within the next few decades,' it read.

One of my ministerial friends, Leslie Newton, had recently commented that as membership secretary for our district at that time, he had struggled to get some membership returns from churches. When he rang Methodist Church House for advice on this, he was told that if he sent in the returns for those churches who had responded, that the others would simply have "the usual rate of decline deducted from last year's membership figure". Lesley was horrified to hear that there was an assumption that churches would naturally decline! But when he checked the statistics he found that there had been a twenty percent decline of membership in the last eight years.

Lead Academy looks for innovative churches and leaders who are committed to reversing this downward trend. Rather than succumb to what some see as an inevitable slide to decline and eventual death, it is important to seek to further the work of God's Church and His kingdom rule and reign across the nation. It was great to join with others from a similar ministry context and to benefit from participating in a highly creative learning environment.

There was the opportunity to explore how the Church could grow both numerically and spiritually in a very demanding current context. We could explore what a 'missional' church looks like and work through the main issues that we were facing in terms of vision setting, culture, leadership, discipleship and mission. For me and a few members of our leadership, it was an opportunity to receive top quality teaching and expert coaching. And it gave us time as a team to think through the things that really matter such as purpose, values and strategy, whilst we also heard what was happening in other places and began to learn from their experience – some were similar and others very different to ours.

We began to explore together the church's culture and how it needed to change, how to release leadership and how we could restructure to become more missional. It enabled us to refocus as a church and to develop our discipleship in a way which engaged the local community.

It was an interactive journey which benefited from some of the most innovative Christian thinkers and practitioners currently available, who challenged our ideas and provoked us to think differently as a team. The process also recognised that sixty to seventy percent of the information needed was already present in the teams sharing together and that through good facilitation we could benefit from one another's experiences, knowledge and passion.

The outcomes expected were that we would become a focussed and united leadership team with clarity of vision and strategy. It was anticipated that our church culture would then be committed to supporting that vision as a mobilised congregation which grows and makes a positive impact upon the local community. Only time will tell if each of these outcomes are achieved, but being able to then take a large proportion of the church membership through the Lead Academy process in workshops has guaranteed that we have all been on this interactive journey together and continue to be so. There has certainly been a fresh impetus to seek God's vision for our church and a real sense of excitement about the future mission and ministry of the church in our community.

Proverbs 28:18 reads, 'Where there is no vision, the people perish.'[21] The fresh sense of vision will no doubt enable growth in people's lives and in the church, so that any talk of decline can be forgotten and we can focus upon offering our very best – even greatness or excellence – for God and for our local community as we seek to journey 'from good to great'.

---

[21] KJV.

19

The People's Princess and the Queen of Hearts

On a typical Tuesday market day in our town, two young men, Peter Williams (nineteen) and James Brodie (twenty), went into the Time Centre jewellery store in Arnold to steal money from the till. They aimed a pistol at Xanthe Bates who was serving in the Front Street shop; her mother Marian rushed into the store to save her daughter's life but was murdered as she was shot in the chest in the process.

It was a defining moment in what was normally a fairly trouble-free market town, where you would not expect this sort of thing to happen. It was devastating for the family and friends of Marian, especially for her husband Victor (who had run out of his office to rescue his family). Marian was the heroine of this story. She was a grandmother of sixty-four preparing for her retirement with Victor, and a lady who had worked in the town for years, who had done charity work for orphanages in Romania. She became the queen of many hearts.

I arrived back home that day from Alder Hey Children's Hospital in Liverpool, where my son Timothy had recently undergone major surgery, to find a message asking me to ring the church office – something to do with a gun incident in the town. I rang the church and was asked by Maureen Carter, our church administrator, to come immediately as there were two television lorries with their crews outside the church reporting on the crime.

How can an ordinary church respond to a tragic situation such as this, when the incident becomes national news and the town is reeling with shock in total sympathy for the family? How can the church leave the comfort of the building to engage a community in appropriate ways, to bring hope in the marketplace of life and to actually be alongside people when there is a real need?

The nearest to this that we had experienced before was when the church had become the focus of community grief after the people's princess, Princess Diana, died and books of condolence had been made available for people to sign. In our context of Arnold, we felt it important to respond to the grief which people felt in our community. In our Sunday morning worship, we mentioned that the church would be open for prayer. On the Monday we put displays of Diana Princess of Wales in the church windows around the marketplace of Arnold, calling people to join us in praying for Diana's friends and family during the week and particularly at a prayer celebration on the Friday (the eve of the funeral). On Tuesday morning we opened our doors for people to sign the books of condolence for the two young princes (William and Harry) and then later we had sheets from Gedling Borough Council for signing too, as they realised that the church was where people were choosing to respond, rather than making their way out of the town to the Civic Centre. The sheets were later bound and presented by the Lord Lieutenant to a representative of the Queen. This was a recognition of our role in the situation by council officers and an early example of partnership with the council in working together for our local community.

We wanted everyone in the community, if possible, to have the opportunity to express their sympathy and to have somewhere to do that as a local community together. We asked the market owners if we could make an announcement on the marketplace tannoy and were able to announce, "If anyone would like to express their love and concern for the family and friends of Diana at this sad time, please come to the Methodist Church to sign the books of condolence." Articles in the local press followed, as did radio announcements and interviews. We were amazed and almost overwhelmed by the response; large queues became commonplace outside the church and a small group of volunteers kindly responded to oversee everything.

People of all ages and backgrounds came into the church to sign, to pray their prayers, to ask their questions, to talk of personal loss, to weep their tears and to lay their flowers at the communion rail and beneath window displays. The church suddenly became the focus of our community grief, with two thousand people coming into church in just six days and over five hundred more at least in the following five days. The volunteers became quite weary with the constant flow of people and the need to support them as they came. In the late evening, we had to put off the lights, just to allow other business meetings in the back rooms of the church to continue without interruption.

The death of Diana had triggered all sorts of emotions and responses within people. People had been surprised by the impact her death and the mass media coverage had upon them. For some, it had brought back the memories of the death of a loved one or friend, and it was almost as if they were experiencing the grief all over again. Some had been involved in an accident and they were now reliving the trauma of that event. Many different experiences were being recounted, some seemed totally unrelated, but this was their opportunity to talk to someone to find hope in their personal situations. The church was the listening ear that they needed and had waited for, in some instances, for quite some time.

In one incident, two young men dressed like punks came into the church looking like really rough characters. The lady looking after the church was quite afraid of them and feared trouble. They made their way to the book of condolence and as the first young man sat to write, he just burst into tears. The lady simply held his hand as he said, "I just keep thinking that it could have been my mum!" She comforted him as he sobbed. She did not say anything profound; she just held his hand. Holding people's hands through this experience became a powerful symbolic picture of the church being alongside people at a time of need.

This whole period left me with many questions as to what was happening in our community, with everyone suddenly smiling at me or acknowledging me in the street when they would not normally bother, as they saw my clerical collar and knew me to be the minister at "the church in the marketplace". It was all very strange and unnerving. Could this be a turning point in the life of the local community – even a turning point back to the church at a time of crisis in people's lives when they needed to discover hope?

We began to wonder at the time if we would ever see anything like this again in the life of our church and the local community. Would we be more prepared to respond to need in the future? Would people's perception of the church change, leading to a better relationship with the community as a whole? With all of the different challenges and the myriad of spiritual choices offered in the marketplace of contemporary society, only time would tell. In actual fact, it was to be the situation at the Time Centre, our high street jewellery store, which would reveal the answers to some of our questions in this situation.

The place of the church in today's society seems to be very much on the sidelines. It is deemed to be an archaic institution which has little or no significance to the modern day, with no viable contribution to make to society as a whole. The presupposition of this chapter is that church, faith and the Bible still have a major part to play and that society would be all the poorer without the contributions of the past and the ongoing work within local communities.

Carl Burke in his book *God is for Real, Man,* which was first published in Great Britain by Fontana Books in 1967, quotes Lord George MacLeod of Iona with some challenging words:

> *I simply argue that the cross be raised again at the centre of the marketplace as well as on the steeple of the church. I am recovering the claim that Jesus was not crucified in a cathedral between two candles, but on a cross between two thieves; on the town garbage heap; at a crossroad so cosmopolitan that they had to write His title in Hebrew and in Latin and in Greek... At the kind of place where cynics talk smut, and thieves curse and soldiers gamble. Because that is where He died, and that is what He died about. And that is where the churchmen ought to be, and what churchmen ought to be about.*

My understanding of this quotation is that the cross, here representing the gospel of Christ and the love of God for His world, should be raised again at the very heart of the life of today's society, bringing real hope. The marketplace of life in the main street can be a very challenging, daunting, demanding place to live out your existence, and the temptation for the Church is to withdraw to safe ground where people can feel secure and concentrate on the things which are of most personal importance. The problem is that in focussing upon the agendas of the Church, we can so easily be considered irrelevant and have no place at all in the agenda of the world. That is why the Church partners with organisations such as Bible Society who are still working today to make the Bible available around the world, more accessible to the culture of today and to resource the church in understanding and communicating its credibility.

Bible Society's aim is to both affirm the Church in its mission and to challenge leaders and those interested to consider new approaches as we seek to engage society as a whole with God's Word; to raise up once more the good news of the Cross in the marketplace of life. This can be a challenge to the thinking of many within Bible Society's partner audience, the Church, who have come to accept a maintenance model of ministry. But for others the hope is that they will be inspired to pioneer new approaches in mission and to discover new emerging models of Bible engagement and church in the community. It was a privilege to work for Bible Society for eight years. This particular chapter is offered humbly as a contribution to an ongoing pilgrimage of discovery for the church from my own experience and is my way of disciplining myself to share honestly with others some of my own reflections so that we might have constructive conversations during our future journeying together.

During one interview after Marian's death I commented, "Seeing all the flowers today is reminiscent of when Princess Diana died, and a lot of people are making that connection here. This is a time when we come together to grieve as a community."

The fact that we had experienced a public outpouring of grief at the death of Princess Diana in Arnold and had been able to respond quickly and appropriately, in some ways had prepared us to know how we could also respond for our community when Marian Bates died. After speaking with the family, a book of condolence was made available for people to sign and write their personal comments. The church was made open for prayer and we had the privilege of supporting the Bates family through a traumatic time of loss and the incredible media pressure that ensued. They were amazing, I admired their resilience and at the time I became a friend.

The challenges were immense for the family and for those of us supporting them. With complete disregard of the grief and anger about what had happened, a reporter sneakily crept closer to us so that he could overhear what Victor was saying as he shared personally with me about his feelings in the church. He was quickly removed. Another reporter tried to get into the church through a fire door just after a service for Marian so that he could interview the family. I personally was doing around fifteen interviews each day for national, regional and local TV, radio, newspapers and magazines at this time. I had never realised how many different news agencies there were and I very much appreciated the support and advice of the Southwell diocesan media officer at this time. And *The Sun* newspaper offered a reward of £50,000 for information leading to the arrest of Marian's killers and asked me to have a photograph taken whilst putting up the wanted posters!

The whole church in Arnold responded to the situation with all the individual clergy leaders supporting the Methodist Church, and me personally in hosting a service of prayer and thanksgiving for Marian's life exactly one week after the incident. Commander David Robertson of the Salvation Army (now a leader at Kingsgate Community Church in Peterborough) led the worship, my good friend singer-songwriter Freddie Kofi sang the family a moving song, *Come by Here,* and the whole thing was filmed by more than sixty TV cameras and broadcast live on Radio Nottingham. There was the opportunity for me to challenge Vernon Coaker MP to raise questions in the House of Commons about gun crime which influenced the political agenda at the time. But it was the relational unity of the Church and the council, built over a number of years working together, which enabled us to influence the media agenda from revenge to justice, to respond to the needs of the whole community and to care for the Bates family at a very difficult time.

During the service I was able to say, "Our hope is that Marian's story – the story of a heroine in the town of Arnold – will not be forgotten, but will inspire us to continue working for change in our lives and in this community."

It was in this context, the very same week, that Bible Society's pilot billboard campaign to culture had begun, seeking to relate a story of revenge and forgiveness in the soap *EastEnders* with people's everyday experience and an issue of local concern, namely gun crime. The question, "Is Lisa right to seek revenge against Phil Mitchell?" was posed, with the image of a gun alongside it and the opportunity to vote. "The stories in soaps explore themes first dealt with in the Bible. If one grips the nation, why dismiss the other?" read the reveal billboard a couple of weeks later. The agency who had helped to develop the creative for the billboards had wanted to be relevant to the culture of Nottingham and to address the real concerns of people. I had been asked to serve on the steering group for this campaign, but I had not been aware of the images to be used on the billboards or of how relevant they would now be to our current context.

The billboard media campaign question changed because of Marian's death to, "Should Dirty Den's kids forgive him for faking his own death?" And an image of a bunch of flowers replaced the gun, to be pastorally sensitive to the situation, despite Victor Bates' personal support of the attempt to address gun crime. The campaign became very poignant for the church in Arnold and throughout Nottingham, as we were working through issues of revenge and forgiveness.

Amazingly, as part of Bible Society's campaign festival of events exploring life, culture and spirituality, a debate had already been organised in Arnold's Civic Centre entitled *Rebuilding Community in the 21st Century*. The idea was to show how stories have power to shape and influence our lives in the context of Arnold. The debate was facilitated by Rev. Dr. Chris Sunderland of Agora (the Greek word for market-place), who is very gifted in facilitating conversations, and at this very significant time in the history of our town with councillors and community leaders all present, it was good to have his expertise in handling the situation sensitively. At the back of the room sat Victor Bates, less than a fortnight after Marian's death, but before he left quietly, he said privately to my wife Carol, "I want to thank everyone. This night has helped to restore my faith in human nature." There was hope even in those dark days of loss and concern about the future. As people brought their concerns to an Agora marketplace of thinking and ideas, fresh hope was birthed for our town.

This was a real situation, a live context in which to run a campaign, and it was certainly a steep learning curve for the staff of Bible Society. A Radio Nottingham law and disorder debate on gun crime quickly followed, in which I was a panellist alongside the chief constable of police and Vernon Coaker MP. I was not an expert but the church had proven itself caring and credible, so apparently, I was suddenly a relevant person to speak on this and related matters. My overwhelming sense of inadequacy was overcome by the fact I believed that if the Church had nothing to say at a time like this, then it has nothing to say!

Peter Williams was arrested and imprisoned for Marian's murder, but James Brodie has never been found or imprisoned, though many believe that he was killed for overstepping the mark in killing a grandmother in such a cold-blooded way. Victor Bates has never fully been able to feel a sense of closure because there is no actual proof that Brodie is dead! We can only hope that some sense of closure will one day come.

Our calling as Christians is to passionately share the love of God in whatever ways we can, wherever and whenever we can; to bring hope where there is devastation, hurt, loss and even despair. All around our nation and even our world, there are examples of ordinary Christian people bringing their love and compassion to people at a point of need, through individual churches and Christian organisations, many of which are working collaboratively together with other agencies to respond most effectively and efficiently. Our society would be all the poorer without this simple offering of God's love in practical ways.

These are just a couple of stories from my own personal experience, where hope was brought through the church in the marketplace of Arnold at two defining moments in our nation and in our town. Standing alongside people, speaking into a situation and actually holding people's hands at a time of need (sometimes quite literally) is the most important and appropriate loving action to bring hope.

20

Prayer Reducing Crime

Once upon a time, there was a group of Christians led by my friend Geoff Sadler who met for prayer and worship at the Arnold Hill Youth Centre each week. As they prayed together, a group of young people began to gather outside and were wondering what they were doing. So after the prayer meeting they would chat with the youngsters.

This then developed and they started to cook some pizzas and give out some orange squash whilst they talked to the youth about their faith. They played a few games together and the relationships developed, so that special outreach events with a speaker or band were also included in their programme. The team were made up of friends from different churches, but predominantly Geoff had the support from his own church: Arnold Christian Fellowship.

At the same time, local Police Chief Inspector Alan Stuart, who is also a lay reader in the Church of England, began to notice that on the night of the prayer meeting and youth club there was a reduction in juvenile crime locally. Funny that!

Nottinghamshire Police then appointed a police officer to set up a project to reduce juvenile crime. He was part of a Pentecostal church and therefore started by coming to speak to local church leaders. He sang at an evening service at Arnold Methodist Church and he then contacted Inspector Stuart to discuss the possibilities.

As a result, I was asked to host a meeting of local Christians at Arnold Methodist Church to explore what was achievable. I booked the Wesley Room as I did not expect many more than twenty people to attend this sort of meeting, such was my faith! But I was pleasantly surprised if not shocked to find that around sixty people arrived! We quickly relocated the meeting to the small hall and certainly there was a feeling that by discussing the issue of juvenile crime, we were "scratching where people were itching"! There was also a sense of knowing the favour of God on this project right from the outset. How exciting it is to be in step with God's Spirit!

A Saturday morning workshop was planned and was also well attended. But the key thing that people felt able to do initially was to pray. And so PACT (Police and Arnold Churches Together) was formed and each month Inspector Stuart would raise juvenile crime issues of concern with a group of us confidentially and we would meet with him on a Saturday morning to discuss and pray about them.

This was also an important time for church leaders and their key leaders because as we met in this regular pattern with a shared vision for our town, our relationships grew closer and we became friends and colleagues. The unity amongst leaders and churches gave our shared mission and ministry more of a focus, trust and a strong basis on which to build. God would present other possibilities to us in due course and this unity enabled our response. Psalm 133 became a key passage of scripture for us: 'How good and pleasant it is when brothers live together in unity! For there the Lord bestows his blessing, even life for evermore.'

This was also an opportunity to affirm Inspector Stuart and the other local police for the work that they were doing. In particular it became a priority to come alongside those police who were working closely with the local community, so Arnold Methodist made a table available at the Tuesday coffee morning to allow the community policemen to talk to people about their concerns, almost offering a weekly surgery for the community. We considered Adopt a Cop as a project for the churches, but the main focus was upon Inspector Stuart and the community police.

There was then a register of youth activities produced in all of our churches which was made available to young people through the schools and library so that they were aware of what they could get involved in. Alongside this we were made aware that when juveniles are arrested by the police there has to be a responsible adult present before they can be interviewed. This is needed because some parents are not always available or willing to attend. At the time there was only one person prepared to serve as a responsible adult. So the churches put out an appeal and around twenty people registered for this role.

The strange thing was that as we prayed about the crime issues, there were clear answers to that prayer. If there was vandalism in a particular area, it quickly stopped. If there was a spate of thefts from garden sheds, the thief got caught. It was quite remarkable how the crime began to fall. In fact, there was a thirty percent decrease in juvenile crime at this time.

Inspector Stuart then made the bold assertion to some local press that "prayer reduces crime". This was quickly picked up by BBC Radio 4 with both Alan and me being interviewed live on air, followed by Radio Nottingham and Trent FM, who after interviewing us did a rather cool mix of my comments interspersed with a current dance track. This felt quite a credible thing to hear on the radio.

At one point, the *Nottingham Evening Post* wanted to do an article about the work with young people and the feature included comment on what Geoff had been doing at the youth club alongside our church-based youth work at Arnold Methodist. At that time we were hosting Chips 'n' Chat at our home with almost forty young people loving Carol's chocolate cake, the chips, chatting together and a few silly games. It was a relational way of getting to know the young people and became foundational for much of the youth work at the church. So the *Evening Post* needed a photograph of young people eating chips to go alongside the article, but the only young people available at short notice were our children Sarah and Steven. A photo was taken of them eating chips in the church, which was in some ways symbolic of our work with youth, so we have a rather good photo of our children to remind us of this chapter in the story.

This, however, was followed by a CNN film crew coming to visit from the United States who were doing a news report on the story and a Dutch film crew who were doing a full documentary on the prayer project. The latter crew were quite a wacky group of people. They filmed me as we travelled in the car around Arnold and bursting out of the fire door at the church to speak to the young people, who were totally bemused by the invasion of people from Holland wanting to film them.

There was correspondence from churches in Holland as a result of this documentary being so well received. Our small project became famous in Holland for a few weeks, which seems rather bizarre. But there was also a high level of interest from churches around the Nottingham area and also farther afield. Inspector Stuart was asked to speak in Manchester at an early point in the development of PACT and it is interesting to note how the praying relationship between police and church has developed significantly in some areas. Redeeming Our

Communities[22], under the leadership of Debra Green, have now developed a national strategy of relating to the police, local authorities and other community groups, starting Redeeming Our Community Cafés in a number of regions around the country.

Redeeming Our Communities has become a recognisable and credible brand which offers support and advice as groups of Christians seek to engage their local communities effectively to bring hope into some very challenging situations. Debra Green has recently been awarded an OBE for her contribution to local communities.

---

[22] The main aim of Redeeming Our Communities is to bring about community transformation by creating strategic partnerships between statutory agencies, voluntary groups and churches.

21

Soap Stories and the Bible – Engaging Culture Today

The trustees of Bible Society had headhunted James Catford to be their chief executive in an attempt to deliver on their agenda to engage the culture of today and to make the Bible known in a post-Christian Britain. After a successful photo shoot entitled *The Prodigal Daughter* which had been published in Vogue magazine, followed by window installation displays of the story complete with the relevant texts in Fenwick's Store, London, a campaign strategy emerged. The appointment of James was deemed to be key to enabling Bible Society to effectively rediscover its campaigning heritage, having been founded by William Wilberforce (amongst others) whose Christian faith was outworked in the public square campaigning against slavery.

After his appointment, James in turn headhunted Ann Holt OBE to head up a Bible Advocacy team and Peter Meadows to head up the marketing team. After the media campaign in Nottingham, I was recruited for Bible Society's campaign in Bristol and later became the senior campaign manager for a campaign to Greater Manchester. In the first instance, my role was to share the vision with local churches of a media campaign to engage the general public with stories from the Bible in a way which would put a blip on their spiritual radar.

A liaison group was created of representative church leaders from around the Bristol area, who had been nominated by their denominational heads. Our meetings were held at Müller House, the headquarters of the Müller Foundation (whose founder George Müller had cared for ten thousand orphaned children in the nineteenth century) where Tim Dobson (one of our key contacts) had an office. I had previously been invited to speak to a group of church leaders by Chris

Sunderland about our work with the local community in Arnold. This had been a great opportunity to share about engaging contemporary community and had helped to introduce me to some key leaders including Right Reverend Mike Hill (Bishop of Bristol) and Rob Scott-Cooke (senior leader of a network of twenty-first century churches).

Having Bishop Mike and Rob Scott-Cooke commending me and the Bristol campaign to other church leaders ensured that I was welcomed by them as I sought an appointment to share the vision of a Bible Advocacy campaign to culture in the Bristol district. It appeared that some leaders were very wary of an alternative agenda for Bible Society, but I was quickly able to diffuse their fears and to ensure them of genuine partnership and investment in the city. Having a fellow church leader involved who had experienced a similar campaign in Nottingham, who had got the tee shirt, borne the heat of the day and had the scars of church leadership, seemed to help the mobilisation of churches. The campaign gathered momentum and was launched at the United Reformed Church on Whiteladies Road, Bristol where Dougie Bradbury (liaison group member and key contact for the URC church) was the minister. Our planning meetings were hosted by Derek at Fishponds Baptist Church, with Tim Harrison and George Nuttall as the Methodists on our liaison group.

The concept of these early campaigns was to think of a vehicle which the general public would be already interested in, because to start with a conversation about Bible stories would be a real turn-off! The marketing agency advising our team were very clear that to promote the Bible to the general public was a very hard sell, with lots of barriers to be overcome in people's hearts and minds. Research had suggested that when people heard about the Bible there were negative stereotypes which came to mind of the Bible being an "old, dusty book", irrelevant to contemporary society, full of contradictions and basically untrue. Similarly, the perception was that faith was some sort of crutch for vulnerable people, only of interest to senior citizens or the very young who will "grow out of it"! Religion was perceived to be the cause of conflict and wars, with recent terror attacks currently exaggerating this perception! The challenge of communicating Bible stories with the general public was therefore immense.

Identifying a vehicle of interest to engage people creatively resulted in the agency suggesting that Bible Society use stories in *EastEnders* to engage people with stories in the Bible. The constant refrain from church members as I introduced the campaign vision to them was, "But we don't watch *EastEnders!*" And yet research had informed us that *EastEnders* was the most popularly watched programme on TV in both Nottingham and Bristol. To educate the church to understand that they were our partner audience, but that the general public were the actual audience of the multimedia campaign, was key in getting churches to host events as part of a kaleidoscope event programme, during which the biblical themes of the campaign could be explored in greater depth and they could also have informed conversations with friends, neighbours and contacts.

EastEnders producers had certainly said some fascinating things about the significance of the Bible in informing their soap storylines.

Devising the Bristol multimedia campaign to culture was certainly challenging for our team, but we had some excellent people working with the help of the agency Farm. The team consisted of Helen Flower (head of marketing), Steve Basset (creative consultant), Beth Lane who is now Beth Openshawe (campaign administrative co-ordinator), David Spriggs (theological consultant), Chris Sunderland (consultant), all of whom worked under Ann Holt (director of Bible Advocacy).

The campaign launch was intended to model the aims and ethos of the campaign and featured creative installations, music by Freddie Kofi, storytelling by Chris Sunderland, with contemporary dance and music from a team from NGM (New Generation Music) based in Thornbury, Bristol. The NGM girls shared impressive testimonies about their work in schools before dancing and singing, then photographs were taken of their presentation for publicity purposes. These images were used as a front cover of the Bible Society publication *Word in Action,* but some of our more conservative supporters felt that an image of girls dancing was too provocative and therefore immediately stopped their support of Bible Society!

At one church envisioning evening shortly afterwards, the vicar's wife said that she was appalled that we had used "semi-naked young ladies to launch the campaign". Thankfully I had the magazine cover in my case and could reveal that the phrase 'semi-naked' only referred to the dancers having bare arms. The looks of horror amongst the people attending soon changed to smiling amusement at the descriptive exaggeration used. The lady concerned did have to retract the statement and said, "Well, I have to admit to being very impressed by their testimonies and the schools work they are doing!" This whole saga seemed to emphasize the challenge of mobilizing the more conservative church audience to engage contemporary culture in relevant ways. We were certainly taking some people out of their comfort zones, if not into uncharted territories.

In thinking of possible events for our kaleidoscope programme, the possibility of having some street performances by the circus training school Circomedia was being explored. The circus training school had recently acquired the redundant St. Paul's church building in one of the tougher areas of Bristol and were due to launch the centre at the time of our campaign going live. So the question was asked, "Could you perform a circus show based on the story of the prodigal son?" The problem was that they had not even heard of the story. So two of our team did a basic Bible study with the circus directors, who loved the story – so much so that they said, "This is a great story, have you got any more where this came from?"

My colleagues then told them the parable of the good Samaritan, which seemed to send the circus guys into a creative spin as they said, "How would it be if the prodigal, on the way home to the father, gets mugged and then is later helped by the good Samaritan?" This was not quite what our team had in mind but at least the people concerned were beginning to engage with Bible stories in a way which meant that they began to own the stories for themselves. And this was certainly in keeping with the aims of our campaign: to enable people to engage with scripture for themselves. If ever God was to speak to them through His word, then they had to at least read it, so to be given their own copy of the Bible to prepare for a circus performance was an important piece of Bible Advocacy engagement.

In preparing for the circus The Full Circle, church leaders commented that it was the easiest ever invitation that they had given to non-Christian friends and neighbours – people were so intrigued by the whole concept. Certainly, the national press coverage was impressive with the launch of the new circus school venue as part of our campaign and the innovative use of a redundant church building. Freddie Kofi sang before and after the circus performance.

A homeless guy selling *The Big Issue* was happy to talk to us about faith and the Bible and was pleased to accept our invitation to the circus. He went to a charity shop to buy himself a suit and brought his mother to see the production. It was a proud moment for him to be able to do this and for both of them to be welcomed by members of the team. I was then asked to do an interview with the editor at *The Big Issue* who seemed intrigued by our approach to sharing Bible stories and why we felt it to be important. She was particularly interested and surprised to learn that the Bible dealt with justice issues and had important things to say on the current issues of our day.

There was a very credible season of films at The Watershed cinema exploring faith and spirituality, plus a very striking piece of graffiti art on the prodigal son produced and then displayed on an advertising lorry. This was later used at other community arts events for display and also engagement of passers-by as I (or another member of the team) explained the meaning of the story as people stopped to view it.

We sponsored a play about the gospel writers called *Five Sides of a Circle* which was performed to packed houses at The Tobacco Factory theatre in Bristol. In fact, the box office said that it had been that season's bestselling theatre production alongside which we had the premiere of a pop opera *Luv Esther* about the life of Esther performed by NGM. I had insisted that we book the Colston Hall in Bristol as I was confident that with the support of local churches and NGM's schools promotional opportunities, we could fill the venue. In actual fact, we had to put on a second night as we sold out the premiere well in advance. There was a very young and enthusiastic audience for these shows which extended the reach of the campaign incredibly.

There was also an excellent Agora[23] conversation led by Rev. Chris Sunderland in the Council House with Bishop Mike Hill and other local politicians participating, which featured a very dramatic piece of drama on justice issues in scripture, which certainly grabbed everyone's attention.

During the preparations for the campaign I had been struggling to arrange an appointment with Luke Walton (curate at Christ Church, Clifton) who was very busy launching his latest Alpha courses. So I offered to take him out for lunch and Luke said, "Well, we both have to eat sometime!" This was a very strategic meeting because Luke and I became firm friends, with him hosting a number of very creative events from a Family Fun Day on the green outside their Clifton church to a film night with the theme *May The Fourth Be With You*. Yes, he is a *Star Wars* fan. But the showcase event for Luke was with Oscar award-winning Nick Park of *Wallace and Gromit* fame. Nick was such a very gracious guest and he even brought his Oscars with him as part of his presentation about his life and faith in the film industry.

---

[23] The Greek word for marketplace.

There was wine and cheese served to guests at the reception beforehand and Luke had written to the cheese factory that produces Wallace's favourite cheese – Wensleydale – as a reference to the films. The cheese factory had so appreciated the publicity that the films had given their cheese that they sent a rather large roll of cheese free of charge to the event as a thank you to Nick Park.

Later, after the campaign had ended, I approached Luke about a vacancy at Bible Society for a creative officer to work on our campaigns. Luke jumped at the opportunity to apply and was successful in being appointed. This appointment and the work that he is still doing to this day are an important part of the legacy of this campaign.

But the major part of this high profile, citywide multimedia campaign to culture was the erection of brightly coloured magenta billboard banners all around the city, with posters on bus shelters, the back and interior of buses, beer mats in the city centre bars and even a taxi with the campaign question featured. There were radio jingles produced by a commercial radio station and event programmes were widely distributed through many mainstream venues and local churches.

Trying to anticipate what the current storylines would be at the time of our campaign going live was something of a nightmare. But then there was also the challenge of linking the soap story with a Bible story in a credible way. It was a tease and reveal strategy, meaning that a question on a soap storyline would be posed for people to engage with and to vote upon. Initially the general public may have thought that it was a BBC advertising campaign, which two weeks later was revealed to be something quite different.

At this point in the history of *EastEnders* (2005), Kat had cheated on Alfie (her partner at the time) and after a break from the show was about to return. It was a story of betrayal, trust and the possibility of forgiveness. The question posed on the billboards was, "Can Alfie ever trust Kat again?" We also explored the story of Judas betraying Jesus in the garden of Gethsemane with Freddie Kofi even releasing a song, *Kiss*, in conjunction with the campaign.

Pat Butcher had had four husbands in the soap and had also worked with young prostitutes as a younger woman, but when a character who knew her history was threatening to reveal everything to all of Pat's friends and neighbours, the relevant question to be asked was, "Can Pat ever put her past behind her?" But the story of the woman at the well offered an incredible insight into the approach of Jesus to a woman who had had five husbands and lived a sinful life. To her He offered living water to quench her thirst for satisfaction. To have such a story of personal transformation which was so comparable was amazing.

The lookalike of Pat Butcher who then came to Bristol to help us launch the billboard campaign was great fun, but also very scary in taking her Pat Butcher man-eater persona a little too seriously! I have to be honest and say that I felt quite nervous when asked to pose for a photograph with her, but I think that the burly motorbikers of the Christian Motorbiker Association who were helping us with this media event were probably of far more interest to her!

There were many very creative and engaging community things happening as part of the kaleidoscope event programme, but the billboards were the things that really grabbed people's attention. So much so that *BBC Points West* invited me to do an interview on the early evening news to explain about the innovative approach of using soap stories to engage people with Bible stories. This was a nerve-racking experience and when asked about the tag line of the campaign my mind temporarily went blank! The campaign tag line which we had worked on for months suddenly escaped me, so I had to glance quickly to refresh my memory, before thankfully recovering to answer all of their other questions live on air. It is surprising, however, how once there is some media coverage on TV, the campaign becomes more credible in people's perception.

However, the independent research done both before and after the campaign demonstrated that there was a slight shift in the general public's perception of the Bible and there was certainly a very strong recognition of the billboards which achieved significant recall in the memory of those interviewed. This was a fabulous campaign to be part of, with over a hundred creative engaging events, effective Bible advocacy and strong church relationships which I still value more than twelve years later. But alongside this campaign our team were also developing the next campaign in Greater Manchester, which was certainly going to be a major challenge.

22

The Riddle of Life

For a major charity such as Bible Society to be taken seriously as a campaigning organisation, it was clear that our team would have to tackle a major UK city and develop the sort of partnerships that would be strategic in making a significant impact on the culture of our country.

At this time, the churches of Manchester had been organising an event called Real Christmas under the leadership of Sue Green, a gifted communicator and networker who had a real heart for Manchester and seeing churches work together in unity. Sue was someone who had a real grasp of contemporary culture and how to communicate effectively. She had particularly good relationships with Radio Manchester, but also with many key church leaders. Sue was certainly well respected for all that she had achieved working with many different churches, leaders and organisations. It was therefore key to have Sue working alongside myself and the team in developing this campaign and inviting the right people to form a steering group to assist in this process.

Early in my appointment at Bible Society, David Spriggs and I were invited to do a presentation to the presidents of Greater Manchester Churches Together, which was a meeting of the Anglican and Roman Catholic bishops, Methodist chairs of district, moderators from the United Reformed Church, Commander of the Salvation Army Battalion, overseers from the Baptist Church and other officers of Churches Together. It was hosted at the home of Rev. Keith Garner whom I had known years earlier as a student from Cliff College doing a mission in the Cheadle circuit (now Staffs Moorlands) and Chick Yuill (then Area Commander of the Salvation Army) chaired the meeting.

This was a very challenging gathering as forthright questions about the intentions of Bible Society were asked. But the truth was that Bible Society were offering to make a significant investment of time and resources, partnering with the church in Greater Manchester. However, any campaigning could only be effective if real partnership at a local level was in place, so securing an invitation from this body was very strategic. Allaying people's fears about Bible Society asking for money was easily achieved as that was not our responsibility, but agreeing to the condition made by these leaders that the campaign had to be for the whole of Greater Manchester was later to prove to be too much of a challenge!

In some areas of Greater Manchester where urban churches were struggling through lack of resources, they were thrilled to have any support and encouragement offered. In fact, the charity Urban Presence, who worked hard to equip and resource some of these churches, were very helpful in the advice they gave, but anything done in these local communities had to be in keeping with the ongoing life and mission of the churches.

We had formed the steering group of people nominated by the presidents of Greater Manchester Churches Together and therefore they were representative of the whole church and key organisations within the area such as Urban Presence (Paul Keeble) and The Message (Matt Wilson). Sue Green was also very much involved, alongside Rob White, Roger Sutton (Altrincham Baptist), Chick Yuill (Salvation Army), Phil Mason (Bolton Mission) and Dave Martin (Cheadle Hulme Methodist).

There were those challenging meetings when I was invited to speak to the Bishop of Manchester's team, one of whom was very wary of "outsiders" coming to do any form of mission on their patch. He was certainly clear in what he thought when saying, "We don't want some rabid evangelical telling us how to do our mission!" He did not know me and this comment was certainly not based on anything that I had said; it was just rude, offensive and a real test of my limited grace. I certainly did not repeat the comment in my report back to Bible Society as it may well have jeopardised much of what we had a vision to achieve in partnership with others.

On other occasions, having meetings cancelled at the very last moment when train tickets and accommodation were already booked and paid for, was certainly very frustrating. Travelling many miles from Nottingham, via London, to Manchester, only to stand waiting in a very cold and bleak Bury Bus Station, when a vicar had cancelled the Churches Together meeting anyway, was something of a low point!

Keeping a sense of vision at times of tiredness and frustration was enabled by some of the people I met in Bristol and Greater Manchester, plus those who supported me through offering accommodation and meals. Whilst Ann and Douglas Holt had welcomed me into their Clifton home in Bristol, George and Elizabeth Nuttall had also hosted me in Patchway, near Filton, Bristol. But a lovely Methodist couple, Carol and Brian Barratt in Swinton, were a real God-send during my travels around Greater Manchester, offering their home to me and other team members as a real ministry to us.

We hosted a number of launch events at the Nazarene Theological College (where our steering group would also meet), Bolton Wanderers Football Ground, a Catholic church and a Methodist church north of Bolton! Being able to invite church leaders for breakfast at a football stadium ensured a high level of response and ownership of the campaign. The free hire of the venue was offset by the cost of the catering, but having a team photo overlooking the football pitch was a real highlight of our campaigning journey together.

We were keen to develop a media campaign theme around homecoming, with the story of the prodigal being key, and we did a number of training events exploring the theme of roots, as we encouraged churches to assist people in exploring their family trees. Rev. Dr. Chris Sunderland was key in facilitating these workshops, but certainly the technological challenges of getting online in some church contexts meant that the offering of this possibility to people proved too demanding for some. However, at the time of the campaign events programme, there were some very creative church displays of local and personal history which included marriage and baptismal registers being available. Many local people requested copies of certificates as they explored their family history in a faith context. It was certainly an opportunity for people to reconnect with their personal story.

This theme of homecoming was also explored in devising *Home,* a fashion show in partnership with Iron Army, an American fashion company, and Massive UK, led by Hannah Latty (nee Atkins). Hannah was able to recruit the models for this fashion show and to assist in the creative development for this showcase event at the Urbis. Telling the prodigal son story to a bunch of models who were not familiar with it was part of the challenge of this project, but also handling the negotiations with models who decided at the last moment that they wanted a larger fee were also good reasons to have Hannah's input.

Hannah also hosted another more grass-roots fashion event in The Northern Quarter, Manchester, as part of a series of events there too.

There were those who assumed that because we had done a media campaign on *EastEnders* previously, we would obviously have to devise a campaign on *Coronation Street* for Greater Manchester. However, this view was not shared by everyone and rather than being predictable, we continued to work on a media creative around the *Homecoming* theme. But none of the marketing materials produced really seemed right and therefore, very late in the day, we were switching media agencies and looking for a different creative idea.

David Ashford was at this time our media consultant and as a highly intelligent, astute theological thinker, he began to help our campaign team to head in a completely different direction, engaging people's fascination with scratch cards and the Lottery. This was a radical departure from anything that we had attempted before, but it won the support of our team and, more importantly, the steering group.

The Riddle of Life was devised as a media campaign using seven questions based on Bible stories on large billboards with a key word blanked out – looking rather like a modern-day scratch card. The clues were the Bible references for the stories, so it certainly encouraged people to read the stories to work out the missing word. The incentive to do so was that we were offering £7,000 as a prize to go to a charity of their choice.

Examples of the riddles posed were:

Freak weather flattens house built on (SAND)

Brothers rage as (FATTED CALF) killed for party

Man recovers at local (INN) after brutal attack

Gold-digger's sneak peek at farmer's (FEET)[24]

Alongside large billboards around the city, there were taxis, bus shelters, buses and trams with the creative on them, but whilst the 'opportunities to see' supplied by the media agency sounded very impressive, the Greater Manchester area was just too large to get the level of public recognition that we needed to achieve a change in perception or culture shift.

---

[24] Referring to Ruth.

However, the events programme was rather impressive with the likes of Rob Bell hosting an event at a packed-out theatre which would later be the venue for a full week of the Riding Lights production *Winter Snow*. There was a host of community events which brought together local churches who had never worked together before and where there was already a level of unity this was certainly strengthened. Areas such as Bolton worked well together, as did the churches of Ramsbottom, who supported the local Steam Weekend based around the railway and engaged the many visiting tourists.

Shane Lynch of the band Boyzone, who had been desperate to be part of the campaign, came to speak at an event in the Rossendale Valley, despite the fact that they were outside of Greater Manchester. NGM performed *Luv Esther* to a packed 02 Apollo, and English comedian, actor and singer Bobby Ball spoke about his life story with exceptional hilarity at a Didsbury church whilst also enabling around thirty people to respond. The Message had their whole staff team hosting a tent on Cathedral Green complete with bands such as LZ7 performing for the youth who gathered, with our special events officer Jamie Hill assisting. The Message also hosted a concert with several bands at Methodist Central Buildings in Oldham Street for around seven hundred young people, over fifty of whom responded to their appeal. Whilst these appeals had never been envisaged as part of a campaign to culture, they were a by-product of the wide level of partnership achieved and hopefully lives were transformed as a result.

We also had a short film competition, *Big Story Little Film,* which was entered by many amateur film-makers who attempted to tell a story from the Bible in a film of around seven minutes. The entries varied incredibly, with different categories enabling young first-time entrants to compete against a similar age group, whereas others with very real ambitions of breaking into the film industry delivered much more technically elaborate films.

It was great to have our friend Nick Park *(Wallace and Gromit)* in attendance to speak and to award some of the prizes at the Showcase Awards event in the Lowry Centre's Red Cinema. His attendance through friendship with Luke Walton enabled this event to become much more credible. But this competition also gave Luke a platform to go on and develop a larger-scale film competition: *The Pitch.* This competition has inspired many hundreds of people to prepare a pitch to make a short contemporary film on a Bible story, the winners of which have visited

Hollywood and even shown their finished film at international film festivals. As a piece of Bible advocacy it has impacted many individuals, with TV stars such as *The Bill's* Graham Cole (PC Tony Stamp) and even Hollywood Actor David Alewelu *(Planet of the Apes)* participating in the films produced.

The Pitch means that, along with key relationships between churches and leaders, the legacy of the Greater Manchester Campaign continues today. There was certainly extensive independent research done after this campaign which revealed this.

Personally, the fact that *The Pitch* has grown to be a credible film competition which has enabled Bible advocacy with so many people, both those involved in the film industry and audiences who enjoy film, is very gratifying and part of a wonderful legacy from our campaigning journey.

23

Unchosen – A Popeye Moment?

After working hard with a group of church leaders who were the steering group for a media campaign in Bristol, I had become friends with a number of them. Dougie Bradbury had represented the Congregational Church on the team and had been a key person in contributing to the creative energy for what proved to be a very successful campaign. Dougie had kept in touch with me and one day asked if Bible Society would be interested in underwriting a Bristol performance of Paul Field's musical *Cargo* which commemorated the bicentenary of the abolition of the Slave Trade Act.

Paul Field had presented a whole range of multimedia presentations with my friend and mentor Rob Frost. *Cargo,* whilst being a commemoration, was also a campaigning piece about the modern-day slave trade and the importance of fair trade. Paul's sister, Marion White, had also been involved with taking a group of women to do some research into slavery and so I was aware that Cargo would be properly researched and professionally presented.

Cargo was well received at the Bristol performance and I was pleased that Bible Society had been instrumental in making the presentation happen. But what is even more pleasing is that the story did not end there because as a piece of campaigning it made an impact on people. One lady, Trish Davidson, was very moved during *Maria's Song* which told the story of a young girl whose family were tricked into letting her go overseas to work, only to find that she was sold as a sex slave. In fact, I am sure that many would have been moved by such a poignant story presented musically and visually. But Trish found the words describing Maria as feeling 'unchosen' very challenging, in that no young girl should be made to feel rubbish, or second rate.

Trish began to wonder what she could do to respond and to address the issue of a modern-day slave trade. Hearing Cargo gripped her in such a way that she just had to do something. But then, there was such ignorance about the issues that maybe simply raising awareness was where she needed to start. And so the vision began to formulate in her mind of hosting a film festival which would highlight these issues. Trish spoke to Dougie, the host of the Cargo event, who then invited me to help a small group to devise a festival programme drawing upon the experiences of organising a festival of events as part of Bible Society's media campaign in Bristol.

A series of meetings were held at the home of Trish, and the Unchosen Film Festival was gradually developed with the help of some small grants including £3,000 as seed corn money from my Bible Society Hope budget. A helpful logo was designed with a tear dropping from an open eye; and certainly, the festival would prove to be an eye-opening experience for many people. The marketing of the festival needed to be effective and therefore the publicity materials needed to be attention-grabbing and widely distributed. Alongside this, I was able to invite a graffiti artist called The Love Pusher, who had done some campaigning work with us earlier in the year, to create a piece of art at The Watershed shopping area in Bristol to promote the festival. Having The Love Pusher produce a large graffiti installation on a relevant Bible passage enabled us to have many conversations with Bristol people and to invite them to festival events. Luke 4:18-19 reads as follows: 'The Spirit of the Lord is on me, because he has anointed me to preach good news to the poor. He has sent me to proclaim freedom for the prisoners and recovery of sight for the blind, to release the oppressed, to proclaim the year of the Lord's favour.'

The graffiti art was painted whilst standing on ladders with the canvas on a large lorry used for promotional campaigns. The art was visually eye-catching and drew people over to it to find out what was happening. The image was of people being released from chains of bondage with key words such as 'slavery', 'debt' and 'freedom' being illustrated. People seemed genuinely surprised that the Bible could be depicted in such a contemporary way, but also that it had anything to say on modern-day justice issues.

A number of people came to take photos of the art which they then shared with their friends, all of which helped to promote what we were doing. But the opportunity to invite them to the festival obviously increased awareness of the festival activities and increased the numbers attending.

A selection of mainstream venues were explored alongside the Elim church 'E@B' as a credible theatre-styled venue for the launch event. *Ghosts* is a film about a group of cockle-pickers who were stranded when the tide came in, a number of whom died. The film director, Nick Broomfield, had researched the film carefully and had also made a number of other Channel 4 documentaries. He was therefore a very credible person to invite to launch the festival and to discuss his film. He accepted the invitation and was certainly very charming as he met with other guests at a reception beforehand. He also spoke passionately about the cause of campaigning against slavery and later agreed to become a patron of the Unchosen Film Festival.

The launch was also further enhanced by the inclusion of the footage of *Maria's Song,* complete with the soloist from the original presentation. It seemed wholly appropriate to show this part of *Cargo* as it had been instrumental in bringing about the vision for Unchosen.

Cathy Come Home was an iconic film in the 1960s which campaigned against homelessness by telling the story of young Cathy going to London in a way which brought the issue to the attention of the general public and politicians alike. The film director, Ken Loach, who was instrumental in highlighting homelessness as a major problem and brought it onto the political agenda, had recently turned his attention to sex trafficking in one of his latest films. We therefore contacted him and he agreed to have me host an interview with him at a theatre within a Bristol hotel and conference centre. He was so politically aware that he responded clearly and at times provocatively to the questions raised. This level of engagement with gifted speakers and high-profile film directors created a media interest and credibility with a number of relevant charities that ensured the future of the Unchosen Film Festival.

It is exciting to think that a musician such as Paul Field can write a song about something which he feels concerned about, and by offering that to others as part of a presentation can make a difference in addressing the very issue of concern. A church leader or individual such as Dougie Bradbury can mobilise people to help him to host such an event. A lady such as Trish Davidson can go out to watch a multimedia presentation and can be inspired to proactively launch an initiative which, at different levels, has responded to educating others, campaigning in the media and publicly on issues of sex trafficking, slavery and fair

167

trade, alongside raising money for a number of causes which help to bring hope into people's lives.

The Unchosen Film Festival has since grown from strength to strength with festivals being held in a number of major cities and more recently a short film competition being launched as a way of engaging young film-makers with these issues.

Whilst some people can feel overwhelmed by the problems of our society and the challenges that we currently face in our world, others are mobilised into action and this activity can bring hope where there is despair.

In reading Bill Hybels' book *Holy Discontent,* I was reminded that when I was a young lad, I used to enjoy watching cartoons on TV and in particular Popeye. If you are a similar age to me, then maybe you can remember the theme tune somewhere in the recesses of your brain right now. How good it was to sit watching this unlikely hero of a sailor engaging in his next amazing adventure.

Popeye had a girlfriend named Olive Oyl with an odd-looking nose and very thin arms, whom he seemed to think was quite beautiful. But, Olive Oyl had another admirer in Brutus, who could make both their lives difficult. Popeye would always try to stay calm in these circum-stances, but when he felt that his darling was in danger, his blood pressure would go sky-high and his anger would get the better of him. Popeye would then always say the familiar words that we were all expecting: "That's all I can stands, and I can't stands no more!" This was not the best of English, but then, Popeye didn't come from Staffordshire; he was just a sailor!

Popeye would then tear open a can of spinach and swallow the green mass in just one big gulp. He seemed to immediately become superhuman with the supernatural strength which flowed through him. His muscles bulked out and he became an unstoppable superhero who was going to right all that was wrong in the world. He would conquer any challenge set before him and obviously save his beloved Olive Oyl. Then, of course, he would casually sing the closing refrain of, "I'm strong to the finish, 'cause I eats me spinach. I'm Popeye the sailor man!" How amazing!

If only it were all that easy, I hear you say! I wonder how many of us wanted to be eating spinach after watching Popeye? Apparently, the sales of spinach did increase as a direct result of the show, which no doubt did a lot of people a favour medically. But, the more important legacy of the show was the catchphrase, "That's all I can stands, and I can't stands no more!" Because I wonder what happens when we reach that point as individuals (or as a church) where we 'can't stands no more'; when we actually say that something needs to be done about this, or something needs to change? Have you ever had a Popeye moment?

Bill Hybels refers to this experience as "holy discontent", when we feel that there must be more to life than this for other people and for ourselves. A Popeye moment could be when you feel that you want to lead a purpose-driven life, a fulfilled life in the way that you live out your God-given opportunities and experience God's love and power at work in you and through you.

For young David the shepherd boy, he hated to think that the giant Goliath could humiliate the Israelites and their God; he was so incensed about it that he just had to act. Even though others (like his own brothers) thought that he should just go home to work in the fields with the sheep, he decided to approach King Saul to seek permission to kill Goliath on behalf of the nation. David was experiencing holy discontent; he was not happy with the situation; he felt that enough was enough; he could not stand the thought of this obnoxious giant ridiculing his Father God.

David was in tune with the heart of God. *What you care about, God, I care about. What stirs your Spirit, God, stirs my spirit too. And however you want to use me to help solve the problem that we both see – use me!*

There were others there that day – bigger, stronger men. But David was in tune with God, he had the heart of God and then the anointing of God was upon him. God's purposes were fulfilled through a scrawny little shepherd boy, a smooth pebble and a slingshot. There may be giants facing you right now, but I wonder if God is calling you to face up to your Popeye moment? What is God saying in your heart right now? Are you in tune with God? Do you have the heart of God, knowing the anointing of God upon you?

For Paul Field, his Popeye moment resulted in him writing songs and presenting Cargo. For Dougie it resulted in him hosting Cargo and then helping Trish and others host a film festival. For Trish Davidson, her Popeye moment as she listened to *Maria's Song* resulted in her devising the Unchosen Film Festival and having a new passion in her life. For some of you, your Popeye moment was many years ago and it could have been to do with people's health, education, politics, well-being, employment, care, business, spiritual nurture, poverty. It could be to do with South Africa, Thailand, India, Tanzania, The Welcome Café (a Fresh

Expression[25] outreach launched by Knutsford Christians), or a town like Knutsford itself. It could be to do with some problem out in the world, or in your local community that needs to be addressed, or to do with your own work, or sense of vocation, but when we come to that point where we say, "That's all I can stands, and I can't stands no more!" something has to change. There must be something done about this! If Christ came that we might know life in all its fullness – His best for us – then maybe we need to know God's purposes for our lives and for the lives of others today. Certainly, when people respond to their holy discontent, their Popeye moments, God is able to use them to bring hope into areas of darkness and hopelessness.

---

[25] A fresh expression of church is a new gathering or network that engages mainly with people who have never been to church. There is no single model, but the emphasis is on starting something which is appropriate to its context, rather than cloning something that works elsewhere.

24

Biblefresh and the Proper Bible

Bible Society commissioned some independent research a few years ago into the Bible-reading habits of the Church in Britain, called 'taking the pulse'. Michael Pfundner was the project manager responsible for this research which revealed fairly startling results about the lack of Bible-reading and engagement amongst church attendees. Bible Society had long been aware of the challenges with scripture engaging the general population in the culture of today, which was why we had been so committed to the citywide campaigns to culture, but if the Church itself was biblically illiterate, then that in some sense was even more alarming. Was it any wonder that there was a lack of confidence in scripture if people were not even reading on a regular basis?

This issue was highlighted to the Evangelical Alliance Council on which I had the privilege to serve for a few years during my appointment at Bible Society. A campaign was devised by Evangelical Alliance to celebrate the four hundredth anniversary of the King James Bible with a Year of the Bible by re-engaging people with a love for scripture. I was seconded by Bible Society to work with Krish Kandiah (missions director) and his team at Evangelical Alliance as the network manager, developing relationships with key partner organisations and denominations.

I was keen that the Methodist Church should make the most of this opportunity and so I contacted Martyn Atkins, who was then serving as the general secretary of the Methodist Conference, for some advice. Martyn arranged for me to speak to the senior leadership team at Methodist Church House about the vision and so I was able to speak of the need to address the poor levels of Bible literacy and of the organisations who were likely to be involved and the Christian festivals who would profile the campaign.

Thankfully, with Martyn's help, advice and support, Methodist Church House set aside a budget to enable the campaign to be profiled properly within the denomination, and staff were assigned to develop the campaign strategically with the denomination under the leadership of Jenny Ellis and with the full support of the media officer and media team. Pete Phillips (a contemporary from Wesley College days), who became part of our campaign steering group, and I would meet regularly with the Methodist team working on the campaign.

I felt that Grandad Fred Cotton would have been really pleased with my involvement in this campaign as he had always referred to the Authorized King James Bible as "the proper Bible". "Read it from the proper Bible, lad," would have been Grandad's refrain. It is rather ironic that whilst I do have Grandad's personal Bible to treasure, the one photograph I have with him is of my recognition service as a Methodist local preacher in which I am being presented with a Good News Bible!

Also, alongside the Evangelical Alliance led campaign to the Church, Bible Society had also formed The 2011 Trust as a more culture-facing campaign to celebrate the King James Bible's four hundredth anniversary. I was invited to be a trustee and to attend my very first trustees' meeting at Portcullis House (opposite the House of Commons), where most Members of Parliament have their offices. After going through all the security, I nervously sat in a meeting chaired by Frank Field MP, to have a scribbled note passed under the table to me from my colleague Luke Walton (like a couple of naughty schoolboys) which said, "The man sitting next to you is one of the richest men in Britain." I smiled as politely in his direction as I could and introduced myself to Robert Salisbury or, to give him his full title, Robert Michael James Gascoyne-Cecil, 7th Marquess of Salisbury! I began to wonder what on earth I was doing in such a place, attending such a gathering of the great and good. The Dean of Westminster Abbey, a former Poet Laureate, and my two most significant bosses at the time, James Catford and Ann Holt, were all present. I would have to be on my best behaviour and also make a significant contribution. My references to another campaign (Biblefresh) to celebrate the four hundredth anniversary were perhaps not always deemed to be the most appropriate!

But on my way to London prior to one meeting, Freddie Kofi had referred to an invitation to sing at the Prince's Trust service in Westminster Abbey when Prince Charles would be in attendance. And so, when there was a conversation about achieving national profile for the commemorations of the King James Bible, I simply asked if there could be a service at Westminster Abbey to which the Queen could be invited and I wondered if Her Majesty might consider referencing the Bible in her Christmas Day speech? This seemed like an outlandish comment, but for the people in the room, they had meetings planned with the Queen's advisors and the Dean of Westminster Abbey had already had the same thought! Suddenly it appeared that more could be achieved through this campaign than I had ever dreamed possible.

It was amazing sometime later to watch Her Majesty visiting a school in one of her beautiful outfits, having two children – one boy, one girl, one black, one white – read from the King James Bible to the Queen, which was then followed by a special reference to the four hundredth anniversary and to the importance of the Bible to Her Majesty's own faith and service to the nation.

To then have a small role in helping to host a service at Westminster Abbey was a real privilege. Carol and I were tasked with a team of people to examine everyone's passport as part of the security checks when they entered the Abbey. Giles Brandreth arrived; many invited Bishops were in attendance, as were a good number of clergy friends from around the country who had been involved in our campaigning journey and the Year of the Bible.

But sadly, a number of guests were delayed in traffic and had to enter the Abbey through a side entrance which we were then still staffing, which resulted in us being delayed in getting to our own seats. As we made our way to the front row reserved seats only a few metres away from the royal family, the Queen began to enter the Abbey and so the stewards would not allow us to go to our own seats and we just had to find seats which were nearer the back to avoid the embarrassment of arriving at the same time as, or just before, Her Majesty. I often think of this experience as I read the Bible stories of people striving to get the best seats at a banquet (Luke 14:9) and the first becoming last (Mark 10:31).

There was also the minting of a commemorative coin when the Mansion House, Westminster, launch was attended by Prince Phillip. There were those who unkindly commented that whatever we did, we should not allow him to give a speech. But he simply spoke to the assembled guests he was introduced to and shook their hands, listened to the short speeches and watched the young people's presentations as requested. His attendance, however, gave the event a media credibility that would not have been achieved without him. It was good to be able to host and to take Jim Wallis to this event during his visit for the Justice Now tour before going to dinner at the Houses of Parliament with Bishop Mike Hill (Bristol) and the Bishop of Bath, followed by a brief meeting with Bishop James Jones for drinks nearby.

Undoubtedly, Bible Society was able to profile the Bible's contribution to society and its influence in shaping our values and culture during 2011 in a way which would not normally be possible. The high-profile lectures, cathedral exhibitions and TV coverage with celebrities such as Melvyn Bragg were all very credible and created a platform from which conversations and debates could be held at the highest level, whilst also increasing confidence in local churches through the opportunities that Biblefresh presented.

Being involved in both the 2011 Trust and Biblefresh gave me a unique oversight opportunity to network in ways that I had never experienced before. However, chasing around the country to speak at Churches Together launch events whilst recovering from a heavy cold (sometimes referred to as man-flu) resulted in my getting shingles and being unable to preach on a few occasions. I was relieved to have friends such as Paul Wilson (Knutsford) who could deputize for a preaching engagement at short notice. Having recovered, I then had an exciting year of amazing opportunities for Bible Advocacy, particularly within the Methodist Church who, with the connexional (national) structures, a team led by Jenny Ellis and communication networks, were able to make Biblefresh a very significant year of Bible engagement for Methodism as a whole.

In particular, the *Handwritten Bible* was a very ambitious nationwide project, where people in various community settings were invited to write out a prescribed passage of scripture on a manuscript which was then bound into volumes in each regional district of the Church. These were then displayed in prominent locations around the country.

At Evangelical Alliance the campaign had begun with a branding process, which resulted in the name Biblefresh being chosen. But sadly, the agency had not checked to find that the name was already owned and registered by Robert Hicks, a publisher living in Bath, who had been very instrumental in launching the Back to Church campaign a few years earlier.

I was tasked to go and visit Robert to request the use of the brand and I feel that it is important to mention here just how gracious he was in donating the brand to our campaign consortium, in giving advice and in making resources available to the local church. His passion for the Bible was clearly evident and in his working relationship with Steve Brady (Moorlands Bible College) he provided a credible and affordable commentary to festivals and encouraged me personally in whatever way he could.

Biblefresh had four tracks to the campaign: Reading, Training, Translation and Experience. The number of Christians who were reading the Bible personally other than in church worship was so low at this point that it was important to inspire them to engage with scripture in fresh ways individually, in groups and as whole churches, particularly making the most of new technology and resources.

Research had shown us that only half of church leaders and a seventh of churchgoers were feeling confident about their Bible knowledge, plus forty percent of Christians felt that militant atheism had undermined their confidence in the Bible. There had been a lack of Bible training for Sunday school teachers and house group leaders as to how to teach scripture or how to apply the Bible to everyday life, so there were major needs to address in this stream.

With over two hundred million people without the scriptures in their own language and over two thousand language groups yet to even have their own Bible, we felt it right to ask churches to financially support a joint translation project of Bible Society and Wycliffe Bible Translators during the Biblefresh year. The focus of this project was Burkina Faso. It was also hoped that the campaign would enable Christians to translate the message of the Bible into their own culture and lives.

Bible experiences were devised to whet the appetite for biblical engagement by using all manner of things from drama to films, music to pilgrimages, all designed to draw people back to reading and living out the Bible daily.

How wonderful it was to participate in several projects during this year. For example, it was good to take a few New International Bibles to an event such as ECG in Llandudno, placing them under people's seats as part of the Viral Bible project. People were invited to highlight an important verse, or their favourite verse in the Bible, putting their postcode in the margin, before logging on to *www.viralbibleproject.com* to register where they had then placed the Bible for someone else to discover. The Bibles travelled around the world, with many people participating in this significant project. It is interesting to hear Bud Foster from Knutsford refer to finding a Bible under his chair at ECG and to relay just how significant an experience it was for him at the time. It is funny that in God's grand scheme, the culprit who placed the Bible is now his minister!

Bible Society was keen to offer a project which could engage the general public during the year and so *The People's Bible* was devised; a digital Bible which everyone could contribute to. A road trip was planned beginning in Scotland and then touring Britain, with even the Queen and Prime Minister David Cameron contributing a verse, alongside several actors and Christian celebrities writing on the digital screens the verse selected by them.

The challenge was that alongside our media officer, Rachel Rounds, who coordinated the interviews and media coverage, we also needed someone to manage the logistics of the tour. So I asked Mary Corfield (now Acland), who had so ably helped me with Hope Nottingham, to consider this opportunity, which she thankfully grasped and so ably managed. I think that she has now forgiven me for landing her with this incredible challenge.

It was great to host *The People's Bible* at Arnold Market (Nottingham), Calverton Car Boot Sale and Lord Street (Southport) as part of Firefest. In Congleton local church leaders and Fiona Bruce MP all took part after I had spoken at and helped to launch their very first Bible Week earlier in the year. On one occasion in Southport, we assisted an elderly gentleman to a chair and cared for him whilst he wrote his verse, before getting him into his daughter's car. A few days afterwards, we received an email thanking us for our support. The gentleman had died later the same day and the family wanted to thank us because they were able to see online the verse that he had written even on the last day of his life.

Touring in that year to festivals and hosting church concerts on the final tour that I did with my friends, Sons of Korah (supported by Freddie Kofi), the Australian band who had set the Psalms to music, was a real highlight. People around the country had a Bible experience with the band which took them on a journey into scripture and it was quite unforgettable, particularly the narrative of the prophet Nathan with King David. Driving our tour bus from place to place and being on tour with a band was quite a challenge, but it certainly delivered in providing a relevant Bible experience during Biblefresh.

Carol and I also led a pilgrimage to the Holy Land with a gifted team of leaders including Pam Rhodes *(Songs of Praise),* Dave and Pat

Bilbrough (worship leaders and songwriter), Phil Gough (Leyland), Martin and Biddy Turner (MCHW[26]), Tony and Frances Miles (Premier Christian Radio), and Ann and her late husband Tim Hall (Linacre Mission and Southport Circuits). This was a Bible experience of 'walking in the footsteps of Jesus' which I have written about in another chapter of that title, but I need to make reference to this profound experience which I shared with many friends and my late father Charlie and stepmother Mauveen at this point. To say our pilgrimage was a highlight would simply be an understatement! My good friend Colin Smith, whom I had travelled to South Korea with during our college days, and his Anglican colleague Richard Watson also led a Biblefresh parish pilgrimage in the June of this year, which similarly was a significant experience for all who participated.

In writing about the different campaigns that I have been involved in, it is always hard to quantify what has been achieved and I would never want to make unrealistic claims about my personal role, but undoubtedly many people were blessed during this Year of the Bible and re-engaged with scripture. How can you overestimate the importance of individuals reading and studying scripture in a way that they had not done previously? What a transformation occurs in people's lives bringing tangible hope to them personally, and to their churches and communities, when they have relevant Bible experiences and when the Bible is actually translated into a person's own heart language, whether that be in Burkina, Faso, or wherever.

On a personal level, whilst the year was one of blessings, opportunities and challenges, the greatest challenge I felt was that I was being called back to serve in the local church. Whilst I had certainly enjoyed the many opportunities that Bible Society, Evangelical Alliance, Hope and other organisations had given me, I began to feel that the primary call upon my life after being a husband, father and son was to be a local church minister.

Initially I explored with Bible Society and the Methodist Church the possibility of retaining a part-time role at Bible Society alongside a circuit appointment. But after much prayer and a failed attempt to be stationed into a viable appointment, I reluctantly had to accept that this season working with Bible Society was coming to an end. I therefore accepted a different role for an interim period working with Andy Bissex and his

---

[26] Methodist Central Hall Westminster.

church relations team in sharing at local churches and Christian festivals about the work and ministry of Bible Society. This was a good way to end my appointment productively, whilst preparing myself to be stationed to the Alderley Edge and Knutsford Circuit.

In addition to this, Nottingham East Superintendent Paul Worsnop helped me to transition back into local church ministry by allowing me to assist the leadership of a fresh expression called Church@Community which met at Blue Bell Hill School, to think through their future missional development. This was primarily through helping Paul to lead a series of studies with them and preaching there on a monthly basis alongside my commitment to preach at our local Calverton Methodist Church.

It was great to be part of such a growing, dynamic, fresh expression as it became a church in its own right. Nic Williams and a small team of around a dozen had left Mapperley Methodist Church after becoming increasingly frustrated with traditional models of church but were now meeting with over fifty and sometimes up to seventy people! The potential for mission that had been unlocked through engaging the local community and school was certainly a great catalyst for hope in that area and certainly in the circuit churches.

A new season was approaching, but with the hymn-writer I could meaningfully sing, "I will praise him for all that is past and trust him for all that's to come." I will always be thankful to Bible Society, Hope Together, Evangelical Alliance and the Nottingham East Circuit for all the opportunities that I enjoyed during this season of my life and for all of the friendships that I have shared and continue to value to this day.

25

Bear Town or Bible Town

In the preparations for the year of Biblefresh, I was contacted by Rev. Keith Jervis, a retired Methodist minister whom I had met during his appointment as the superintendent minister in the Cheadle Circuit, now known as the Staffordshire Moorlands Circuit, inviting me to speak at the very first Congleton Bible Week.

I felt privileged to be helping to launch the event and was focussing upon the book of Acts for my studies. It was, however, quite poignant that during the Bible Week the town were launching the Bear Trail as an attempt to bring tourists into the town. This was the brainchild of Dawn Gibbins who in 2009 appeared on the TV show *Secret Millionaire*, helping three community projects in Bristol with donations of £250,000! The experience had totally changed her priorities in life!

As you research the history and spiritual heritage of Congleton, you soon discover that in the early 1600s the most important event in the town each year was the Congleton Wakes. This was an opportunity for local people to relax from the humdrum of their working lives and to have some well-deserved family fun. The unlikely star of the Wakes was the town's dancing bear and sadly, sometime in the 1620s, Congleton's bear became seriously ill and actually died just before they were about to begin!

This caused major panic amongst the organisers, as the dancing bear was the highlight of the wakes, which everyone came to see, and it also generated a good amount of money for the town. So they contacted the town alderman to see what could be done.

Strangely enough, at that time an amount of money had been budgeted to buy a new Bible for the town. The old Bible had become quite tatty and obviously needed replacing. But, seeing the desperation of the townspeople in what seemed to be a time of emergency, the alderman proposed that they borrow the money for the Bible to buy a new bear and that at a later date they buy a Bible with money raised by the bear during the Wakes week! It was therefore intended to be a loan to be repaid as soon as possible.

However, we are not sure when or if the Bible was ever actually bought and, in fact, one idea for Biblefresh was to buy the town a new presentation Bible, but I am not sure that agreement was ever reached on which version of the Bible the local Council felt able to accept. Folklore has meant that the tale has been told and then retold quite differently over the years, with the facts being changed to make it more interesting. Some have suggested that the town Bible was sold to raise money for the new bear, but this is clearly not the case!

The Congleton Partnership suggest that the people of Congleton showed great entrepreneurship by taking out this loan and used it for the benefit of the town at that time. That same strong sense of creative thinking is still evident in the town today, as they strive to put Congleton on the map with initiatives such as the Bear Trail.

However, for some Christians in Congleton, this part of the town's history seemed rather embarrassing and when it was suggested that the Churches Together not only participate in the Bear Trail but actually sponsor a bear, that seemed to be fairly contentious. There were certainly those who would rather forget this part of the town's spiritual heritage and so they were not keen to highlight it in this way.

Therefore, it was a rather forward-thinking and courageous step for church leaders to sponsor a bear and to profile the launch of the Bear Trail, alongside which Fiona Bruce MP sponsored Justice Bear. It was so profound, and in some ways ironic, to see Justice Bear with extracts of Micah 6:8 written on his sash: 'And what does the Lord require of you? To act justly and to love mercy and to walk humbly with your God.' It was certainly good to see this positive biblical engagement and advocacy during the year of Biblefresh in my role with Bible Society and also Evangelical Alliance during my secondment to work on this campaign at the time.

So it was into this context that I was then invited to attend the launch of the Bear Trail with other local church leaders as I led the teaching at the Congleton Bible Week, led assemblies and classes at Congleton High School with Jeff Cutts' team and lived briefly with Steve Hodgkinson, the senior elder of New Life Church. It seemed right that I had the opportunity to encourage the churches of Congleton in this defining moment of a strategic week in the history of the town.

I felt that the book of Acts had much to offer as I attempted to speak into the life of the church at that time. Why do I love the book of Acts? Because here we have the stories of what happens in a kingdom community when they experience the power of the Spirit, and there is certainly some key teaching that should help to shape the way in which churches engage their local community. For example, in Acts 17 when Paul is in Athens, he was distressed to see the city full of idols. It was a marketplace of the latest ideas, with the Stoic philosophers and the Epicureans all waiting to hear what Paul had to say.

So here you have the intellectuals of his day, meeting together to discuss the latest thinking. There was a sort of snobbery about them; they would like to think of themselves as rather clever, knowing what is what. Here are a group of people who intellectually could potentially run rings around Paul. So as Paul begins to share the good news about Jesus, the Stoics and the Epicureans start to ask, "What is this babbler trying to say?" It is actually a way of being a bit snobby and of putting Paul in his place. Intellectually they are looking down on Paul, because in calling him a babbler, not only are they saying that he is not being clear, but they are also alluding to a little bird called a babbler. The babbler used to feed on scraps of food, a little here, a little there, from the gutters – scavenging around for a few morsels where it could find them. They are suggesting that Paul probably doesn't know much of what he is talking about but has just got a few scraps of information from here and there and is trying to sound like a man of understanding when actually he knows very little.

So Paul has a challenge ahead of him. He is distressed to see that the city is full of idols – and maybe as we reflect upon modern society and culture, with people being preoccupied with making idols, we have a similar challenge today. Modern-day values portrayed in the media are not what we would want for society, so we could feel distressed or despondent. And even in places such as Congleton, as the Bear Trail was launched for those with concerns about the way society is generally going, this story seems rather apt. Some of us might want to challenge something of what is happening in society today, or at least to be a prophetic voice into the life of our local councils politically and into our community.

But in Athens, rather than lambasting the people for having all of these idols – as I might have expected, encouraging Paul to sort them out!

– Paul commends them for being "very religious" and he seems to pat them on the back. So he gets around all of these pompous intellectuals by commending them for being religious. He affirms them! And then he draws their attention to an altar with an inscription 'to an unknown god'. It is interesting to note that they were so intellectually determined to identify all of the gods that they even had an altar with such an inscription, just in case they had missed one. So Paul comments, "Now what you worship as something unknown, I am going to proclaim to you." He immediately has them intrigued and totally engaged in what he is saying, because they need to know about this 'unknown god'. He has them eating out of his hands (so to speak).

What a masterful way of communicating to them – and not the way the Church communicates much of the time. The Church has had a reputation for telling the local community, the society around us, that all it is doing is wrong, of standing in judgement and tut-tutting as it has condemned people, politicians and society. And then we wonder why they do not want to listen to us and do not want to know us – because that is the image they have of church. They will never hear us if we are perceived as sitting in judgement. We are supposed to be *good news* and that is what God calls us to be. Here in Acts 17, Paul in Athens, we have one of the most important passages to inform us in our mission and ministry!

Paul began where they were, speaking at the Areopagus (which was almost like a court when it met formally and sometimes was used to settle disputes). He quoted their poets, using the arts to engage them. Paul engaged people in the public square, where they were, in a way which was most appropriate to the culture and setting in that place, at that time. It is true to say that not everyone accepted all that Paul was saying; we read that some of them sneered as if to mock him, particularly when he spoke of the resurrection of the dead, but then I am reminded of the saying, 'You cannot please all the people, all of the time.' Some asked if they could hear more from Paul on this subject and others became followers of Paul and believed.

In a multicultural context, and in what some would describe as a post-Christian society, it is important that we engage in appropriate ways that are sensitive to who people are, where they are and what their needs are. This is particularly true as churches prepare to participate in Hope Together, but also as we seek to bring hope into the community of which we are a part. Certainly, this has always been important as part of my local church ministry, but also of the many campaigns that I helped to co-ordinate during my appointment at Bible Society. Whilst we always worked hard to listen to the partner audience of the local church, it was key that we always remembered who were the target audience of any campaign! In that sense, there were always two audiences for every campaign: the partner audience of the church and the cultural audience of the general public. I feel that Bible Society invested significantly during my appointment working for them and continue to do so in equipping and mobilising the local church through Bible Advocacy and also in its mission of campaigning to the culture of today. I trust that the relevant chapters of this book reflect something of that investment, but also that the local church can continue to explore how best to apply the teaching of biblical stories to mission in their cultural context.

Certainly, I feel that the church in Congleton and all of the church leaders should be applauded for their forward thinking in this strategic participation within the Bear Trail. As I mentioned earlier, it is a very positive example of Bible advocacy and engagement. It was good to return later in 2011 to Congleton with *The People's Bible* project and then to invite Congleton's church leaders to Westminster Abbey, when Her Majesty the Queen attended a service commemorating the four hundredth anniversary of the King James Bible. Twenty-six thousand people participated in the Bear Trail between May and October 2011, plus £10,000 was raised for local and international charities. The initiative still continues to this day.

26

Hope 08

There have been times during my ministry when I have been accused of having some daft ideas! As part of the creative 'blue sky thinking' that I have openly engaged in with church stewards, leadership teams and occasionally church councils, I have to be honest and recognise that not every idea I have shared has been credible! But when three good friends met together for coffee during a festival and decided that rather than just organise a future campaign for another city, they would do a campaign for the whole country, that was a *really* daft idea! However, when the three friends concerned are Roy Crowne (former CEO of Youth for Christ), Andy Hawthorne MBE (CEO, The Message Trust) and Mike Pilavachi (Soul Survivor), the daft idea has to be taken seriously.

Conversations were then held with key organizations who would eventually be invited to partner with them to collaborate and own the campaign collectively, and all of the major church denominations and streams were consulted in an exploratory envisioning process.

During this time, I had been tasked to write a proposal to James Catford (Group CEO) and Ann Holt (Bible Advocacy Team Director) about our future campaign strategy. My proposal shared the principal of collaborating with other major organisations to launch a national campaign through Hope 08, engaging a much broader audience with the Bible. The aim was to achieve synergy, in that the results realised in unity would be far greater than any outcomes achieved if we all continued to work in isolation. Bible Society became a key campaign partner and I was seconded to work as part of the national leadership team, with representatives of mainstream church denominations, streams and other major Christian organisations.

One of the challenges I had to overcome personally was juggling the different demands upon me during 2007. I was still managing a major campaign, The Riddle of Life, in Greater Manchester, which then had to be properly researched afterwards, but the experience of attending Hope leadership teams always inspired me. When there was no money in the kitty, you would have Andy Hawthorne saying, "I really love it when we have no money, because then you just have to step out in faith." We called it 'squeaky bottom time' at The Message and the whole team would just burst out with laughter. Finance was an issue, but also the setting of targets was a challenge as we tried to define what success would look like. We decided that if five hundred villages, towns and cities participated in Hope 08 to engage their communities in word and action to meet local need, this would be a great success. We were to be totally overwhelmed as one thousand five hundred actually took part!

The targets that we prayerfully dreamed up in our team meetings skilfully chaired by Steve Clifford (general director of Evangelical Alliance) were designed to be credible with the media, so that the churches' role in bringing hope to local communities could be profiled and discussed on a much wider platform. A million hours of 'random acts of kindness' and a million pints of blood to be supplied at Easter during a national shortage of blood donations were just two of the target challenges given to the Church nationally. Both targets were of course exceeded.

The envisioning process took various members of the leadership team around key towns and cities, plus all of the major Christian festivals came on board to offer platform profile, speaking opportunities, seminars and displays, all of which were essential if we were to effectively mobilise the Church nationally. I had the privilege of representing the leadership team on many occasions, particularly when Roy, Andy and Mike were otherwise engaged. Speaking at Grapevine, Lincoln, at the main celebration to between five and six thousand people in the largest marquee I had ever seen, immediately followed by another young adults' celebration of over a thousand, was quite breathtaking. However, on other occasions I travelled many miles to be greeted by a handful of people who equally needed to be envisioned, if the campaign was to ever have the reach that we felt was required.

I was certainly indebted to John and Debbie Wright (Trent Vineyard, Nottingham) who allowed a member of their staff in Mary Corfield (now Acland) to assist me with the logistics of Hope Nottingham which I chaired during this period. Hope 08 had an envisioning visit from Roy, Andy and Mike, which was to be later followed by a launch celebration with Roy preaching at the Trent Vineyard Warehouse. It was really good to have so many church leader friends together in unity, praising God and committing themselves to work together. Many of them had encouraged me during my ministry in Nottingham by praying with me and for me, so I felt confident that Hope Nottingham would be well supported.

Launch events were held in numerous settings around Nottingham from the leisure centre in Beeston to a Boys' Brigade Centre in Chilwell, in parish churches around the diocese, in synods and chapels and in rather lively black majority New Testament of God churches with Bishop George Beeston and other friends. It was an incredible time of opportunity, preaching to large gatherings of Churches Together groups who had gathered their people with a shared vision of reaching out to meet need within their village, town or city.

There were significant civic and community events to either speak at, host a stand or just attend. It was good to host a schools' art competition, Images of Hope, in a number of settings, with several hundred entries having to be judged and then Bibles donated by Bible Society to be presented to the winners. The exhibitions of the pictures produced by children were proudly presented to the wider community and to the children's families at the community events. It was certainly interesting to see how youngsters had engaged with Bible stories of hope in their attempts to produce a credible 'image of hope'.

The culmination of the various area events was a Hope Nottingham festival in the market square with a couple of thousand people attending an act of morning worship which I had the privilege of co-ordinating, led by worship band Trent, with other key church leaders participating, alongside singers Paul Field and Freddie Kofi, followed by Bishop Tony Porter preaching. The afternoon festival then featured local Christian bands alongside Paul and Freddie, food stalls, displays of literature and a graffiti art lorry displaying an alternative 'image of hope' by graffiti artist Lovepusher.

People just walking through the market square were able to seek information, or to talk to the Christian Listening Point from Arnold Methodist and it was good to hear of positive conversations leading to prayer being requested and a few being enlisted onto an Alpha course.

But all of this activity and the profile that resulted also led to two of the highlights of my ministry: there was an invitation received from Prince Charles to Clarence House for afternoon tea and then to meet

Gordon Brown the Prime Minister at the time, as I have recounted in the chapter *Does Our Nation Need a Prophetic Voice?*[27]

However, an agreement had been reached that Hope 08 was to be a one-off campaign and I think that it was probably a relief to most of the leadership team when it was all coming to a satisfactory conclusion as we received the independent review. However, Mike Pilavachi was not convinced that it was right to draw a line under Hope, feeling that there had been a real sense of the favour of God upon it and he even wondered if God might be calling us to do it all again! At which point, one member of the leadership team said, "That's because you didn't do it the first time!" referring to the fact that Mike had missed a number of our meetings and had delegated the campaign to members of his team. However, in fairness to Mike, his contribution as one of the figureheads of Hope 08 and as a gifted speaker/communicator had been invaluable to the development and credibility of the campaign.

And actually, he was challenging the leadership team to think the unthinkable at the time, in such a way that Hope Together has since developed in ways that we could never have imagined. There have been so many developments with large-scale community lunches (The Big Lunch) in many towns and cities and a distribution of gospels for the Queen's Diamond Jubilee, followed by special *Silent Night* events in football stadiums for the centenary of the ceasefire in the trenches during World War I. There has even been an excellent booklet specially produced for the Queen's ninetieth birthday, *The Servant Queen and the King She Serves,* with a foreword actually written by Her Majesty.

A *Hope Christmas* magazine featuring Mary Berry (of *The Great British Bake Off)* sharing her faith story and a free Christmas recipe, alongside Bear Grylls talking about the greatest adventure of his life being his faith journey, was widely distributed in November 2016 with an invitation to Christmas services.

All this has prepared the Church for a nationwide Hope campaign in 2018, ten years after a rather daft idea actually became a reality. If young men see visions and old men dream dreams, I am wondering what daft ideas you might conjure up to bring 'hope in the main street' of your village, town or city?

---

[27] See page 39.

27

Sheep 'n' Shops

I had arrived in Knutsford only a couple of weeks earlier, when a local councillor came to visit me. "I have come to see you to notify you that the council are closing Princess Street for the town's Sunday Artisan Market in just under two weeks' time!" This was the main street on which our church was based and the date in question was our Harvest Festival Sunday.

I was a little taken aback that the council had not consulted with us earlier, but it was also going to pose an immediate challenge for the senior citizens in gaining access to the church, particularly those who needed to be dropped off at the door and for those with wheelchairs!

I looked at the councillor and asked him, "So are the council thinking of stopping the senior citizens and people with disabilities from attending their church on a Sunday?" He suddenly looked very concerned; he had not taken into consideration how this might be perceived by the general public and how the church might react if the council just tried to ride roughshod over us without any proper consultation or notice.

There was a choice to be made at this point: were we as a church going to object strongly to the council hosting such an event on our doorstep without any proper consultation, notice or consideration for people with disabilities, or pushchairs, and senior citizens? Or should we try our best to work collaboratively and, despite the frustrations, seek to see this as an opportunity for partnership, rather than a major inconvenience and hassle?

"We want to be a part of this community, to support you in what you are doing and to partner with you in some way," I heard myself say! "We could open up the church and give people a free cup of tea, coffee or juice. People could see the harvest displays, or just have a moment's rest in the church. Do you have any live music as part of what is happening because we have a number of musicians?"

The church secured access up the wrong way of Princess Street (Top Street), with council marshals escorting cars transporting older members up the road in safety. The water boilers were on overtime with the many visitors we had throughout the afternoon and people came into the church for the very first time, to see the Harvest displays, have a drink and to use the facilities. Our worship leader Graham Boler performed mainstream music with a couple of contemporary Christian songs thrown in for good measure on the street arts stage as part of a programme of events. It was great to see a jazz band accompanying Graham as his backing band at one point, with church members singing along to a few well-known pop classics to support him with his set.

What could have been a difficult, stressful day of conflict with the council and local traders was a very positive day of engaging numerous people in conversation from the local community, with real collaboration and partnership. On another occasion, I would want to have a larger band supporting Graham in playing on the music programme, with free literature ready to give out other than just the church magazine, but Carol and I walked away in the late afternoon, buzzing with a sense of excitement of what could be achieved in the community of Knutsford.

There was a meeting with the town clerk and town mayor shortly afterwards to arrange the local church involvement on Armistice Sunday and at the Advent crib service. The first comment was to thank me for the support of KMC in making the Artisan Market (later to become Makers Market) such a positive experience and for working with them in solving the access issues on that particular Sunday. This was the start of a very positive relationship with Knutsford Town Council, which would be important for future ministry in the town. There are so many negative perceptions of the church, the Bible and faith in general, that it becomes strategically vital to avoid affirming negative stereotypes of Christians and the church as an institution.

I was then able to secure an invitation to the council meeting where the Artisan Market was to be reviewed and the Christmas tree light switch-on was being planned. Our children's worker Jenny Mossman had already discussed an idea of doing a messy church Sheep 'n' Shops activity on the evening of the light switch-on to engage local families, but I realised that the council also had a similar 'stranger in the window' idea!

The conversation was fruitful because the feedback of our collaboration during the Artisan Market had been so positive. Having previously spoken with the town clerk and mayor about our partnering with the council, I was able to offer the church's support of the lights switch-on by organising Sheep 'n' Shops for the council and free cups of tea and coffee for the shoppers.

Sheep 'n' Shops is a treasure hunt style activity where young people and their parents go around the town to find 'lost sheep' which are hidden in local shops. In Knutsford we had twenty-one shops partnering with us after Knutsford Town Council kindly agreed to write to them asking for their support for a fun activity which was designed to generate greater footfall through their shops during a community event. The shops would name their toy sheep something appropriate, so the Pudding Club fashion shop named their sheep 'Banoffee'.

Jenny Mossman (children's worker at the time) had attempted to make a toy sheep for this activity, but Jenny is not the greatest at knitting and so her sheep Norbert seemed to have an identity crisis in that it looked more like a camel with lumps where there were not supposed to be any! A jokey story developed after a few of my 'unkind remarks', which was that Norbert had been so upset by my comments that he ran away from the church to a local shop where he was now lost waiting to be found. He was actually at Roberta's, the beauty salon, trying to get a makeover. The *Knutsford Guardian* kindly printed the story and it became a good talking point for our church members and great fun affirming Jenny's ministry. Welcoming Norbert back to KMC a few weeks later and offering a stuffed sheep (who looked like a camel) a public apology, the prodigal sheep who returned after going astray was an amusing family service just prior to Christmas.

But to create a focal point of the church I had asked Mark Walton (a lecturer at Reaseheath Agricultural College) if he could provide me with three live sheep and a pen to put at the front entrance of KMC. Pete Thompson reminded me how you should never work with children and animals. I had the joy of working with children, animals and Jenny Mossman!

Mark kindly obliged with the sheep, which Jenny suggested we call Ba-a-a-arbara, Ba-a-a-arnaby and Ba-a-a-aarnabus! This was a corny joke which made a good number of people smile as they came over to inspect the pen of live animals. It was an amazing opportunity to speak to people, take their photos with the sheep and to invite them to our Christmas services.

In delivering the toy sheep to the shops partnering with us, I was able to introduce myself as the new Methodist minister in Knutsford and talk to them about partnering together in the future. The businesses had been pleased to get people through their doors as a result of our fun activity and all of them were keen to partner again in the future. It is likely that the activity will be repeated for a few years to come but developing the theme in such a way that ensures more people, both adults and children, are able to participate, with a proper marketing strategy in place a few months in advance. Cheshire Life were also hoping to run a feature on a future Sheep 'n' Shepherds project which we hope will more effectively draw people into the Christmas story.

In talking to some clothes shops, I mentioned a fashion show that had been produced during my campaigning work at Bible Society in the Greater Manchester Riddle of Life media campaign. I was able to tell them the story of the prodigal son and how the Heavenly Father always welcomes us back to Himself when we come to our senses and return to Him.

The *Home* fashion show had been a successful attempt of recapturing the spiritual heritage of Bible Society in engaging the cultural audience of today with a credible presentation of Bible. It had been a particular desire of mine to have such a presentation during this campaign, because the story of how Bible Society did a fashion shoot in *Vogue* magazine to launch their campaigns to culture, followed by a window display in the major London store Fennick's, had inspired me a few years earlier.

Luke Walton was the creative director who had met a couple of young fashion designers who helped us produce the show. And on one occasion when Luke had all but spent the show budget on the venue, models and food, he came to discuss the possibility of a further £4,000 to bring a band over from America to perform at the show. Their songs *Apologize* and *Prodigal* were to be the soundtrack for the fashion show production. But I knew that we could not justify the further expense on the show and so Luke had to say no to the possibility of the band One Republic coming to perform. Within weeks of our show, One Republic were top of the British charts with *Apologize,* produced by Timbaland. Showcasing a chart-topping band would have been a great campaigning story, but on this occasion it was not to be!

However, years later, being able to discuss a fashion show at the Urbis in Central Manchester with people in the fashion business was a credible conversation which enabled perception to be changed and future partnership possible. I look forward to one day hosting a charity fashion show in Knutsford in the not-too-distant future.

One principal to learn here must be that positive collaboration is important in opening doors and to securing future possibilities, alongside enabling credible engagement with a local community, businesses and the town council. The partnering with Knutsford Town Council enabled the collaboration in writing to the local shops and in demonstrating that we are people of good will, which has resulted in others demonstrating good will to us. The second principal is always to be open to possibilities of what could happen with the right partners and resources, no matter how unlikely they might at first appear. Acquiring the sheep enabled conversations and profile. A third principal would be to tell the story of what has happened in other situations in such a way as to draw people into the story. Allow them to see how they could have their place in the future story. Allow their imagination to join the dots for them. We wait to see if a Knutsford charity fashion show is a real possibility. A fourth principal is to use the Bible in your storytelling whenever possible, because it has the capacity to connect with people at a much deeper spiritual level. Going into the shops collecting a toy sheep to loudly joke, "I've come to round up my lost sheep!" drew people in to share in a joke and a spiritual truth. I *was* actually looking for lost sheep as I was on my travels!

This interaction with people was just the first chapter of what could be many. But it will be exciting to see how the story develops, particularly as the next campaign, Hope Together, unfolds in 2018.

Knutsford Town Council decided to host a monthly Makers Market[28] for the foreseeable future and we have enjoyed partnering with them in offering hospitality with free teas and coffees. The church is being mobilised to work with the community, partner with other agencies and build credible relationships by offering relevant facilities and provision for children and young families. On the first Sunday of each month there is now a wonderful community feel in Knutsford as people travel many miles to explore the Makers Market.

---

[28] See *http://www.themakersmarket.co.uk/markets/knutsford*

28

'Get in the Nativity Picture' and 'The Real Nativity'

After three years of doing Sheep 'n' Shops, it felt time to do something different, as the concept began to feel a little tired. We needed to raise the bar a little if we were going to keep people's interest and engage the local community.

During the campaign Biblefresh, I remembered a project called Get in the Picture. The concept was based on the idea of having a large board at a seaside resort near the beach, on which there would be pictures of a large woman in a swimming costume and a skinny man in his trunks. The faces of these characters would be missing with two holes instead, so that people could put their own heads through the holes and pose for an amusing photograph.

The Get in the Nativity Picture concept was to have a painting of the Nativity story with the faces omitted, so that whole families could pose for a Christmas Nativity photograph. Members of a family could be Mary, Joseph, a shepherd, angel or wise man. Alongside this picture, we would develop a Nativity scene with real animals to create a very authentic experience of entering into the Christmas story.

I put the idea to Peter Freeman (children's and family worker) in the summer of 2015, asking that he develop the project whilst I was away on sabbatical. Peter enthusiastically pulled a small team around him and was able to produce a large piece of scenery with the Nativity characters all in place, but with a shutter where their faces were, so that a photograph could be taken of any number of family members, with a painted face of those characters missing from the photo!

All those ladies who had always wanted to be Mary in the school play or the church Nativity would now have the opportunity to play the part.

Likewise, those who ended up as a donkey (or worse) could be Joseph, a shepherd, angel or wise man. The possibilities were endless.

When I first saw the Get in the Nativity Picture board I was really pleased by what Peter had produced, but very excited about the obvious potential that this gave us to engage with people from the local community.

Having spoken to Anna and Mark Walton the previous Christmas, they were keen to be involved, as Mark had kindly provided the sheep for Sheep 'n' Shops for the previous three years, from Reaseheath Agricultural College. Anna thought that she would be able to get a miniature pony as part of a Nativity scene, which would be very endearing for people to see. However, only a couple of weeks before the Christmas lights switch-on event in Knutsford, when we hoped to be hosting Get in the Picture, we found that the miniature pony was pregnant and that she could not travel!

Initially, I thought that we would end up with the sheep again but, undeterred, Anna asked if we could loan a donkey from Tatton Park Farm Estate. Thankfully the estate manager kindly agreed to loan us Sparkle the donkey who came complete with her Christmas hat and coat with her name on it. She was a real star as hundreds of people all came to stroke her in the pen that we had erected just outside the entrance to the church. As people came to see Sparkle the donkey, they were invited to have a family Christmas photograph taken free of charge.

People were asked to sign a permission form before having their photograph taken and we then sent them a copy of their photo, along with an invitation to all of our Christmas carol services. It was great fun, inviting everyone into church, where they could have a free coffee whilst they waited for their photograph to be taken, giving all of the children a goody bag with sweets and a booklet with the Christmas story in it. This was a very positive piece of advocacy for the Church and the Bible, as we invited people to enter into the Christmas story for themselves.

A large number of families then attended a Christingle service a few weeks later, but our Christmas services were all well attended too. This concept will now be developed for next Christmas because it was considered to be such a great success. The town mayor Councillor Tony Dean and his wife were great fun and joined with me to 'Get in the Nativity Picture' for a Knutsford Town photograph, but we also had the President of the Methodist Conference Rev. Steve Wild join Jackie Betts,

Ben Clowes, Carol and me in forming an Alderley Edge and Knutsford Circuit photograph.

However, not everyone was so pleased with this particular project, as they worried that we were dishonouring the holy family by allowing others to pose in a Nativity scene. Some apparently felt that it should not be in the worship area as it was a fun activity. But what a great opportunity it was to have people come into church, some of whom were doing so for the very first time, and have a positive, fun experience. I think that when explaining the project, my speaking about the seaside photos in swimming costumes had seemed too frivolous for some people and therefore this explanation had proved unhelpful! Hindsight is a wonderful thing! The fact that the *Methodist Recorder* then published a photo of Steve Wild and our circuit staff team alongside reports of Bramhall Methodist exploring the concept for the following year, meant those with reservations were enabled to change their viewpoint.

Raising the bar for the next year included exploring the possibility of hosting a dramatic presentation, *The Real Nativity,* actually on a farm the week after the Christmas lights switch-on, using the Get in the Nativity Picture concept with animals to engage the local community initially with publicity in the town. At a time when the Christmas story is no longer valued in society as perhaps it once was, we need to be creative in the ways that we tell the story, so that people can be enabled to enter into the story for themselves. As people begin to enter into the story, suddenly it becomes their story too.

Biblical literacy is probably at an all-time low and therefore we can no longer assume that people can engage with the stories of scripture as they once did. Therefore, I feel that the challenge to share Bible stories in culturally relevant and appropriate ways must be grasped by the Church today. Some might feel able to go into schools as part of an Open the Book team, but others may feel that this is beyond them. I therefore would encourage churches to explore ideas such as Get in the Nativity Picture as a fun way to engage people effectively, even if it is only on one particular weekend in the year.

In Knutsford we have now begun to combine the open-air crib service with a candlelit procession around the town to create another significant community event with our town council. This includes favourite Christmas carols accompanied by a brass band together with local school children singing along and a short seasonal message. There is even an arts theatre company who run workshops for families to build rather impressive lanterns. I particularly enjoyed sharing *The Chocolate Nativity,* with youngsters spotting the chocolate references in my alternative retelling of the Nativity. It certainly seemed to engage everyone present and the *Knutsford Guardian* was keen to run an article on the event afterwards.

Christmas is still the highlight of the year for many villages, towns and cities around our country and I feel that alongside hosting charity Christmas fayres and the like, which see hundreds of local people enter our church halls and premises for Christmas presents, bargains, good cakes and coffee at affordable prices, we have a responsibility to share with others the real meaning of Christmas.

The whole season of Advent is manic at KMC with many carol services, concerts and pastoral visits, but the highlight is still Christmas Eve and Christmas Day, coming into the presence of the Christ child once more and knowing Immanuel, 'God with us'. Christmas Day's family celebration is something that I look forward to each year as an amazing worship event for all the family and to share something of a Christmas gospel message with everyone. Some regard themselves as regulars in that they come to church every Christmas Day!

How wonderful it is to know Christ was born not just as a point in history, but also born into our hearts, and to celebrate that fact together.

We have experimented each Christmas with the use of different animals outside the church, whilst the Christmas Fayre and meals are available inside. Having Sparkle the donkey from Tatton Park in a pen at the front of church was certainly an attraction. But in 2016, the combination of small heifers in a pen outside church, the Get in the Nativity Picture board, and an invitation to attend our multimedia drama presentation *The Real Nativity – The Prince of Peace* complete with sheep and a donkey in the cast, was certainly successful in terms of engaging people with an interesting and appropriate event for young families.

KMC worship area had to be quickly reinstated in preparation for some of our Christmas carol services afterwards, but the following day, there was an invitation to worship in the stable!

The church had been converted into a stable for *The Real Nativity,* with pens for the sheep and 'Donk' the donkey who had starring roles in the specially written presentation. We had originally thought of using a local farm, but it was decided to bring the story into Knutsford town centre so that we could invite the whole community to experience the story for themselves actually in the stable. They could hear, see and even smell the story unfolding before their very eyes.

The concept was devised by Peter Freeman who asked Liz Howden to write the script and Anna Walton to direct the presentation. The actors were all church members, as were the sound, stage and lighting crew. We were also very grateful to J.F. Richardson for the loan of the sheep and to D. Heath for loaning the donkey, all of whom performed their lines very well!

There were those who felt that this was a very risky project because they believed you should never work with animals due to the possible accidents that could occur! However, we wanted people to have a realistic experience of the Nativity, with all the sights, sounds and smells of a stable. The God we believe in is not some old man sitting on a cloud, remote and distant from the muck and mess of the stable or our world. The God we believe in became vulnerable as the Christ child, He became flesh and dwelt amongst us, even in the mess and challenges of our world. Our God can enter into the mess, pain, struggles and darkness of our lives and of our world. He can empathise, help and even bring comfort into the most difficult of experiences.

Nativity Live presented the message of Christmas in an unforgettable, joy-filled way, which enabled people to have a real experience of the Nativity story for themselves.

For an interview and edited clip of *Prince of Peace,* please use the following links.

- Interview:
  www.youtube.com/watch?v=L43jyEWe0rk&feature=youtu.be
- Two-minute highlights clip:
  www.youtube.com/watch?v=GLc_GeIGy8A&feature=youtu.be

I would strongly encourage every church participating in Hope 2018 to make the most of the opportunities that Christmas gives us to present the message in credible, engaging ways. These are just some of the ideas we have tried in order to bring a message of hope during the season of Christmas.

29

Real Lives

After an amazing Real Lives festival in 2013, I found myself asking a few critical questions about the experience. It was undoubtedly a success with large numbers attending and very gifted communicators sharing with us, including a lovely guy called Paul Hinton as the evangelist, but I was left with a whole range of questions which I needed time to reflect upon.

For example, having invited so many unchurched people to events which were undoubtedly credible and presented in a very professional way, why was it that only a handful of forms were handed in by people wanting to do the Alpha course in a few weeks' time? And the honest truth is that those who wanted to enrol were people that we were already in contact with.

The festival had been envisaged by members of St. John's Parish Church, but their leadership had felt that KMC would be the best venue to host the events because it was more flexible, appealing to people who would not usually attend a church, in addition to which they were thinking of re-ordering their building which could have made it unavailable.

I received an email about the idea a few months prior to taking up my appointment as the minister of KMC to see if I had any objections to the mission/festival taking place in our building during my appointment, possibly in October of 2012 – literally weeks after my arrival! I felt that this would be a good start to my appointment, although I did have a few reservations as it was too early really after starting in a new post. I would be possibly hosting a mission in a town I did not know, as minister of a church I did not yet know, in partnership with another church I did not know, with an evangelist I had never heard of! However, I did know that if a mission was to happen in our church building, then it should be a partnership of churches working together in unity. I also knew that to say no to such a mission before actually even starting my appointment would send all the wrong signals to my future church and to other churches in the town whom I would hope to work with.

In writing back to the people seeking my feedback about the possibility of the churches working together, I was unwittingly starting the two churches down a path that had not yet been anticipated. Whilst there was a growing relationship between individuals at the churches, they had never done a major project such as this together.

The response to the mission being a joint project was positive, although I was later to find that most people in the early days of discussion still saw it as a St. John's mission. There were a few emails about the proposed speakers to check that I was happy with their preferred options of celebrity guests, all of which sounded quite exciting and the vision of a mission with these celebrities and an evangelist speaking alongside them really appealed to me. I also knew that as a result of all of my experiences of festivals and of campaigning, I ought to have some creative ideas to offer to the planning process.

So the email planning process began with the evangelist Paul Hinton being invited to lead the mission and three celebrities selected to share at a chat show event each evening. The first guest was the former police Chief Constable Robin Oake whose son Stephen had been tragically murdered. The second was Fiona Castle OBE who could speak about her life, fame and the tragic and untimely death of her husband, the entertainer Roy Castle who was possibly best known for the show *Record Breakers* in my childhood. The third was Dan Walker, the BBC TV sports presenter of *Football Focus* and other sports programmes in addition to hosting the occasional quiz, *Songs of Praise* and more recently *BBC Breakfast*.

However, after more careful consideration, it was decided that because the proposed October dates clashed with half term, the mission should be postponed until March 2013. This was an incredible relief to me, as I then felt that I would have more time to settle into the new appointment and to prepare both myself and the church for the mission.

On beginning life in Knutsford, I had to hit the ground running, as there were so many immediate challenges to face in leading a medium-sized church where expectations were high and there was so much to adapt to, having had eight years of work and ministry with Bible Society. The exercise of walking to and from church and doing most visits on foot, alongside a low cholesterol diet, meant that very quickly I lost weight – two stone and four pounds in six months to be precise!

An early meeting with the clergy and then the representatives of St. John's, Knutsford who were responsible for the mission was then arranged, but although the speakers were booked, there was still much to do. This was really helpful because I then felt able to own the process with the team and select those people from KMC whom we needed to be involved. Having the right creative people alongside those with a problem-solving, logistical mind and those with a 'can do' attitude was a must to develop the strategic plan and to have a timeline which was realistic and deliverable.

I needed a credible person within the church who could co-ordinate other people, standing beside me in the process of envisioning the church. Pete Bowler was the right man for the job. The creative people were Steve Benson (creative design, lighting and production), Phil Bland (staging and project-planning), Sue Cussons (prayer), Stuart Kirkham (marketing) and Marion Barker (publicity and presentations), with Henry Waters being co-opted later to build a set for the events.

The first core team meeting involved representatives from St. John's including Nigel Atkinson (vicar), Richard Reeve (head of mission and project leader) and Debbie Woods (a key lay leader), alongside the above-mentioned people. Time was of the essence; we were all getting to know each other, building relationships with each other, but it was important that we agreed on the purpose of the mission and how best to plan.

It was agreed that the main focus would be the adult audience, with each evening having a different age profile targeted, hopefully reaching the broadest possible audience. There were also conversations about the music that should be played both before the start of the events and after a short interval. I suggested that we consider having a musician play live and singer-songwriter Freddie Kofi was the person I had in mind. Those members of KMC who had heard Freddie sing when he supported Australian band Sons of Korah during their tour in 2010 were very supportive of the idea and this encouraged the St. John's contingent to agree to this in principal.

Paul Hinton came to preach at both churches in December, bringing the key message of *Be a Bringer,* giving church members the confidence in him as a person and also as a communicator. I suggested that whilst Paul was with us for the day, that we also have a core team meeting to discuss the vision for the mission with him and to ensure that we were all on the same page.

We met at The Angel public house on King Street, and Paul had a very clear idea of how each evening would run and the timings of the events. A meeting I had with Steve Benson the previous week was also important in having creative ideas of hosting and staging events credibly to discuss as a core team. Steve's experience of other similar situations while working with the BBC on *Songs of Praise* came into play, with his expertise raising the bar considerably in aiming for the highest production values. Whilst the ideas sounded sketchy at this point, it was helpful to have a nod of approval from all parties so that the creative process could move forward.

The marketing of the mission depended upon having a strong theme, and after conversations with Paul Hinton, it was agreed that Real Lives would be the right title, as the speakers were sharing of their real-life experiences and how their faith had brought them hope in the most challenging of situations. It was quite late in this process that we discovered that Paul and another evangelist, Roger Carswell, whom Paul worked in association with, had actually used this theme on a number of occasions. This then gave us the opportunity to see the artwork that was being used for a similar mission in Sheffield and we therefore decided to develop the ideas with the same company who had done the creative for their publicity. As we discussed the publicity, I strongly felt that if we referred to Real Lives as a festival, rather than a mission, that this would help to communicate our events with a wider audience in a more friendly and acceptable way.

Alongside the publicity materials and a marketing timeline which Marion and Stuart helped me to develop, teaser posters with three characters in a silhouette and a question mark on their chest were created to get the church members thinking about which three people they would invite to the festival. This was very much in keeping with the message of *Be a Bringer,* which Paul shared at both churches in December 2012, and therefore enabled people to pray for their friends, neighbours and colleagues as part of a prayer strategy developed by Sue Cussons.

Two prayer gatherings were planned at each church, with a Prayer and Pastries Saturday morning meeting at St. John's in February and an evening Prayer and Praise at KMC in March. Both were fairly well attended and helped again to build relationships within the churches and to recruit the necessary volunteers required for hosting, stewarding, catering, manning the bookstall and being on a prayer team. It was agreed to meet for prayer each night of the festival at 6.30pm to prepare ourselves properly, before the stewards and all of the speakers were briefed each night.

The creative ideas developed quickly for the building of a new stage by Phil Bland and a new set by Henry Waters, the painting of the set by Stuart Kirkham. Steve Benson drafted the plans for the sound and lighting required to give the festival the most professional feel possible within a tight budget! Pete Bowler co-ordinated the various activities and with his help I prepared the church with regular updates of the progress made, also aided by two different promo DVDs which Steve and Phil Benson created. These promos helped to give people enough confidence to invite their friends and were shared extensively on Facebook and on our website, alongside a smartphone card which enabled people to access it directly on their phones.

The week of the Real Lives festival arrived, with the set still being painted, the stage still being built and the media clips for each evening still to be prepared! It was a good job that I had total confidence in the people around me, because I was able to depend upon them totally.

Tickets had been made available for each evening which were free but had to be booked in advance. The first three evenings had a café-style layout downstairs with those bringing non-church friends and family sitting in the priority seats downstairs with drinks and nibbles on the tables. The balcony was made available for everyone else and we also had an overflow facility with a screen in the large hall, particularly with the final Dan Walker evening in mind. On the Sunday, we had the chairs put back into the usual formation used for services so that an extra hundred people could be accommodated, but thank goodness that we had the overflow ready for the twenty people who arrived late and were unable to find seats in the church.

There were stage lights and smaller spotlights on the tables, dry ice and amazing lighting effects to create a very impressive chat show atmosphere. People were amazed by the level of professionalism which had been achieved and particularly by the slick BBC-style production values of each evening. Paul commented that he had never done such a professionally produced Real Lives festival before.

Freddie Kofi performed a concert on the Friday evening which attracted people who possibly felt unable to invite friends to the more evangelistic evenings. Freddie was also able to prepare the audience each evening with a chilled music vibe which changed the feel of the event considerably by making it more relaxed. The other dimension which I had introduced with the help of my colleague Ben Clowes was to launch a Smooth Transitions project at Knutsford Academy. Supported by Julie and Tuesday King, Ben Williams (our youth worker at the time) went into the academy for a period of five weeks to run a choir workshop with young people. Students were selected to participate in the workshop based on who the teaching staff felt would benefit from the experience.

Ben with his team had met with the students to teach them the Gary Barlow jubilee song, *Sing,* in addition to which the students would meet Freddie for a workshop immediately before the event and then support him in singing one of his songs, *Gospel for the World.*

This sounds much easier than it actually was in practice, but the experience of those young people was amazing. They sang their song well in front of an audience of around two hundred people and then supported Freddie to receive rapturous applause. They should have felt pretty good about themselves for what they had achieved in a very short space of time. Each student was then given a download of a recorded version of their song. Parents and friends, as well as the assembled audience, were thrilled with the young people and the concert event as well.

The other evenings focussed more upon the spoken word, with a celebrity interview of around thirty minutes, a short interval, promo DVDs for Alpha and Christianity Explored (the follow-up courses offered by each church), a couple of musical items by Freddie and a preach for thirty minutes by Paul Hinton. Coffee and cakes were then served afterwards as people mingled and bought books from the bookstall, and a few spoke with the prayer team made available each night.

The 'hook' to attend for non-church members was definitely the celebrity guests, and certainly the publicity in the *Knutsford Guardian* articles each week for a month beforehand on each guest was key to engaging a wider audience of people. The relationship that had been developing with the paper through reports on the visit of Darrell Tunningley a couple of months earlier and through my monthly column *Rev. Rob Speaks* had enabled this to be achieved. I found the local paper very supportive of what we were doing in the community.

The dilemma I felt when reviewing the Real Lives festival with people afterwards was that some of their guests seemed genuinely surprised to sit through an evangelistic sermon even though the publicity clearly stated that Paul would reflect with us each evening on what the celebrity had said. Whilst we felt that we had been clear in our communication and publicity, we wondered, did it lack integrity to invite people to an evangelistic event on the basis of hearing a celebrity interviewed?

The consensus that I began to hear from people was that they would have preferred to hear more from the celebrity in an interview format, rather than have a combination of interview and preach. Certainly, there were those who strongly felt that this would have been more in keeping with where we were at as a church, or what they felt comfortable with as individuals. Some certainly felt that the gospel had been clearly communicated through people telling their story in a very open, honest, direct and, at times, humorous way.

The guests had all been well received and were communicators of calibre, but even with the profile of some of them and the relevance of their area of interest to some of the church members' families, it had still proven difficult for some of them to get their family and friends to attend. For example, football-mad husbands and sons still felt unable to come despite the presence of a TV celebrity in Dan Walker. I began to wonder, just what did you have to do to secure a positive response to an invitation?

For some people who had been unsuccessful in getting a son or husband to attend the Dan Walker evening, they were really disappointed when hearing just what a good interviewee he was. Dan was fun, entertaining, and informative and people commented, "You felt like you were mates chatting in his front room." But he was also very clear in sharing his faith and it was communicated with warmth and sensitivity. However, the same people felt relieved not to have their relative attend, when afterwards Paul proceeded to preach a fairly direct evangelistic message for up to forty-five minutes! This just may be where those people are currently at with sharing their faith with family, but some obviously felt relieved that non-attendance had protected their ongoing sharing of faith with loved ones. A few others, who had managed to get someone to attend, had actually taken their friends home during the interval to avoid the 'embarrassment' of having them preached at!

There is obviously a balance to strike in all of these experiences in wanting people to hear something of the gospel. The following Sunday evening, I hosted the Real Lives review chat show, when I interviewed a young student, Vicky Royal, from our church about her experience as a Christian in university and her vision to work with young people in

Tanzania. I then interviewed Billy Ainscough, a Liverpool fan who shared about his experience of being caught up in the Hillsborough tragedy and the impact that this had upon him. Billy spoke in a moving way of having a very real encounter with God just moments before he thought he was due to die, with dead bodies under his feet and alongside him in the crowd. He came to faith later as a result of the experience. Having Vicky and Billy share fully about their experience of coming to know Jesus in very different circumstances and then interact with people's questions seemed to effectively communicate to the people present. They were both inspirational and yet very different, sharing of their real-life challenges and of how God had guided them through to each attempt great things for Him. This approach seemed to work well.

It is true to say that the audience present were mostly church members, but one comment afterwards was that it had made someone's perception of Real Lives much more positive, in that they could now see the potential of us doing something as a church in an ongoing way. This had been an experiment to do a 'home-grown' version of a Real Lives chat show event which had worked, at least at a low-key level. There was the set, some basic stage lighting, two interesting guests and coffee afterwards. It had the brand identity of the festival with some of the elements of interview and hosting; it therefore offered a credible follow-up event.

To be absolutely clear, if I could turn back the clock in a Doctor Who tardis-style machine, and was given the choice to host such events again, I would still jump at the opportunity of having exceptional celebrity guests communicating well, with a gifted evangelist preaching the gospel effectively. My post festival critique is more a case of my wrestling with how best to offer such events in the future, with the benefit of insight gained through the experience. Real Lives has been an amazing experience of engaging large numbers of people with credible events, excellent guests and the highest quality presentation in a way which has raised the bar for us as churches in Knutsford. Anyone who attended Real Lives could not fail to be impressed by what had been achieved and I am full of admiration for the small core team who delivered an amazing festival.

Real Lives certainly informed my practice of launching the Alpha course with celebrities.

I am reminded of the words of St. Paul in Romans 1:16, 'For I am not ashamed of the gospel, because it is the power of God for the salvation of everyone who believes; first for the Jew, then for the Gentile.' And in reviewing some of 'my issues' after the experience of Real Lives, I would like to feel that Christian people were more confident in the gospel and that non-church friends would be open to hear more about it after the event. But the honest truth is that for some people, I would need to be very clear about the content of any event I was expecting them to invite their friends to. If it was going to have an evangelistic talk as part of the presentation, then I would obviously have to be very clear that this was the case, without dressing it in any other guise. Integrity is an important value for me personally and for the Church. The gospel is good news and needs to be shared with people, so that everyone has the opportunity to respond personally to God's love demonstrated for them in Jesus. As churches and individuals seek to share God's love in their local communities, there is also the responsibility to 'always be prepared to give a reason for the hope which we have in Jesus',[29] as St. Peter writes.

As I wrestle with 'my issues' there will be those who do not understand my dilemma, but I feel that the communication of the gospel is such a priority for the Church as we seek to offer 'hope in the main street' that it is worth exploring how to do so in the most effective and culturally sensitive way which is credible and has integrity. Word and deed mission has to have biblical content communicated at some point. The Real Lives festival and similar initiatives within a community as part of the ongoing relational ministry and mission of the Church offer insights to this conversation.

---

[29] 1 Peter 3:15.

30

The World is My Parish

For many clergy today, they are so consumed with the business of local church, trying to spin all of the plates a local church expects them to keep spinning, that 'parish becomes their world'. It is all-consuming! But Wesley confidently proclaimed, "The world is my parish."

Whilst I personally might find that spinning all of the plates in the local church can sometimes feel all-consuming, I would like to also live on that bigger map with Wesley and consider how the world can quite literally be our parish. Certainly, with the advent of social media and global communications, we live in a global village and I wonder if John Wesley would even need to get in a boat to America or ride his horse many thousands of miles to effectively communicate with people today.

I was recently invited by my former employers at Bible Society to join a group of church leaders on a visit to China. When we met for our briefing meeting at 77 Great Peter Street in London, the headquarters of the public think tank Theos, it was a privilege to hear from the Bible Society Group CEO James Catford (prior to his departure from Bible Society) of his experience working with both the government and Church in China over a number of years.

James commented humbly that he was "sharing ignorance" with the assembled group of leaders. He then urged us to forget what we knew and to consider that China was experiencing the biggest revival that the world has ever known. Following World War II there were possibly around eight hundred thousand Christians in China, whereas today there are officially thirty-eight million and unofficially at least double that, if not nearer to one hundred million. That means one tenth of the Chinese population are Christian. This level of growth has never been seen before, not even in the early Church! The Welsh revival cannot compare with such growth.

But quite probably this revival might not look like you would expect. Some of our preconceived ideas of what a revival might look like in China are certainly wide of the mark, partly because when Communism came into China, time in some sense stood still. In fact, rather than modern contemporary songs, you are more likely to be singing traditional hymns in many of the largest churches in China! The hymns tend to be very European and archaic in nature.

When the Archbishop of Canterbury, Justin Welby, visited China in 2015, he was apparently surprised by what he experienced and contemplated on whether you need to see certain features in the worship for it to be truly revival? And yet the Church are very earnest, orderly and there is a certain expression of pain amidst their experience of revival. Certainly, many of the older generation of church leaders have experienced great persecution and imprisonment in the past and maybe they are rightly very mindful of this fact still. In actual fact, in James Catford's view, this is probably what revival does look like! Whilst much of what you experience there does confound your expectations and defies what you think you know, God is very definitely at work.

Our visit to China was deemed to be strategically very important, because of our exposure to the situation in China, the culture and all that is happening there, whilst sharing something of our own experience in the UK. The Three-Self Patriotic Church is obviously patriotic to the country, as the name suggests, and the government want the Church to help keep the peace in a time of religious unrest (as far as Islam is concerned), despite the fact that it is a regime of power and control. The question which they must consider is whether Christianity is going to help create and maintain peace in the nation. Alternatively, does it bring some unrest? The Bible should be seen as part of the answer, not part of the problem. There are five religions living in relative harmony in China, which do not include Judaism. And as Christians we should be the very first to bring reconciliation and to campaign for social justice.

There are obviously tensions, with examples of government officials ordering that crosses be taken down from churches in some provinces, partly because the Church could be seen as becoming too influential. However, other officials are keen that the Church is instrumental in caring for the frail and elderly. So therefore the situation can be rather confused and varied, with one foot on the brake and another on the accelerator!

The truth is that China is just so large, with thirty percent of the world's total population, that whatever you have heard or read in the media may be true somewhere and at some point, but it is not the whole story and certainly our experience was very positive. So I take this opportunity to 'share my ignorance' to hopefully change some of the outdated perceptions that people have of China.

As I prepared for our Vision visit, there were those who were concerned that I might get arrested as a Christian, and when I told them that we were distributing Bibles in the poorer rural areas, some assumed that I was smuggling them in or that I might get arrested and imprisoned for such activity! The following analysis of what we experienced during an inspirational ten days is offered as my contribution to the developing vision for the Church and people of China.

The story of the gospel in China began 'once upon a time' when missionaries from the West brought wonderful things to China, opening schools, hospitals and building churches. But the other side of the story is that they arrived on ships bringing opium to the masses, which is how our government managed to balance the payments being made for the import of tea to Britain. Certainly, the Opium Wars are a sad part of our political history. The missionaries would preach against the evils of opium, whilst also earning an income as translators for some of the businessmen who were embroiled in the trade. This working relationship is hard to reconcile, but then, it is hard to contextualize to a very different time and culture.

The missionary hero that many people still make reference to in China is Hudson Taylor, who as a young man sailed for China not knowing if he would ever see his family again. He is still today a role model for cross-cultural mission, in that he began to dress like the Chinese, eat and live like them. This was judged to be scandalous in that day, but it enabled the Chinese to relate to him and for him to engage them in a way that other westerners could not.

The China Inland Mission (CIM) was a faith venture and Taylor went to Changsha in the Hunan province. It was where the missionaries had the least success and so he went to encourage them; it was the toughest place! At one sad point in the history of their mission, there were one hundred and fifty missionaries beheaded during the Boxer rebellion. But when the government later offered compensation to Taylor, he refused because he said that they were going to be forgiven "as Jesus teaches us". This gave further credibility to CIM, with many more people feeling called to serve as missionaries as a direct result and it was also a very clear statement of love to the Chinese. Taylor lost his wife and children in China, but his legacy still continues today and it would not be an understatement to comment that the Church growth seen today is reaped as a result of those who have faithfully sown the seeds of the gospel and even the blood of the martyrs in the past. CIM was renamed Overseas Missionary Fellowship when they were forced to leave China during the Cultural Revolution.

The Cultural Revolution is another sad chapter in the history of China, with the communists closing all Christian churches, schools and colleges, with highly educated people being forced to work on the land in rural areas. Christians were not allowed to meet in public, but many met secretly underground in small groups to pray together and to encourage each other in what can only be described as a time of persecution, with many people imprisoned or disappearing. The Bible and other books were burnt in front of people as something of a statement and a very real spectacle. Those who lived through this period are hesitant to speak of their experiences. It was a dark time, but the younger generation are living in a very different time now that the Cultural Revolution has long since ended.

It is into this context that the Church in China is now growing at a phenomenal rate with the Jiangsu province today experiencing a five percent growth each year, with a new church being planted each week. They are giving believer's baptism to five hundred thousand people a year, though the availability of pastors and very strict teaching programmes limit this number. There is a massive shortage of church leaders to care for these churches, particularly in the rural areas. There are twenty-two seminary colleges training students in preparation for future ministry, but the resources are limited and the partnership with United Bible Societies is vital to meeting the needs.

The Bible is now more valued than ever; it is a precious book for which there is incredible demand, with many Christians never having had their own copy, particularly in the poorer rural areas. On 14th October 1987, Amnity Printing Company began printing the Bible in Nanjing, China for the Chinese people, but also for many other areas of the world. They have printed over one hundred and twenty-seven million Bibles with seventy million Bibles printed for China. To visit Amnity is an inspirational experience as you see Bibles rolling off the printing presses (some of which are British) every second, being prepared and packaged for various parts of the world to the very highest standards.

Certainly, the availability of the Bible in China is a major facet of the Church growth, with it being made available freely to those who cannot afford it through the gifts of Bible Society supporters and also being heavily subsidised by United Bible Societies. Through them the paper is supplied free of charge, enabling Bibles to be sold for less than £1 to everyone else through registered bookstores at local churches. Because the Bible has been a banned or burnt book in the past, it is now treasured and valued. People are genuinely passionate for scripture.

Whilst distributing Bibles in a rural church, we had a queue of mature people waiting for their first Bible and to see their disappointment when we thought that we had run out of Bibles was quite heartbreaking. One of our team offered a lady a bookmark as consolation, but her crestfallen face seemed to communicate, "I haven't walked miles for a bookmark; I want a Bible!" Thankfully another box of Bibles was collected from the minibus and she had her heart's desire as a Bible was presented to her. On another occasion, we were surprised by a lady who had journeyed with us as a guide around the Avatar tourist site suddenly declaring that she wanted to become a Christian. Apparently, she had watched us every step of the way and was surprised by us. When given a Bible, she said, "I will cherish this Bible as I cherish my life!" which seemed to communicate what others seemed to be expressing in their tears of joy as we presented Bibles in many remote rural villages.

Two pastors, having travelled two hundred kilometres, arrived at a Bible distribution centre having heard a rumour that we were visiting. They wanted Bibles for the new Christians in their churches, so we were able to provide one hundred and eighty Bibles for them. Their joy was replicated on many other occasions during our visit, with poor Christians walking two hours just to meet with us, and yet their hospitality was always generous. Whilst it was a privilege to take God's precious word into these situations, I always felt that we were receiving far more than we were giving.

During one church visit, I felt that I had never heard a church choir sing so flat or a piano player make me feel so much like Liberace or Jools Holland! I had to conclude that any growth experienced in this context was not as a result of human factors or musical excellence; it would be 'just God'. And certainly, as you spoke to church leaders, they constantly mentioned God's grace and Him being at work in surprising ways. So for those of us who would like to analyse, explain or understand the Church growth and to apply the lessons to the wider Church, I have to say that there is a sense that God is at work, it is 'just God'. Church leaders were very clear to us when they spoke of the work of the Holy Spirit to explain why the Church was growing.

It is true to say that God never works in a vacuum and the context is very important in understanding what is happening. The freedom since the Cultural Revolution means that there is now the favour of the government, which we saw in the appreciation and support of government officials during our visit. In fact, after our reception with one official in the Zhangjiajie province, he then rang ahead to his contemporary in the next province who spontaneously arranged a banquet for us and for an official photographer to capture his presentation of a commemorative gift to our group. Having government officials then drive through the early morning rush hour traffic with their staff just to bid us farewell and to wave us off from the hotel seemed to be a measure of favour that we had not expected and certainly contrary to what the media would have you believe.

Young people who have been to university are also said to be dissatisfied with materialism after the economic boom and are looking to the Christian Church to satisfy something of the spiritual vacuum that they are feeling. Particularly in the city areas, large numbers of young people are joining churches. It was great to visit Jinling Seminary where young students who were from all over the country were accepted because they were capable of speaking English to a higher standard. They were then trained and empowered to lead worship each week. They and other students in the Hunan Seminary (mostly under the age of forty) were empowered to lead churches and to secure the future growth of the Chinese Church.

The Church is offering social welfare to the elderly and blind in their locality, which makes them attractive to their communities, but also to the government as the alternative social welfare service provider. The Church brings added value and benefits to the government and society as a whole, in bringing hope to people in times of need. In this context it is the USP[30] of the Church.

Personal testimony of people sharing their faith with family and friends was seen to be an important factor in the growth of churches. In

---

[30] Unique Selling Point.

fact, there were repeated mentions in people's stories of the quality of individual Christian's lives impacting their own, because of the difference that could be seen as a result of the personal transformation. Changed attitudes and behaviour attracted people's interest and desire to know what had made a difference in people's lives. It was described as a mysterious thing during a visit to the China Christian Council and the National Committee of the Three-Self Patriotic Movement of the Protestant Church in China.

Public evangelism is still not allowed in some areas and leaflet distribution is deemed to be ineffective, but people are invited by friends and family to evangelistic gatherings at the church and the fruit of their faith means that this invitational approach is very successful. Social media is also used effectively to communicate, with radio and the internet offering good ways for the Chinese to interact with Western culture and Christian internet content specifically.

The importance of the healing ministry should not be underestimated either, particularly in the rural areas, with numerous stories of people being healed: one of a tumour on someone's shoulder, others needing a kidney transplant and the most spectacular being a man whose wife was given up for dead after an accident but was later found to be alive! They had even placed her in a body bag, and as they were about to move the body to the mortuary, they realised that the body was still warm and that there was a pulse. He had not even recognised his own wife when he initially visited her at the hospital, but as the church prayed, a miracle of healing was experienced. He later introduced his wife standing at the back of the church, who shared her testimony with us.

The commitment and sacrifice of church leaders who were totally sold out for God was also an impressive facet of our visit. The high level of commitment gave an authenticity to their message and ministry. Certainly, the way that they were received during our visits demonstrated a deep love. They were obviously hugely respected, which was not just because of their role, but because of who they were. It was obvious to our team, having spent time with some of these guys, that they were the real deal!

All of this is undergirded by prayer and it was always good to hear the amens or hallelujahs repeatedly spoken by the members of churches during any act of public prayer. The whole church engages and prays. In Britain, it is almost like we are going to the theatre or opera when we pray; there is a respectful silence with the risk of people being disengaged;

we watch and observe. Whereas in China, it's more like a football match: we participate, people shout encouragement and get involved actively; they are totally engaged in the prayer; there is an ownership of the prayer; it is *their* prayer.

In fact, in China, you see the Word (Bible) and prayer working together, with an emphasis upon scripture memory, as many did memorise whole passages of scripture when it was a banned book. That way they could recite to themselves and others the Word of God. God's Word was very definitely taken into their hearts and as a result it impacted their whole being and certainly they would never take that for granted. Scripture, therefore, formed part of their prayers too.

I do not want to write a romanticised account of what is happening in China, as there are so many aspects of the situation that I am still struggling to get my head around. I am merely 'sharing my ignorance' with you in an attempt to re-educate readers about the current reality of the situation in China, as I have not been arrested for distributing Bibles and I did return safely to the UK!

I do not know if it is appropriate to call what is happening in China 'revival' as it is all so new. It reminds me more of the early Church than anything that has happened in Wales or the Hebrides or elsewhere! People are coming fresh to Christianity rather than being renewed or revived and the statistics are outstripping anything that has been previously experienced.

There are undoubtedly some mistakes being made by the Chinese Church along the way in their efforts to keep pace with the growth they are experiencing with limited resources available. I do feel that as new church buildings are built, that the wider community use of the building should be considered and that pews are not the best seating option in most situations. The need to be more Chinese and less Western in the worship styles offered should be explored, alongside a legitimately Chinese contemporary worship, rather than choir-led services appealing to a younger age group. But having young Korean Chinese Christians Li Mei and Mam Fi Hua lead worship songs so passionately will stay with me as an abiding memory of our Vision visit.

However, I feel that it is important for the Church in the West to humbly take seriously what is happening in China. Whilst the importance of the Chinese economy for the rest of the world, and certainly Britain, should not be underestimated – if our former Chancellor of the Exchequer's fairly recent comments about a golden era and running towards China should be taken seriously – the spread of Christianity and growth of the Chinese Church must also be considered. The need to invest resources responsibly where there is need should be a priority for churches in the West to ensure that global kingdom growth continues. Whether this is in training new leaders, making the Bible freely available to even more poor people, or in praying for the Church and people of China, each church and leader should decide, but hopefully what I have shared will enable these issues to become known and to be discussed and responded to.

I have been greatly encouraged by all that I experienced in China; it has given me fresh hope for global Christianity and certainly I look forward to welcoming the Chinese who will no doubt come to our shores to share their faith, as Hudson Taylor and many others did in China many years ago. When they do arrive, we need to welcome them hospitably in humility and learn from them.

31

Thin Places and Holy Ground

My wife Carol and I have a special place, a place that over the years we have ventured to whenever we have important life choices and decisions to make. 'Our place' (not that we own it, you understand) is situated nicely between the village of Alton (with Alton Towers nearby), where Carol grew up as a child, and Whiston village where I grew up and where a number of my family still live today. I refer to the beautiful picturesque woodland area of Dimmingsdale.

Dimmingsdale is where Carol and I have walked together, kicked leaves together, had time to talk properly together, prayed together, and taken our dogs Poppy and Tammy. We have stood on the footbridges watching the calming waters running by together, appreciated the birds and wildlife together, but also been aware of God's presence with us and felt near to Him there. We have felt a sense of peace about those big decisions and even felt God's guidance in what we have discussed and done. And we have nearly always rewarded ourselves with a coffee and cake, or even a meal at the Ramblers Retreat coffee shop, afterwards.

Dimmingsdale is 'our place', our special place, and no doubt it is probably other people's special place too if the number of people frequenting Ramblers Retreat is anything to go by! It is a place where people can go for a walk around the lakes and woodland, to relax and find peace as they enjoy the beautiful Staffordshire Moorlands countryside. Maybe they even feel close to God there, as we certainly do.

During a recent sabbatical, when I began to reflect upon my own spiritual journey, I was able to travel to some places that have become very important to me in my spirituality, places which have taken on a significance for me personally which others might also appreciate. Whilst their appreciation might be different to my own, places do become significant in special ways.

I had always wanted to visit Iona, Scotland ever since we had a Bible and Theology Week during my theological training at Wesley College, with John Bell of the Iona Community. Our college lecturers at the time wore suits, shirts and ties, but when our guest lecturer arrived wearing brightly-coloured jeans, large cowboy boots, a chequered shirt, neck scarf and a hat, we wondered who this guy could be! It was to be the highlight of our theological training when John Bell made us laugh, cry and stretched our comfort zones theologically, whilst also singing together as he shared with us in a very personal and challenging way. A college community of lecturers, students, guests, evangelicals, liberals, feminists, young, old, black, white, university graduates and the rest of us, all became one together. We were a community of Christian family together.

But the journey to Iona was horrendously challenging, plus the expense of this journey and the abbey accommodation was such that any sabbatical grant began to look a little inadequate. Carol and I both began to think and feel that it had better be worth it! And it certainly was. But the challenge of just getting there was quite a pilgrimage/journey all by itself, especially when I was confronted by the number of people begging on the streets of Glasgow and in particular a young girl whose eyes I mistakenly looked into. So I wrote the following meditation:

She could have been my daughter,
As I looked into her eyes,
And I felt so helpless for her,
Wanting to help, but how?
Limited time and no resources,
So I end up walking by.

She could have been my daughter,
As I looked into her eyes,
So I asked the hotel waiter
'bout the beggars on the street.
"Don't know why the police don't move them on,"
He said. "It's quite a problem this year!"

She could have been my daughter,
As I looked into her eyes,
I wonder where she sleeps at night,
Or how she ever gets fed?

Wonder what her story is?
I'll never know – I just walked by!

She could have been my daughter,
As I looked into her eyes.

Reflection on My Journey – Give the Man a Medal

From Knutsford via Stockport,
To Manchester Piccadilly,
On train to Glasgow Central,
Then on foot to Queen Street,

On train to Oban,
Then quick to the ferry Oban to Craignure,
Then coach across the Isle of Mull,
Travel sick to Fionnphort,
Then ferry again to Iona,
Luggage on a trailer,
And walk up the hill,
Arriving at the Abbey,
Give the man a medal,
But he only gets a cup of tea,
I've arrived at long last – he thinks – I've arrived!
But the journey – has only just begun!

For many years, Iona has attracted pilgrims who are in search of the sacred. This desire to find holy ground is no new thing, you can trace this journey back to the sixth century voyage of Saint Columba, but today's pilgrims who arrive on the jetty are quite literally from every corner of the world. George MacLeod, the founder of the Iona Community, described the island as a "thin place" – only a "tissue paper" separating the material from the spiritual.

MacLeod, as a parish minister working in Govan, Glasgow, realised that the Church was failing to engage seriously with the poor and their concerns. In 1938, he had the vision to rebuild the Iona Abbey Community and in doing so to also rebuild the sense of community in urban contexts such as Govan and to see the re-engagement of church with everyday life. He brought together young ministers, students and unemployed craftsmen to rebuild the cloisters at the abbey. The whole abbey community accommodation has since been completed, enabling guests such as me to stay at the abbey for a week and join in the rhythm and pattern of life. Worship and work flow together as part of this pattern, fostering a sense of community. So whether people do their chores, attend worship, seminars, courses, go on trips to Staffa or share in the pilgrimage, they are enabled to engage with each other and with God. We did not actually meet in the chapter house to discuss a chapter of the Rule of Benedict as the Benedictine monks did, but we certainly could appreciate something of the experience in the programme of activities.

The Iona Community has for many years run a weekly pilgrimage around the island, stopping at places of significance – some historical, others religious, or simply just thought-provoking. The Iona Community's witness of perceiving a close connection between the spiritual and the material is reflected in this pilgrimage: with one stop taking you to the prayerful inspiration of Columbian times, while the next may highlight the struggle for justice and peace in the developing world. The pilgrimage is led by staff from the abbey and MacLeod Centre and is never the same twice!

The off-road pilgrimage is seven miles long and takes you around the island, but you do need proper walking boots with good ankle support and waterproof trousers and coats, so it is a challenge both physically and spiritually. Doing the pilgrimage with people of different nationalities, cultures, backgrounds, theologies, churchmanship and spirituality certainly adds another dimension to the whole experience. Being aware of the spiritual heritage of the setting alongside the promptings to make a fresh start by members of the abbey staff team, who become your spiritual directors for the day, enables you to make the most of this particular journey.

Our first stop was at the nunnery which had been founded by the Augustinians in the early thirteenth century and we were asked to think about those unknown women (and men) who never make the history books or major platforms and yet they influence our lives by their example and contribution. The pilgrimage included a crossroads where we were invited to reflect upon those times in our life journey when our decisions take us down new and unfamiliar paths. In my mind's eye I was back in Dimmingsdale kicking a few leaves with Carol by my side.

The personal highlight of our pilgrimage was St. Columba's Bay where it is said that Columba and his followers landed in the year 563, on what is a very pebbly beach, from Ireland on their leather-bound boat known as a curragh. Here, not only did we get to eat our sandwiches after a long morning's walk, but we were asked to consider the things which hold us back from making a fresh start, or that weigh us down as we journey forward. We were then invited to pick up two stones, one which would be symbolic of that which we wish to let go of – something we need to leave behind – and then, having thrown this into the sea, we would pick up a second stone without turning back as a symbolic sign of a new direction or commitment that we have made, before continuing our journey.

I picked up a large stone to represent the expectations of others, which as a minister I have foolishly tried to live up to. And then, greedily, I picked up a second stone to represent my own feelings of inadequacy which hold me back in life and ministry. I threw them both into the sea as far as I could and then picked up a small third stone as a commitment to do ministry differently and to make a new start as part of my sabbatical journey.

Later, I rang home to keep in touch with Carol, only to find that the new Chair of District Rev. Andrew Lunn wanted me to go on three different residential courses if I was to supervise a new probationer minister in our circuit. We later welcomed a recognised and regarded minister Rev. Scott Manning and his family from South Africa. But ironically, I needed to be booked on these courses before this appointment could be made. I felt like going back to St. Columba's Bay to fish the largest stone out of the sea again! So much for my commitment to a fresh start of not succumbing to the expectations of others. I am, after all, a man under authority and it is great to have Scott as a colleague too.

We enjoyed the beautiful scenery on our pilgrimage and were reminded of the importance of community as we journeyed together. We also visited the Hermit's Cell, a simple circle of stones representing the place where Columba and others would escape the busy life of the monastery to spend a period of prayer and reflection. As we walked over stepping stones, through the mud and over the stiles, it was a reminder of our role in the world with all of its different challenges and conflicts, particularly as the need becomes even more apparent with the number of refugees, asylum seekers and vulnerable people appearing on our TV screens in the recent past. We do have a prophetic role in becoming a voice for the voiceless, building bridges where there are only boundaries and borders, helping dialogue wherever and whenever possible.

Having already visited the Holy Island of Lindisfarne on a few occasions, it was helpful to build upon those Celtic experiences and to be able to learn of Saint Columba alongside the stories of Saint Cuthbert. I have stayed during both of my sabbaticals in The Bothy at St. Cuthbert's Centre, where there is accommodation for just one, which was ideal for my purposes. It was also good to share morning prayer with the congregational warden, lunch and night prayer with members of the St. Aidan and Hilda Community, the possibility of evening prayers at the Parish Church, and conversations with Andy Raine (a founder of the Northumbria Community) and his wife Anna. I was also able to visit the Northumbria Community's retreat centre Nether Springs which is a lovely prayerful place.

The rhythm of prayer, walking, reading and writing formed a powerful spiritually enriching experience, with the tidal times ensuring that the tourists would have to leave at a particular time, leaving those of us staying and living on the island to our own devices. I began to smugly feel like an islander, rather than just a mere tourist; but in reality, I was only staying for a week, so I was actually in some sense still a tourist even though I felt much more like a pilgrim and in tune with the rhythm of the island. One challenge of our lives is whether we live as tourists or pilgrims!

There are so many things to explore and to experience. The island is indeed a 'thin place', with the opportunity at times to even be totally alone on St. Cuthbert's Islet just set off the island with a cross at its centre. It is believed that St. Cuthbert went for retreat onto the islet and as the seals look at you, wondering why you are invading their space, it is easy to understand why the saint would escape there too.

The silent retreat walk around the island is also well worth trying, but for me the highlight was to do the Pilgrim's Way, despite the strong wind and pouring rain. The awful conditions seemed to make the experience all the more authentic and the mud underfoot meant that taking off your boots to do the latter stages in barefoot seemed the most sensible option. I certainly felt like a pilgrim by the end, but a warm shower and a complete change of clothing was certainly required!

32

Walking in the Footsteps of Jesus

During my appointment at Bible Society, I was seconded to Evangelical Alliance to work with Krish Kandiah, Steve Clifford (General Director of the Evangelical Alliance), Alexandra Lilley and their team to develop the Biblefresh campaign.[31] One stream of Biblefresh was to give people Bible experiences which enabled them to engage with scripture in new and creative ways, to bring God's Word alive for them. What better Bible experience could they have but to walk in the footsteps of Jesus and to hear scripture in the actual context and setting of the reading?

It was Andy Frost (Share Jesus International and son of the late Rob Frost) who first spoke to me about organising a pilgrimage to the Holy Land. Issa Tahhan of Special Pilgrimages had approached Andy about hosting a pilgrimage, but he asked me to meet with Issa and to explore the possibility of hosting it myself. I had met Issa when he was assisting Rob Frost in sorting out all of the accommodation for the Easter People conference and therefore he was someone I knew that I could work with and rely upon. We met on a few occasions and the vision for a Biblefresh pilgrimage began to develop, with a team of leaders being invited to assist me in hosting coaches, events, worship celebrations and visits to pilgrimage sites.

Pam Rhodes would be the consummate professional in hosting our very own *Songs of Praise* gathering at Caesarea Maritima, with singer-songwriter Dave Bilbrough and his wife Pat sensitively providing the music. Phil Gough, Methodist minister in Leyland and team leader from Summerfire's Firefest events, worked alongside me in hosting one of the coaches. Martin Turner, superintendent minister at MCHW (at the time), with his wife Biddy, worked alongside his colleague Tony Miles

---

[31] See the chapter *Biblefresh and the Proper Bible* on page 171.

(supported by his wife Frances) who also presents at Premier Radio and regularly does *Thought for the Day* on Radio 2. Ann Hall (superintendent at Linacre Mission at the time) was supported by her late husband Tim Hall, who sadly died quite prematurely in 2015. He was ministering in Southport. And we were also joined by Gail Hunt (minister in Knaresborough), her husband David, and a whole group from their church, as well as Neil (Studge) Rees (Bible Society) and his wife Kirsty, who had incredible knowledge of Bible translation and was a great support throughout the pilgrimage.

We went for a recce tour in October 2010 with a few of the leaders to develop the sense of team and to orientate ourselves to the places that we were due to visit. It was very special for Carol and me to celebrate our wedding anniversary on the shores of Galilee with a few good friends. We were hosted by members of Issa's family and his contacts whom we would be working with throughout the pilgrimage. It was a wonderful experience, with some of our group renewing their baptismal vows at Yardenit, the baptismal site on the River Jordan, the same waters in which Jesus Himself was baptised by John the Baptist. There were those moments when we were particularly aware of God's presence with us, in the boat on Galilee and also in the prison dungeon where it is believed Jesus was put before His crucifixion. But the whole experience prepared us to have more confidence to invite others to join us and in actually leading a pilgrimage ourselves.

My friend Colin Smith, superintendent minister in Barnet at the time (now in Cambridge), and his Anglican colleague Richard Watson, who was serving as the area dean of Barnet and rector of St. Mary the Virgin, East Barnet, led a very successful parish pilgrimage in June 2011 as part of Biblefresh.

The logistics of then leading a pilgrimage with one hundred and seventy people in November 2011 on three coaches were certainly challenging, but Special Pilgrimages handled the arrangements admirably and our team worked well together, with each leader having an opportunity to speak or lead one of the celebrations. In inviting Martin Turner to preach at the garden tomb, I simply said, "If you can't preach a great sermon on resurrection at the garden tomb, then where can you?" It was intended to be a joke, but I had every confidence in Martin and each of the other leaders that we would be blessed by their ministry.

How great it was to have Pam Rhodes interviewing people at our *Songs of Praise* service and to have Tony Miles interview members of

Bible Society staff based in the Holy Land about the challenges of living out their faith amidst all of the troubles and conflict that they have seen. For all of our pilgrims it was certainly challenging and moving to hear first-hand these accounts of their personal struggles and opportunities to share their faith with others.

Having two boats together on the Sea of Galilee to lead an act of worship, along with Dave and Pat Bilbrough, Pam Rhodes and Tony Miles speaking, was a great way to experience the beauty of Galilee. And it was poignant that we particularly remembered our friend Maureen Wenn back home in Calverton who had wanted to be with us on the pilgrimage. Sadly, her husband David had been seriously ill in the lead-up to the pilgrimage and his funeral coincided with the day that we were on Galilee. As Maureen and her daughters prepared for David's funeral, they had chosen the hymn *Dear Lord and Father of Mankind*. It includes the words, 'In simple trust like theirs who heard, beside the Syrian sea, the gracious calling of the Lord, let us like them, without a word, rise up and follow thee.' It continues, 'O Sabbath rest by Galilee, o calm of hills above.' So it seemed appropriate at the time, as we prayed for Maureen and all of the family, that we also sang the hymn actually on the Sea of Galilee.

There were many very special 'God moments'. Singing a cappella in some of the churches was certainly spine-tingling in poignancy; certain carols will never feel quite the same again and will always transport me to the Holy Land. And it was also very special having my dad Charlie, who was with me on the pilgrimage, reading about the shepherds, as a modern-day shepherd, in Shepherds' Fields. I will also treasure the photograph we had together immediately afterwards.

After assisting with the renewal of baptismal vows for many people at Yardenit, it felt appropriate to ask Phil Gough and Ann Hall to assist me in renewing my own baptismal vows. A dove fluttered down from a nearby building as I came back up out of the water and I was quite overcome by God's presence and power. It is impossible to put into words the experience, or the way in which I personally encountered God in that moment. Such was the power of the experience that I just had to remain standing in the water as I could not move, it was just so awesome! I urged Phil and Ann to leave me and to attend to themselves and other members of the party. I just needed time alone to capture the moment and to be in the presence of God for a while. Whilst the pilgrimage was organised to give other people a Bible experience as part of Biblefresh, I was also personally blessed and had my very own experience.

Some of you reading this might feel quite cynical or sceptical about such 'God moments' and certainly one of our pilgrims, Julie Weaver, would have described herself in that way too as we journeyed towards Gethsemane from the Mount of Olives. I will allow Julie to explain in her own words.

Extracts from Julie Weaver's journal written at the time:

Friday 25/11/11 (Wow Day!)

We walked down to the Garden of Gethsemane; cars everywhere, horns, noise! I was very sceptical (as usual) when the guides were claiming these were the actual olive trees Jesus touched!

I went into the church, it was very dark (meant to feel like night/dark place).

A priest was taking a service. I sat down and as I closed my eyes I heard the priest speak in English! He said, "I am so pleased you have come." I was sure I hadn't heard English when I came in – I opened my eyes – he was talking quietly and gently but I couldn't understand; it was definitely a foreign language. I closed my eyes again. I heard him say, "I will help you. I will guide you."

I was shocked, tears rolling down my face. I couldn't stop. (I am glad it was dark!)

I sat for quite a while – didn't know what to do, where to go.

I knew it was time to go soon so I stood and wandered out of the door. I felt really shaky. Was that Jesus? I saw Phil and decided to tell all!

After Julie had told Phil, I noticed that she was rather tearful, so I went over to see if she was alright.

Phil told her to tell me what had happened, so she recounted the story and then said, "But things like this don't happen to me, God doesn't speak to me!"

I simply replied, "He does now!"

I will allow Julie to finish the story from her journal:

I still can't quite believe it! Me, the sceptic! In fact, I think if I hadn't told someone I would have persuaded myself it was nothing by now.

I still have that quiet/gentle voice in my head. What will happen next? Do I need to do anything? How will I be guided?

Sunday 27/11/11

P.S. On the way to worship this a.m. we went by the Garden of Gethsemane as music played in the coach. I had been having thoughts that maybe I had dreamt up my experience there. As we passed the Garden the music was Speak the Language of the Hebrew Man! *A little reminder from God, I think!*

The Biblefresh pilgrimage had a big impact on all of our pilgrims and whilst leading such a large pilgrimage was a challenge, it was a real privilege to work with such a gifted group of leaders and to share in such significant acts of worship. We were able to pray over Jerusalem and, for me personally, to preach before receiving Communion together with Jerusalem as the backdrop was certainly very special.

There were so many highlights, too many to mention here, but leaving the Upper Room to the sound of singing from a Nigerian pilgrimage party was quite heavenly as different nationalities sang in unison together. The carrying of a cross through the Via Dolorosa was very challenging, particularly as a few Jewish people took exception to such a large group having their own spiritual moment and shouted angrily at us, but this seemed to just add to the significance of the experience. You wanted everything to stop whilst we had 'our moment' and carried our cross, but business certainly continued and then as I reflected upon it afterwards, I realised that this was probably more in keeping with 'walking in the footsteps of Jesus'!

It was also always helpful to pray our prepared Prayers of Reconciliation as we made our way through the Wall of Separation around Bethlehem, but it was also important for us that the majority of the group actually stayed at the Bethlehem Hotel so that we were in solidarity with the Christians living in Bethlehem itself and actually experiencing something of what they have to live with.

We had a civic reception with the Mayor of Bethlehem, Victor, and were entertained by the local pipe and drums band followed by young traditional dancers from the local community. This was an important opportunity to engage with local people and to hear their stories, whilst showing our concern and interest in their situation. It was also a real cultural exchange with friends from Knaresborough singing the song *Ilkley Moor Bah Tat*. I was not quite sure what they made of British culture at this point, but the gathered local audience in the council house certainly showed their appreciation.

On one occasion, as our coach was making its way through the Wall of Separation's stop-check, the young Israeli soldier stepped on to ask for our passports.

As Phil Gough and I gave him our passports, the soldier said, "Ah, English, Manchester United!"

Phil, as a Liverpool fan, responded, "No, Liverpool!"

The soldier looked at him as if he was annoyed and said, "Off the coach!"

At this point I was totally horrified and thought to myself, "Phil, what are you doing?" But I needn't have been concerned, because the soldier's expression suddenly changed to laughter at his own joke and sense of humour and he just said, "Have a nice day!" as he stepped off the coach.

We all breathed a huge sigh of relief and laughed, at which point Phil led us all in the singing of *You'll Never Walk Alone*. This was not one of the most spiritually uplifting moments, but nevertheless it illustrates the range of experiences that we shared together.

Having had such a positive experience with such a great team of leaders, it was with some nervousness that Carol and I prepared for a pilgrimage in 2014 with members from KMC and from around our circuit, with a few other friends who had expressed an interest in joining us. But Carol did much of the administration and whilst we did consider other pilgrimage companies, my preference was to work with Special Pilgrimages whom I knew and trusted. It was important that I could rely on their expertise to ensure the safety of our pilgrims and to provide them with the most fulfilling pilgrimage experience we could offer.

Hosting just one coach instead of three did, however, have some advantages, in that it felt like a much more personal experience, with Carol and me having time to spend with each individual pilgrim as we journeyed together. We changed the itinerary based upon our previous experiences and determined to allow pilgrims more time to reflect. We began in Jerusalem and Bethlehem, finishing in the beauty of Galilee, with the Yardenit renewal of baptismal vows on the Sunday becoming a more fitting climax to our time together.

One of the advantages of this pilgrimage, based upon previous experience, was that Dad had visited a small shop business and restaurant whilst most of our party were floating in the Dead Sea. Here the Palestinian family owners had dressed him up in traditional costume and had treated him to tea and cakes. We therefore walked to find the shop on our first evening staying at the Bethlehem Hotel and arranged for groups of our pilgrims to visit each evening to share with the family and to be dressed up and pose for photographs. This was a wonderful cultural exchange as we were able to hear their stories as we ate together and could also support them in a very practical way as pilgrims bought souvenirs from their shop. There was also a lot of laughter as many of our group looked more like Yasser Arafat than British pilgrims!

We were able to visit different sites in addition to the main itinerary with a smaller group and there was less waiting for people and queuing with the group. But visiting the garden tomb was just as special, with Tony Judd preaching and Carol Fleming reading the scripture whilst excitedly wanting to point to the tomb as she read.

Jo and Nathan Brown shared the reading of John 21 at the Church of the Primacy of St. Peter, located on the northwest shore of the Sea of Galilee, where scripture tells us that Jesus appeared to the apostles to enable a miraculous haul of fish. It was here that Jesus asked Peter three times if he loved Him, but for Jo it was one of those lightbulb moments.

As she later sat with Nathan, staring across the Sea of Galilee and reflecting on the reading, she could see in her mind's eye Peter launching himself into the water and scrambling over the rocky shore; she could smell the breakfast BBQ that Jesus had prepared for them and could sense Peter's relief as his relationship with Jesus was restored. But she could also hear Jesus asking if she loved Him too!

Jo had a fresh awareness of God's love surrounding her. In her words:

The phenomenal love which we had all shared in the Holy Land was very real. Jesus had whispered His love to us in the churches and synagogues. He had spoken of it to us, in the garden, on the street corners and in the shepherd fields. He had shouted it to us across the market place, shared, danced and sung it to us on the Sea of Galilee. But firstly, He demonstrated it to us on the Cross and in the empty tomb.

Our daughter Sarah had tragically lost one of her closest friends, Kathryn, just a few months before her marriage to Fintan in 2010.

Kathryn was married to Fintan's brother Ronan and had been due to be a bridesmaid at the wedding, so her sudden death had been a terrible shock to Sarah, her family and all her friends. Carol and I had driven to Sheffield to be with Sarah and Kathryn's parents the night after her death to share in the prayer vigil which was being held at St. Thomas' Church Philadelphia Campus.

Having shared this experience, it was particularly poignant and a real privilege that Kathryn's parents decided to join us on the pilgrimage. We experienced many highlights together, but then as we stood together in the River Jordan and I was about to assist them in reaffirming their baptismal vows, I had the overwhelming sense that God was pleased with what we were doing but that Kathryn was smiling over us too. As I told them what I was sensing, it seemed to add to the poignancy of the moment and yet it also felt wholly appropriate to share in this most intimate of ways.

Walking in the footsteps of Jesus can enable us to experience deep spiritual truths in our hearts as well as in our heads. The very things that we have been convinced of for years in our minds can suddenly become a reality in our hearts too. This was certainly the experience of one of our senior local preachers, Tony Judd. Tony is a very capable and learned local preacher who delivers well-prepared worship and sermons of some depth in our Methodist Circuit churches. I therefore had no hesitation in asking him to preach at a Communion service in the garden tomb and he certainly spoke well.

However, after our service on the Sea of Galilee, he sat quietly and reflectively by himself on the boat. I went to ask him if he was alright, to which he replied, "I just don't want to come down from the mountaintop!" Tony had a heart-warming experience during worship in a boat on the Sea of Galilee and he returned to Knutsford a changed man.

Walking in the footsteps of Jesus is particularly exciting when on pilgrimage in the Holy Land because you are visiting the very places where Jesus walked and talked. The challenge is to also walk in the footsteps of Jesus every day, asking ourselves that old question, "What would Jesus do?" Jesus would certainly bring hope to any village, town or city that He might visit and therefore it is our challenge and privilege to be His hands and feet, His body, the Church, here on earth today. We are on a pilgrimage with Him in our day-to-day lives.

33

Methodism's Best Kept Secret

It was during my appointment in Preston that my friend and Wesley College contemporary Mark Dunn-Wilson invited Carol and me to attend the Southport Methodist Holiness Convention. The convention had been started in 1885, with the intention of spreading the teaching of Wesleyan Holiness, and had seen some incredible heroes of the faith lead the convention and also preach to large gatherings.

There have also been very close links with Cliff College, who would send a team of Cliff College trekkers to do mission in Southport during the convention. Students such as former President of the Methodist Conference, Steve Wild, would sleep in the attic above the tea room whilst female students would stay with local church members. There was a carving in the original beams of the attic which read, 'Hotel De Attic – proprietor Herbert Silverwood' which some students had obviously engraved.

The convention had been renamed Summerfire to give it a more modern feel some years earlier, but still met in a large marquee on a site in Mornington Road owned by the trust. Speakers such as former President of Conference and Principal of Cliff College Rev. Dr. Bill Davies and well-known conference speaker/teacher Rev. Paul Smith would fill the marquee to overflowing, a trend which has continued with Steve Wild in recent years.

I was first invited to speak at Summerfire in 2001 during my first sabbatical, when I did an evening of storytelling and music accompanied by Freddie Kofi. I was then invited by Mark and fellow trustee John Haley to join the leadership team and to become a trustee.

It has been part of our son Timothy's growing up to stay in a caravan with me and to participate in the children's activities and then the youth work with the Dunn-Wilson family and other local young people. After my mother's death, we invited Dad to come with us and to stay in a Southport hotel. It was at Summerfire's Firefest event that he first met Mauveen from Longton Central Hall. A friendship then developed and they later married in what was most likely the first Firefest romance resulting in marriage! It was lovely to see Dad happily pushing Mauveen on a swing, which was part of the play equipment outside the Firefest marquee.

Working alongside Mark in leading the conference and speaking each year with fellow team members such as Phil Gough, Sally Ann Ratcliffe and local minister Peter Knight (who recently became superintendent minister in the Vale of Stour Circuit) has been both challenging and inspirational. The event is only made possible because of a local team of trustees and volunteers who have led with us and facilitated much of the logistical management. John Cass has led this local team, alongside Clifford and Mary Hill, Derrick Chamberlain, Rebecca Gomersall, Paul Gray, Shirley Potts and Chris Hall. John took over the leadership of the team after the sudden death of David Goodwin who died of a heart attack. A commemorative banner made in David's memory has been put up each year at the event since his death.

The conference has generally met for a full week in the marquee up until quite recently, with Bible study leaders including Rob and Marian White, Chick and Margaret Yuill, David Dunn-Wilson, John Haley, Mark Dunn-Wilson, Mike Simmonds and Chris Blake. Many friends and ministers have kindly spoken such as Ashley Cooper, Anthony Clowes, Pete Phillips, Paul Smith, the late Rob Frost, Andy and Jo Frost (Share Jesus International), Paul Wilson (Methodist Evangelicals Together), Roy Crowne (Hope Together), David Spriggs (Bible Society), Lorraine Mellor (President of Methodist Conference 2017-18) and Martyn Atkins (President of Methodist Conference 2007-8).

In his presidential year Martyn reminded the Methodist Church of how God had raised up the people called Methodists in the first place, focussing on mission, evangelism and renewal. But he then went on to say, "Holiness, too, is part of the Methodist heritage. John Wesley famously quoted that '...God's design in raising up the Preachers called Methodists... [was] not to form a new sect, but to reform the nation, particularly the Church; and to spread scriptural holiness over the land.'" I think that it could have been Paul Hayes who described the event as "Methodism's best kept secret"!

Holiness is therefore a major strand of our Methodist DNA, but there has not always been much emphasis upon this within local churches, and at one time when Cliff College explored running a formal accredited course on Wesleyan Holiness, it didn't seem to get off the ground. Former Principal Howard Mellor apparently used to joke that they couldn't find anyone holy enough to lead it or interested enough in becoming holy so as to enrol in it! However, more recent courses do have a real Wesleyan Holiness emphasis.

Therefore, the task of Summerfire is still as relevant today as it always was in bringing the challenge to live out our holiness in everyday life. The values have reflected this, alongside evangelical preaching and teaching which results in radical discipleship and inspiring worship where we have encountered God.

Worship leaders Northern Light who worked with me at Easter People (from Burniston, Scarborough), Paul Critchley (Presence Music) and Phil Nankivell (Swan Bank) have served the event well alongside local musicians such as David Envisage and guest artists Dave Bilbrough, Noel Robinson and Freddie Kofi. We have had great fun forming gospel choirs with both Freddie Kofi and Noel Robinson, with members of the Summerfire family laughing together as we have swayed from side to side, clapping in time to the music. That sense of being a family of people together has been an important hallmark of our fellowship together, eating together, sharing, praying and worshipping together.

The worship has been consistently good and people have been encouraged, inspired and even felt a sense of God's call upon their lives to ministry of one form or another in recent years. There can be no greater privilege in ministry than to call people to respond to the good news of Jesus and to live out His call to follow Him and to serve Him.

In recent years, since my partner-in-crime and team leader Mark moved to minister at Truro Methodist Church, I have had the challenge and privilege of leading the team and seeking to move the event forward. Hosting the event in a marquee had become a major drain on our limited resources and volunteer team, so we decided to move to St. Phillip's and St. Paul's with Wesley (PPW) for a weekend event, with the aim of encouraging a larger number of people to attend in a warm building rather than a drafty marquee. The minister was Rev. Tim Hall (who sadly died in 2015), a man who was very supportive of Firefest, a good friend, and he welcomed us with open arms. There are those who feel that we lost something by no longer meeting in the marquee, as many had very positive memories over the years of being blessed there. Whenever we sang Dave Bilbrough's song *Holy Ground,* it felt very poignant and appropriate. Many people have met with God on that Mornington Road ground.

Weekend speakers have included Deacon Eunice Attwood (ex vice president of the Methodist Conference), Martin Turner (former superintendent, MCHW), Chick Yuill and Lorraine Mellor (returning during her Methodist presidential year).

However, we began to realise that Summerfire was beginning to be thought of as just an event, so I encouraged the trustees to recapture the vision of being a movement by hosting Firefest events in a number of circuits on the Sunday morning or evening of our timetable to ensure that a much wider group of people were able to participate in the worship. We have therefore had Firefest events in Leyland, Wigan, Banks, Chorley, Knutsford and Preston.

Because we no longer hired the marquee, we were able to use our limited resources in a different way. Therefore, the next step was to host a whole weekend in other areas of the country, which began with Mark launching Firefest in Cornwall at Truro, where Steve Wild and I both spoke and Freddie Kofi also shared in the celebration and performed a concert. Some of the trustees even travelled from Southport to share with us. This was a good event and gave us an insight into the potential of once more becoming a movement. This was further developed when I was able to host a small-scale Firefest Knutsford in 2014, followed by a more significant event in 2016 with Keith Garner as the keynote speaker, alongside storyteller Bob Hartman, worship leader Phil Nankivell and preacher Sam Ward (The Message Trust). At this point, with the help of a large local team, it seemed as if the potential of becoming a movement was actually being realised.

When in 2015 Steve Wild was the president of the Methodist Conference, he challenged the trustees to rediscover our spiritual heritage by returning to the Mornington Road site. He also challenged them to hire a better marquee and to meet during the Methodist Conference which was in Southport so that wider Methodism could be engaged by the emphasis on holiness.

We were able to invite back to the event speakers such as Howard Mellor who was visiting the conference from his appointment in Hong Kong and inspired us with stories of church growth both in Hong Kong and China. This was just prior to my sabbatical visit to China with Bible

Society to distribute Bibles, so delegates were able to sponsor a Bible and to sign a bookmark personally which was then handed to Chinese Christians who were desperate to receive their very own Bible. It was also good to have Paul Smith rejoin us.

During the Firefest event, a good number of conference delegates were able to visit, but Chick Yuill (former Salvation Army officer) had been encouraging us to sing the William Booth classic song, *O God of Burning, Cleansing Flame,* which has a chorus of, 'Send the fire today.' A few years earlier we had experienced an arson attack on the tea room attic which had virtually gutted the whole area and ruined all of the contents. Thankfully, this did enable our site tenant Parenting 2000 to begin a complete refurbishment of this area, creating a good office space for their staff. However, having some young boys throw a can with lit paper in it onto the roof of the marquee, ruining a whole panel, was not quite what we had in mind whilst singing, 'Send the fire again,' and it could have been very dangerous!

It is pleasing to know that the Mornington Road site is used by Parenting 2000 all year round to serve the local community by supporting families and shaping futures. There are youth services, parent/carer courses, therapeutic courses, child injury prevention classes and a legal clinic offering advice, all operating from our site. In my mind, this is all kingdom work, with needs being met in many different ways and being made possible by the provision of facilities made available by the trustees of Summerfire.

No doubt the original trustees and Southport Methodist Holiness Convention leaders would have been surprised that such activity even happens on the Mornington Road site, or that there are still annual events happening through the support of the trust. But John Wesley himself said that "there is no holiness but social holiness", so it seems wholly appropriate that such important social works are made possible. And to work out what scriptural holiness and perfect love looks like in the twenty-first century is obviously very much needed and key to the future mission and ministry of the Church if we are to bring 'hope to the main streets' of our villages, towns and cities.

"It's about working out our holiness, not by running away from the world, but by becoming involved in it. We need to take that distinctly Methodist style of holiness and put it to work in our communities day by day," said Martyn Atkins during his Summerfire sermon in 2007 as we prepared to launch Hope 08. Mark Dunn-Wilson, in his sermon a few days later said, "I believe that the Hope@Summerfire event next year is too important an opportunity for us to miss and sits so comfortably with our historic foundations at Summerfire." Another comment Martyn had made was that "Wesleyan holiness on which this event is built, is holiness that gets dirt under the fingernails".

It is my contention that whilst some emphasise personal holiness and others social holiness, actually we need to hold them both together with real commitment, passion and integrity if we are to see true transformation in churches and in our nation. For me this is part of what it means to be whole-life disciples. Our Summerfire and Firefest events have had an important role in mobilising people and churches to work out their faith and discipleship in very practical ways.

Whilst being team leader can be rather challenging alongside the many other demands of mission and ministry, I still hold on to the vision of being part of a movement which is spreading the teaching of holiness and living out our faith in radical discipleship. In fact, Martyn Atkins (superintendent of MCHW), during his tenure as general secretary of the Methodist Conference, coined a phrase to describe the Methodist Church as "a discipleship movement shaped for mission". We certainly need to take holiness teaching seriously if ever Methodism and other churches are to aspire to actually become such a movement once more.

In 2017, we have captured something more of the vision to be a holiness movement when alongside our keynote speaker, Rt. Rev. Mike Hill (Bishop of Bristol), at our Knutsford Firefest we also invited international worship leader Shane Rootes (Washington DC). I had preached at Brookhouse Methodist Church in Lancaster a couple of months earlier as the minister Peter Brown (a Wesley College contemporary) had invited me to do a weekend at the church. After a great time of fellowship together, the leadership team seemed keen to invite Shane to lead a Firefest weekend with me and so Firefest On The Road was born. I preached at Brookhouse on a Saturday evening with Shane leading the worship and then preaching the following day. We then led Firefest events at Aspull Methodist in Wigan on the Tuesday and at Leyland Road in Southport on the Wednesday, before doing a full weekend at Knutsford!

Key to the success of this mini tour was having Peter Freeman handle some of the logistics and also step into the role of Shane's roadie! The challenges with both PA and the visual projection at some of the venues ensured that we would not attempt to do such a tour in the same way again, but we would certainly have a dedicated support team. But Peter's commitment to inviting Shane in the first instance and to enabling the tour to actually work was key in making it a reality. He will certainly have a future role, of that I am sure!

In May 2018, we are privileged to have Calvin Samuel (principal of London School of Theology) as the keynote speaker at our Knutsford Firefest event and John Illsley (Superintendent Minister in the Bury Circuit) leading the Bible Study in Southport. But, I feel that it is also key to again have Shane Rootes leading worship and also to help facilitate the vision of being a holiness movement in moving forward significantly. He returned to Knutsford in October 2017 to share with us again in leading worship, but also to speak into the life of our church and the future of Firefest. We have planned a major Firefest tour in May 2018, visiting Southport, Bury, Leyland and Knutsford. We also hope to do an autumn Firefest tour in November 2018.

34

Four Weddings, a Baptism and the Occasional Funeral

The Church of today still has amazing opportunities to connect with people and to bring hope into their lives. Family occasions such as baptisms and weddings are full of hope for the future and I have had the privilege of sharing them with a number of people. But for me personally, bringing hope at a time of bereavement is also a great opportunity and certainly a privilege.

What greater honour can there be than to share with a family at the most important times in their lives and to speak words of love, encouragement, instruction, comfort and hope into their situation? If I was to reflect upon four weddings prior to my present appointment, apart from the wonderful weddings of our children, then I would first recall the wedding of Bob and Jenny Mayor at Eldon Street, who insisted that I told no one about the ceremony before the actual marriage service on the Sunday morning! To see the look of shock on the faces of church members will always stay with me, but everyone was thrilled for them and I was privileged to share with them.

At Ingol, we had to finish the new church building in time for the wedding of David and Julie Lowes, which was quite a challenge. But to marry a couple of friends whom I went to watch Preston North End football matches with in our newly opened centre of worship and mission was certainly one of the highlights of my whole ministry.

In Arnold, Nottingham, I will never forget making David Keetley go down on one knee at the start of his marriage to Rachel because he had never proposed properly to her. Alongside praying a blessing for them and pretending to wipe Dave's hair gel on his shoulder, this was a very special day. The young man, who was not even in the church when I began to minister in Arnold, rejoined after receiving so much love and care from the church after a violent attack one evening. He now works for the Diocese of Southwell and Nottingham as their youth ministry adviser.

And then there was the wedding of Alyson Edwards complete with white horse and carriage which caused a real commotion in the marketplace of Arnold as everyone came to look at the bride – and the horse! Alyson was so overcome that she burst into tears, so I gave her my handkerchief as a gentleman, only for her to blow her nose very loudly outside the church and then pass it back to me. To which I responded, "No, you can keep that." I had not realised that the whole event had been captured on the wedding video!

Other memorable weddings include that of Robert Buckby and Fiona Berry, who were members of our Arnold youth group and whom we were encouraged and thrilled to see again recently, and the wedding in Leeds of Hannah North, one of our daughter Sarah's best friends, to Rob Walker.

In Knutsford I have had some wonderful weddings followed by beautiful receptions which Carol and I have thoroughly enjoyed.[32] Baptisms and dedications are also such happy occasions, when people's wider group of friends and family are invited to share with us. I love those times when we have the opportunity of welcoming children into the family of the church, whilst welcoming others to hear something of the good news of Jesus' love for them and of how Jesus welcomed the children to Himself. I love the fact that people are constantly surprised that they have actually enjoyed sharing in worship with us at weddings, baptisms and funerals. It is a joy to shatter negative stereotypes and illusions about the Church and reconnect people to their faith, if only briefly!

At a funeral, when people are feeling sad and sometimes a little lost, the church through the ministry of a minister, vicar, priest or pastor with

---

[32] In recent times the weddings of Lauren Brown and Joe Rowland, Clara McKechnie and Rowan Brown, Helen Kerr and Adrian White, plus Laura Freeman and Jack Cureton, have all been very special. It is also great as a church family that we continue to be in contact with young couples Kathryn and Tom Taylor, Margaret and Guy Forman, Ruth and Mike Smith, Luisa and Matt Ashford, Edmund and Amy-Louise Overrill-Chapman, Shavonne and Gareth Erlandson. This is a real testament to the nurture of young people within the family of the church.

a team of pastoral visitors offering bereavement support, can bring comfort and practical help at a time of need, when positive input brings hope. There is good news of a Jesus who understands what it is to lose a loved one, a friend who welcomes us to Himself, bringing His comfort.

Giving a tribute for someone and celebrating their life is a privilege that should not be underestimated. One family were sharing with me about their mother, whose husband had one day said that he would fetch a tin of runner beans for the family's tea. He deserted his family, never returned, and they never saw him again.

In retelling the story to a neighbour, the now deceased mother had been asked, "What did you do?"

She replied, "I opened a tin of mushy peas instead!"

This story seemed to sum up her sense of humour, spirit and determination to provide for her family and to bring them up to the best of her ability. Certainly, in meeting with the family, I could see how she could be very proud of her children. The funeral was very definitely a celebration of the mother the family respected and loved.

On another occasion, during the bereavement visit to prepare for the funeral, the family said that there was a song that their loved one had wanted to be played at the end. There was then a pregnant pause when the family looked nervously at each other, wondering how I would respond to the request. I began to feel nervous myself as I wondered what on earth the song might be!

The son eventually said, "Dad wanted to have *Bat Out of Hell* played at his funeral."

"Why did he want that particular song?" I asked.

"Because he knew that he was not perfect, that he had his faults, but in the song there is a line, 'Like a sinner at the gates of heaven, I come crawling on back to you.'"

I smiled and though I knew that some might not approve of the choice of music, I also knew that in speaking about the deceased father, I could speak with authority about his character without causing offence whilst bringing a clear gospel message about repentance (making a new start) and forgiveness. The song was part of an authentic tribute to the deceased and was very much in keeping with the culture of both the father and the family concerned.

Years ago I was asked to take a funeral in Nottingham of an elderly granny and so I went to visit the daughter to prepare. In the course of the conversation I was told, "I do have a sister but she's the prodigal. Years ago she met a young man and she decided that she would leave her husband and three children for this man, even though the youngest child was only a few months old. Her new partner did not want her to have anything to do with her family, so she has never had any contact with her children from that day to this." The granny was so upset that her own daughter had abandoned her children that she had kept in touch with them and they had all loved her. The daughter organising the funeral then said, "But we don't want any trouble at the funeral, so they will probably not come, because their mother and her partner want nothing to do with them."

So the day of the funeral came, with the lovely daughter and her husband whom I had met, and also the prodigal sister (prodigal mother) and her new partner of fifteen or so years alongside her. As I began the service at the crematorium, the door opened at the back and in walked three young people who sat quietly on the back row. I knew straightaway who they were, but they kept at a safe, discreet distance so others were not aware that they had entered.

The service went well and afterwards I shook everyone's hands and then went to the three young people, aged fifteen/sixteen, eighteen and twenty-one.

"We're not going to cause any trouble," they said. "We just wanted to be at our gran's funeral."

"Do you want to see your mum?" I asked.

"Yes," they said, "but she won't come!"

So I asked them to wait around the corner for a few moments.

I waited until the prodigal mother's partner went into the gents and then I went to shake the children's mother's hand.

She was gushing her thanks, and as I held her hand, I looked her in the eyes and said, "Your children are here!"

"NO!" she said, but I still had hold of her hand as she tried pulling it back.

I kept looking into her eyes and asked, "Do you want to meet your children?"

And to my surprise she then said, "Yes!"

I walked her around the corner and her children burst into tears. They were shocked to see their mum and she just wrapped her arms around them and was totally overwhelmed by their love for her, despite the fact that she had abandoned them.

The family asked me to come to the wake afterwards to make sure everything went well because the mum had invited her children to be with them. I sat with the partner for an hour or so, talking about football and anything else I could think of, just to keep him happy! There was a welcome home of the prodigal mother that day, reconciliation, forgiveness and a celebration party which felt quite different to a wake! And in heaven a granny smiled that day. In her death, she had brought about the reconciliation – just as Jesus died for us that there might be a reconciliation, a relationship between us and our Father God, who runs to meet us, the 'running father'.

It is also a privilege to take the funerals of church members and to celebrate their life and faith in sharing a tribute about them. In recent times it has been good to give thanks for several saints such as Rene Fox, who had taught for many years in the Sunday school at Knutsford Methodist, even teaching one of my former ministerial colleagues, David Griffiths, as a young boy. Rene was always very genuine, a gracious lady who never wanted to be any trouble to anyone. She was a prolific writer of notes, expressing herself clearly; she told you everything. I will always remember her lovely little giggle.

Rene had a very strong faith which revealed itself throughout her life. During her time at The Willows (Methodist Homes for the Aged), Rene was able to witness of her faith to those around her – staff and patients alike. And I do know that we need to thank the staff of places such as The Willows for their care and particularly their chaplain, Jo, for her care of Rene. In the early days when visiting Rene, it was often difficult to get a word in edgeways – she never stopped talking. She used to entertain you – you didn't have to entertain her, but she always wanted to hear what was going on at KMC. She still wanted to be a part of the church which had been her spiritual home for so many years.

Rene never wished to put anyone to any trouble; she was always concerned for the other person. When she was in hospital, she would record the days when her bed was changed! She was even able to tell the nurses which tablets she should be taking, remembering all the long names and what they were for. Rosemary (her lifelong friend) used to say she couldn't keep up with Rene's letter-writing! She kept in touch with everyone including Dorothy and Peter Richards who pastorally visited her regularly, alongside their daughter Jo Wallwork and grandson James who said he would miss Rene as she talked to him about history. Years ago she used to lift Claire, their other daughter, onto her lap to read her stories. Rene was part of their extended family. They will no doubt remember Christmas teas around at Rene's and then later at their home for many years. Rene was an honorary aunt to all the children, part of the extended family and Jo's godmother.

Sadly, as time went on, Rene became more and more frail and was in constant pain. Two months before her death she suffered a stroke which affected her body but not her mind. Her dearest wish was to be with her Lord – but she always said that it would be in His timing. Eventually her wish was granted! Many messages of condolence were received and they all said the same: "Rene was a lovely lady." She loved everyone and was loved by everyone.

What a privilege to share with Rene at The Willows; she was prepared and ready, she knew the peace of Christ and she was trusting in Jesus. "The Lord is with me through the night," she said, "and when I call, He's there. I know He's there for everyone," she added almost apologetically, as if she was claiming too much for herself, "but He's there for me." I said a prayer for Rene, rather like a last rites (my version of it anyway) with my hand on her head, and I made the sign of the Cross on her forehead. She was just so peaceful that I thought she had gone to sleep, so I decided to leave quietly and let her rest, but suddenly Rene burst into this prayer for me and my family: "Lord, I pray for Rob and Carol and their family. I pray that they might all come to trust in Jesus and that you might bless them and keep them safe." It was such a lovely prayer. I'm there supposed to be looking after her and she's praying for me and my family – and then she said confidently, "Shall we say the Lord's Prayer?" So we said the Lord's Prayer and had another chat about how she loved her church and how thankful she was for all the support she had received. Then a nurse came in to see her so I left soon afterwards, with Rene smiling and saying that she will see me again.

Rene was prepared to meet with Jesus and we will see her again one day when we go to meet with Him too. But let's be prepared in our hearts and in our minds, not just for that day but for every day, as we want to serve Him day by day.

When we had the funeral of Millicent Spillman, I was able to speak of her time working as a young nurse in the Oji River Leprosy Settlement near Inugu on the Gold Coast of West Africa. It was a closed-off settlement and Millicent was there with very basic provisions and just a handful of staff (doctors and nurses). Most days she would be assisting with amputations of leprous limbs! It sounded awful.

Her husband Bob was asked by the family one day, how did he know that Millicent was the right one? He replied, "You have to appreciate how repugnant the smell of rotting flesh is and the disfigurement that leprosy causes – you just want to look away. But your mother really loved these people." So as a young man who had recently met her, he asked Millicent, "How can you love that?"

She replied, "Because God looks at the real person inside, not what you look like on the outside – and that's what I do, I look at the person inside!"

This was a powerful testimony of God's love for everyone, but also of Millicent living out her faith. When Bob told his children of this in later years, he would well up in tears because it was actually seeing the demonstration of God's love in Millicent's life that brought him to faith in Christ himself.

It has been a privilege to share pastorally with people in their homes and then in some form of supported accommodation such as a nursing home towards the end of their lives. I take along with me a small home Communion set given to me at my ordination by my godparent Auntie Brenda and Uncle Dennis, to share in a simple Communion service which tends to be very personal and intimate for those sharing.

However, having shared numerous Communion services with Dorothy Crimes and her husband Stanley, my last visit to Astbury Mere in Congleton will always be one of my favourite memories. Dorothy had joined in the music therapy group for the afternoon and so, rather than drag her away for Communion, I joined in the activity for half an hour. Beth, the young lady from Musical Moments leading the activity, was full of enthusiasm and energy, engaging the elderly residents sensitively. I was not too sure what Dorothy thought of residents doing the actions to *YMCA* to improve their mobility, complete with the cowboy hat, Indian headdress, fireman's helmet and builder's hard hat as if we were the Village People themselves. But at the conclusion of the song, I had Dorothy put on the cowboy hat and I wore the Indian headdress for a selfie photograph together, much to the amusement of all the staff present. Apparently, they later asked Dorothy's family if the minister could help with the music therapy session every week!

When Dorothy died a couple of weeks later, it was lovely to share that photo with members of the family and to speak at the funeral of our time together dressed as a cowboy and an Indian, joining in the actions to *YMCA*. I will miss my visits to Dorothy and our sharing together, but wonder if there will be music therapy in heaven?

Even in recent months I have had the privilege of sharing with Josephine Hunns, her husband David and their daughters Helen and Cath as we chatted by the bedside of Josephine's mother, Jane Coulthard. I will never forget the day when Josephine wheeled her mum into CAMEO (Come and Meet Every One – a short service followed by afternoon tea) at KMC after not being able to attend church for a few months. Jane's face was beaming with a smile as she was so thrilled to be back in her spiritual home – KMC.

At the funeral celebration of her life and faith, we reflected on how Jane loved Psalm 121: 'I look to the hills, where will my help come from? My help will come from the Lord, who made heaven and earth.' It was poignant to remember how she used to look out of her kitchen window in Maryport on the beautiful Skiddaw and how the Psalm reminded her of God's faithfulness to her. Psalm 121 concludes, 'He will protect you as you come and go now and forever.' What an amazing truth to be aware of as you wait to go to be with your Heavenly Father.

Noel Patterson had told his daughter Jackie Robertson that he wanted to go home and she had responded, "You *are* home, Dad." He then retorted, "No, I want to go to heaven." On Remembrance Sunday 2017, I was moved to see a rather frail Noel determined to stand for the National Anthem. Nothing was going to stop him showing his respect as a military man. But only a few days later, on the Wednesday, I had an urgent call to pray with Noel as it was only a matter of time.

I talked to him about Jane, whose funeral I was due to conduct later that afternoon. As I then held his hand and read his favourite reading from Philippians 4:1-9, he was totally with me and he was holding on to the truth of that passage: 'The Lord is coming soon. Don't worry about anything, but in all your prayers ask God for what you need, always asking him with a thankful heart. And God's peace, which is far beyond human understanding, will keep your hearts and minds safe in union with Christ Jesus.' It ends, 'And the God who gives you peace will be with you.' I have no hesitation in saying that the God of peace was with Noel to the very end of his days.

In the context of what he had said to Jackie, after reading scripture to him, I asked him, "And where are you going, Noel?" He pointed upwards to heaven; he had the assurance of heaven, a confidence in Jesus, which is why we could later sing one of his favourite hymns (and mine too) with that same confidence: 'Blessed assurance, Jesus is mine, O what a foretaste of glory divine – This is my story, this is my song, praising my Saviour all the day long.'

At Guys Barbers where Noel had his hair cut and beard trimmed, Dan had renamed him 'Lord Patterson' and it was a title richly deserved. This quiet, gentle, dignified man of faith constantly invited anyone who would listen to come to his church and to sit with him. At his funeral, as many as were able came to pay their respects to their friend, a true gentleman of Knutsford, Lord Patterson.

35

Gypsy Kings, Boxing Champions and Rock Stars

One of the most interesting weeks in my whole ministry was when I was asked if I would consider hosting the funeral of a young man, Felix Rooney, who had died tragically, as his family had acquired a burial plot in the nearby Tabley Cemetery. The family had a personal friend, a Baptist pastor, who would speak at the funeral. I was told that they were a perfectly respectable family but there was an Irish traveller connection.

The following day, as I was in a committee meeting, our church administrator interrupted the meeting by knocking on the door. "Rob, there's a police officer here to speak to you. They say it's important; could you come to see them?"

Everyone's eyes in the room turned to look at my bemused reaction! I excused myself from the meeting and told them to continue in my absence, but I'm not sure how much work was done, as they were probably all wondering what misdemeanour their minister had committed.

When I had taken the police officer to a private room, she asked, "Are you taking a funeral for an Irish traveller family in a few days' time?"

"Yes, I am," I replied.

"Do you realise that there could be over a thousand people at the funeral?"

"But our church only seats just over three hundred!" I blurted out. "They said that there would be a couple of hundred!"

I agreed to check with the family, but the police were already thinking about contacting all the local shopkeepers and even closing some of the local roads.

With the welcoming of an Irish traveller family into our church for the thanksgiving on a Wednesday evening, followed by Felix's funeral on the Thursday, we were stepping into the unknown. Imagine with me the front of our church full of five-foot photo tributes surrounded by flowers interspersed with LED lights around them. There were over three hundred people in the church, with many standing at the back in the entrance foyer and two hundred to three hundred people standing outside with the sound being broadcast into the street. Princess Street was closed to traffic, with police at the end of the street to monitor everything.

As a church, we say in our mission statement that we are passionate about sharing God's love with others, so when a young thirty-three-year-old man got killed in a road accident, we had the opportunity of sharing God's love with around five or six hundred Irish travellers from all around the country. I think it's true to say that as a church we did all that we could to care for and share God's love with everyone who came. Some of them were dressed a little differently – some of them were in fairly amazing outfits.

A young five- or six-year-old boy, Jimmy, came to me and said, "Who's in the box?"

I responded, "Don't you know who it is?"

"Is it Felix, my dad?"

The daughter, aged seven or eight, asked me, "Can I have a look at my daddy?"

His wife Winnie and mother Bridgie were distraught throughout the service, sobbing and even wailing, with family and friends supporting them and at times restraining them from rushing to the coffin. We were just offering comfort and God's love in whatever way we could.

The young American Baptist pastor, Derrick (a family friend), was just something else. He preached a very straight and direct gospel message. He would say, "Look at me. Look at me. Look this way," and at the end of preaching his sermon, he asked, "Who here today wants to accept Jesus as their Saviour?" Between twelve and twenty travellers put up their hands.

So in that particular week we were trending on Twitter. There were so many people who were talking about what was happening in Knutsford! We wondered, what was God saying to us in all of this? What were the signs of the kingdom? At that time we knew that the poor were being fed through Hampers of Hope, the good news was being preached... What other signs of the kingdom could we see breaking in, as Christians who passionately share the love of Jesus?

One year later I was asked to meet with the family at the graveside, as the gravestone had been erected, to pray for God's blessing upon Felix and his family. There were around seventy people present, all of whom had a can or a bottle in their hands. But they were very appreciative of everything that I said and did for them. In fact, I had decided not to charge any fee, but the sister-in-law of Felix pressed a £10 note into my hand afterwards saying, "Get whatever you want, Father, a drink or some fags – on us!"

There was gypsy royalty (or so I was told) and even a heavyweight boxing champion of the world, Tyson Fury, present at the funeral. But there were many rumours around the town at the time about what had been stolen and what damage had been done. Yet, the reporter from the *Knutsford Guardian* was not able to find any basis for all of the rumours that were circulating. There were concerns expressed about the policing costs that day and the impact upon local trade, but little acknowledgement of the fact that all the local hotels were fully booked, and cafés and public houses did a roaring trade. No doubt everyone has their opinions about these events, but the priority for the Church must be to share God's love with people in need and to make a positive contribution to the life of the local community it serves and of which it is a part.

The largest funeral that I have taken at Knutsford was that of Howard Kirkham, a church member who was a great man and certainly very supportive of me as I began ministry at Knutsford. For much of his life, Howard was a leader – in his family, in his professional life, in the church and even socially amongst friends. And it was said to me at the time of his death that Howard was a man who was totally consistent, he was the same Christian man who lived out his Christian values at home, at work, at church and with friends. What you saw was what you got with Howard!

Howard had loved sailing with his family and it was certainly true to say that his wife Hilary was his first mate. Howard was the captain on the boat, but he was also a captain at work, in the church and in his family. In fact, his wonderful family are the perfect legacy of the faith that he lived and of the man that he was. Having said this, the redevelopment of the KMC community rooms some years ago was largely made possible by the leadership of Howard in raising the finance, and is therefore also a lasting legacy in the community that was important to him.

When we had a lot of money to raise for the maintenance of windows, the building and the mission work in the community, Howard told me that we just needed to ask the church and the community and the money would come. I could be confident that he knew what he was talking about. We managed to raise almost £135,000 for our Challenge 150 appeal to make the necessary improvements in a short period of time. I just hope that the same will prove to be true as we seek to move forward in our mission and ministry with a strategic five-year plan as part of our 2020s vision!

In recent times, I have taken my first funeral of one of our church members at Plumley Methodist Church, a retired NatWest bank manager and former rugby player, Bryan England. I had got to know Bryan and his lovely wife Christine well in the final months of his life and also their daughter Louise and son-in-law James Maude who had returned to England from America to support Christine in her care of Bryan, as they joined Knutsford Methodist.

However, I had not met Bryan and Christine's other daughter Katie and her husband Bobby prior to the funeral. Katie is a fashion stylist who worked closely with Alexander McQueen and became close friends with Kate Moss as she directed catwalk fashion shows from behind the scenes for over two decades. Her husband Bobby Gillespie is the lead singer and founder member of the alternative rock band Primal Scream who continue to travel extensively around the world. Both Bobby and Katie are still very much involved in the fashion world and their son Wolf looks destined to follow in these footsteps.

I guess that the nearest I had ever been to their world of fashion and music was when Bible Society hosted a fashion show based on the prodigal son featuring a soundtrack of music by One Republic at the Urbis in Manchester as part of our Riddle of Life media campaign.[33]

Bryan's funeral packed out the rural Plumley Methodist chapel even with the Sunday school's room open. The tributes were so affirming of how Bryan had lived out his faith as a safe pair of hands on the rugby field and in the bank and with his family, that I felt moved to ask people to give thanks for Bryan's life and faith with a round of applause. Many people gave him a standing ovation, but everyone applauded quite loudly

---

[33] See page 191.

and for some time. It was the first time I had ever done such a thing and probably it may never happen again.

During the refreshments after the funeral, having circulated around the gathering, I spoke with Bobby before leaving. I began by foolishly making assumptions about him.

"I suppose this is a very different world to you here in little Plumley?" I said.

"Not at all; I'm a very quiet person. I mostly spend my time quietly at home with the family. What I do as a job is different. But I am very quiet!" replied Bobby. This was followed by a very passionate discussion about Bobby's concerns for our world, particularly the rise of fascism and the state of our nation.

I asked him if he had considered a future in politics, but he seemed to feel that he should make his contribution through his music. However, when you consider the work of the likes of Bob Geldof and others at Live Aid, who knows what the future has in store for Bobby, Katie and their family?

One of the challenges for the Church today in bringing hope to a local community, to our nation and even to our world is to identify who will work with you and how you can even broker a conversation with them to develop a credible relationship. The social outreach projects that we launch certainly could benefit by the endorsement of well-known figures in the world of entertainment. Perhaps hosting a fashion show organised by Katie England with a sound track played by Primal Scream might be a little ambitious, but then, the entrepreneur in me can always dream!

36

Hope 2018 in Knutsford and Beyond

The aim for Hope 2018 is that the whole Church will reach the whole nation for a whole year, bringing hope through sharing God's love, as local churches work together meeting needs in our local communities.

This work is based on values of continuing to love and serve people whatever they choose to believe, whilst inviting them to become followers of Jesus by sharing the gospel at an appropriate time, speaking sensitively and in culturally relevant ways. This gives people opportunities to respond to the good news about Jesus and then they are connected to an appropriate local church.

Hope 2018 is rooted in prayer, words and action based upon a very definite rhythm of mission. It should be flexible enough to respond to the needs of any local community, whether in a village, town or city. However, if this results in just a special year of activity and then afterwards the Church just returns to life as normal, then that would obviously be deemed as something of a failure. No doubt, the aspiration is that by modelling effective outreach within a community, the culture of the Church changes to become more missional, attractive and engaging in their local area.

In recent years, we have begun to see that cultural shift at Knutsford Methodist, both within the church itself and in our relationships with the council, schools, statutory bodies and local community. Having had the privilege of serving as the Knutsford town council mayor's chaplain to both Councillor Neil Forbes and Councillor Tony Dean, I have been able to develop good relationships with members of all the parties locally. But appointing my wife Carol as the church and community pastoral worker has resulted in her being able to research the needs of the community and to mobilise the church membership in responding to that need.

A major initiative for us in partnership with other local churches has been the launch of the foodbank with Hampers of Hope. Hampers of Hope (North East Cheshire Foodbank) started in October 2011 as a Christmas project that collected non-perishable food items to make Christmas food parcels for local people and families who were going to struggle putting food on the table at Christmas. Due to the generosity of so many individuals in local churches and organisations, hundreds of lives were touched in our local towns and villages. The demand for emergency food support locally was so evident that the project did not stop after Christmas. And so Hampers of Hope began early in 2012 as an independent Christian charity, with a launch in Knutsford following a couple of years later.

Church members were trained to deliver the hampers to people's homes where, alongside the emergency food, they would be prepared to offer additional support as required and to pray for them when appropriate. All of the churches then acquired a red bin to collect the necessary food after church services, but in our case, we requested a second bin so that those attending our community centre activities throughout the week would also be able to support this venture. Some, however, preferred to support financially rather than to give food, which enabled the co-ordinators to purchase the things which are most required.

The foodbank provides three-to-five-day food hampers to people and families in crisis who are referred by frontline care workers and pro-fessionals. These food hampers are given without prejudice to men, women and children, alongside signposting people to agencies able to support them with longer-term issues.

Carol developed a strong team around her and was very quickly able to pass on the leadership of this project to Jackie Tomkins and Barbara McKenna. This meant that Jackie and Barbara were instrumental in helping to set up The Hope Centre at Knutsford Town Council Offices and to then manage the centre on each Monday morning. The Hope Centre is available for ongoing support and advice, offering debt counselling where necessary and money management courses, amongst other practical help. People enjoy a good breakfast and lunch as they attend the Monday sessions.

Alongside this work Carol has developed a fairly modest furniture store which is available as support in a practical way when people in crisis are referred by the Knutsford Children's Centre or another agency.

Church members donate good quality furniture which is then stored until an emergency situation is presented to us.

We move the furniture with the use of a trailer belonging to one of the church members and we recruit volunteers to assist with the heavy lifting. Particular thanks go to Steve Wilkinson and Peter Freeman for their unstinting support of this work, alongside others who are willing labourers, plus Peter and Dorothy who now co-ordinate. We have recently acquired a container to store the furniture as we required better storage to develop the project.

There have been recent occasions when gardens have needed clearing and homes have needed decorating, so Carol has had to mobilise a much larger group of volunteers! But this has been for particular crisis situations, rather than a regular occurrence, thankfully! No doubt enabling our church members to be involved in these situations has been an important experience for them and part of developing their practical discipleship. Putting our faith into practical action is certainly very much in keeping with the ethos of Hope.

Our latest adventure has involved the launch of a fortnightly Friendship Café for those experiencing dementia and their carers. The personal experience of Carol and other church members of caring for a loved one with Alzheimer's disease and/or dementia has meant that there was a strong desire to respond to this particular growing need within our community.

Originally, we had set up a Forget-me-not Café with MHA (Methodist Homes for the Aged) using a music therapist funded by Cheshire East Council, but when the funding was cut, unfortunately MHA closed the café. After a suitable period of research and relevant training of volunteers, Carol built a team with Paula Lambe, Eve James, Rachel Hills and others who were passionate about running a café which offered support, resources, activities and a relevant safe space for those with dementia and their carers.

There is a lovely welcoming atmosphere as games are played and carers chat as they drink their coffee. But there is also now a very natural link to CAMEO[34], a concept that Carol and I have developed throughout our ministry. Carol is now the driving force behind this, preparing a rather posh afternoon tea with another team of volunteers, complete with

---

[34] Come And Meet Every One – a short service followed by tea, once a month in the afternoon.

tiered china cake plates and matching teapots providing a wonderful occasion for the mature members and friends from our community.

Carol's cakes are legendary. In fact, whenever I have left an appointment, there has always been a campaign to keep Carol, particularly because of her baking and cooking! Carol's hard work pays off when we see the joy of mature people having such an experience, and particularly those who would not normally attend the church because of health or problems with dementia.

Alongside these initiatives, for the last two years during the summer, Carol has co-ordinated and led Holiday@home which is an opportunity for the senior citizens to enjoy a day of activities based at the church with a lunch provided, or a day trip to the Anderton Boat Lift. There has also been a wonderful garden party at the home of Steve and Brenda Wilkinson starting with lunch and followed by a concert, either by my uncle Albert and his friends, The Sounds of Music, singing songs from the shows, or Fiona Simpson singing her own compositions, plus classic and contemporary gospel music.

The rhythm of mission during Hope 2018 will no doubt be enhanced by all that is happening as part of our outreach and ministry within the community. But there will be a particular focus upon Easter and the season of Lent, when we will be doing forty acts of kindness in addition to (or rather than) giving up something. This will be followed by a summer festival including a Pentecost Picnic with other churches, an interactive Harvest experience for local schools, Remembrance Sunday community civic services and special Christmas activities including Get into the Nativity Picture accompanied by local livestock engaging people outside the church's Christmas fayre.

Alongside these festival high points during our Hope Together year, the normal outreach activities will continue and we plan to offer various parenting courses for the community in partnership with the local schools. We also would like to recruit an intern on the Methodist Church's One Programme to help support Peter Freeman and Dan Harris developing our work with children and young people in the local community.

We will also continue supporting our Fresh Expression work at The Welcome, Longridge, Knutsford. The Welcome was started in 1995 and over the years has grown into a fully functioning community centre offering a wide range of activities, services and support to the people of Longridge and Shaw Heath. The Welcome is open to all members of the local community including young children, teenagers, busy parents and the elderly. We offer affordable, good-quality home-cooked meals from our café and provide a variety of free and great value activities to suit a range of age groups and interests.

My former colleague Ben Clowes loved being the minister caring for the fledging Welcome Church which meets in the café and I feel sure that his successor Sue Swires will no doubt love ministry there too. The Welcome is a perfect example of what has become known as the Big Society, and in 2011 was awarded the prime minister's Big Society Award. The community comes together at The Welcome, there's a wonderful spirit, with most of the time and effort being put in by committed volunteers who at the moment number in excess of twenty-five. Without their contribution, The Welcome could not function. In 2013, The Welcome received the Queen's Award for Voluntary Service and a number of KMC members had a proud day at Buckingham Palace to receive the award.

The Welcome is very much about the people and to see the transformation in real people's lives who are now key to the future work in the local community. A local barmaid named Julie King applied for a job as a cook in the Welcome Café and at her interview said, "I don't do God, but I do make a demon chocolate cake!" After working as the cook, Julie came to faith, felt a call to preach and after successfully applying to become a Methodist minister, is now training part-time at Queen's College. She is also still employed at The Welcome as a support worker, serving the community by running groups and supporting local adults, youth and children in very practical ways. In some sense, Julie has become the hands and feet of Jesus on the estate and therefore 'does God'!

The Welcome in some ways reminds me of Church@Community in Nottingham as a fresh expression of church and yet they are also very different. Both are focussed upon the local community, but the emphasis of Church@Community is primarily on being a worshipping church which reaches out into the community, whereas The Welcome is now both a charity and a church and therefore this has affected the ethos considerably to primarily emphasise social outreach. It is, however, true to say that The Welcome church has seen social and spiritual transformation in some people's lives (Julie's included) and it is this holistic transformation that we long to see in the future.

The challenge during Hope 2018 will be to do the social outreach and then to know how to ask people to consider the invitation to follow Jesus!

37

2020s Vision: Church, but
Not as You Know It!

'If you do what you've always done, you will get what you've always got!'

At a meeting of Ministers of Larger Churches, during a conversation about church growth, Manchester and Stockport District Chair Rev. Andrew Lunn said that if our district were to plant a church, that he would look to churches such as KMC to take the initiative – a comment which, at the time, I quickly dismissed because of capacity issues. We were busy enough without taking on other challenges! Andrew spoke about the Chester and Stoke District having a church-planting strategy and wondered if we should consider having such a strategy.

Rod Hill (district resourcing mission enabler) then made very similar comments in relation to what Potters House are doing at Longton Central Hall. Anthony Clowes, who is the minister at the church, had sent a hundred of their members to re-seed a new congregation meeting in Longton, alongside the traditional congregation which meets earlier on the Sunday morning under the care of Geoffrey Short. In a period of just nine months, the adult congregation had grown to one hundred and forty, plus twenty to thirty children. Obviously there have been challenges for both the Potters House leadership and the existing congregation which has met at Longton Central Hall for many years, but the benefits far outweigh the costs involved.

Rod asked if I could identify anyone who could potentially lead a church plant or re-seeding of a church. I struggled to do so at the time. But as I then thought and prayed about these conversations, I became aware that members of our staff team had the potential to plant churches and to engage a much wider group of people than just church members.

During my sabbatical in 2014, I had the opportunity to visit different churches and was particularly impressed by Ivy Church, Didsbury, and was able to have coffee with Pastor Anthony Delaney. They planted a church in Parrswood Cinema (now meeting elsewhere), with the main celebration in the biggest screen, youth work in another, children's work in a third and so on. They are about to run a second service at Parrs Wood alongside having planted churches in warehouses, pubs and other venues. Anthony is involved in New Thing which is a church-planting initiative. At the time of my visit, I began to wonder if the Methodist Church could replicate this concept.

Just after a very busy Christmas in 2016, I had the opportunity to visit the new Odeon Cinema at Baron's Quay, Northwich, and suddenly during a delay in showing the film I began to have something of an epiphany. I found myself counting the cinema seats to see how many people could fit into the particular screen I was attending! I suddenly began to think of how many of our members actually live in the Northwich or surrounding area (currently twenty-seven) and wondered if they could provide a core group to actually plant some form of fresh expression of church? I began to wonder what a missional community of people who began to pray together and seek a shared God-given vision for Northwich would look like, if they did life together and were prepared to serve the community and to share their faith story with others.

Being part of a new development in a local community at the earliest possible point could be strategically very important in collaborating with what the council are doing in the area, and the positive publicity that could be generated in launching a new initiative would undoubtedly engage those who would not normally be interested in a church project.

Having had the epiphany moment at Baron's Quay, I then spoke again to Andrew Lunn, who was very excited by the concept of planting a church in Northwich, despite the fact that it is in another circuit and district. He suggested that we have coffee with the Chair of Chester and Stoke District Rev. Peter Barber, plus Rev. Chris Pritchard (super-intendent of Mid Cheshire Circuit covering Northwich and Winsford).

This was a very positive meeting in which we all committed ourselves to explore this further. The chairs both spoke about districts possibly supporting financially and also of a church-planting advisor, Peter Hancock, being appointed in the Chester and Stoke District. Andrew Lunn commented, "There seems to be something of the breath of the

Spirit behind this!" It is good that there can be porous boundaries to circuits and districts to further our mission. This could, however, be the very first time such a thing has been attempted and achieved.

At KMC, we have been prayerfully exploring our 2020s vision and I have spoken to our outreach team, managing team and church council about the possibility of planting a church, about which they do seem very excited. I then shared the broader vision as part of our 2020s vision in morning worship services and the principal of planting and/or nurturing an existing church.

I had not realised until I shared this part of the vision with the managing team that Town Church in Northwich had closed in the autumn of 2016 and that this had been retained as a mission centre from which the Mid Cheshire Foodbank is run.

The Mid Cheshire Circuit Leadership Team (CLT) met on March 22nd and gave the concept their approval. They then invited me to share the vision more fully on April 26th.

Dan Harris (youth and young adults worker), whom I have identified as the staff member to lead the pilot project, came to support me as I shared with the CLT. We left KMC to travel together to Northwich very much feeling like The Blues Brothers as if we were 'on a mission from God', even posing for a fun photo to post on Facebook, complete with our sunglasses on!

We were welcomed by Clara Brown with some of her homemade cakes, which certainly helped to set the tone of our meeting. People warmly received the account of my epiphany experience in the Barons Quay cinema and the vision to plant a church for the un-churched in the Northwich area.

Superintendent Chris said, "I like to know the details, the nuts and bolts, but let's see where God is leading. God is somewhere in this!" whereas Clara said, "I'm very excited. I feel quite emotional about my church family from Knutsford and my new family at Northwich working together. God has put me here for a reason."

There was a real openness in the meeting, with everyone unanimously agreeing that we needed to move forward together, and Chris writing to the Methodist Churches in the Mid Cheshire Circuit and then to the KMC church council. Rev. Peter Levitt said, "This is so wacky – it must be of God's Spirit; I'm very excited!" Dan and I left with a real sense of God's peace, but with great excitement about what God was about to do. The car stereo volume was cranked up as we drove home, the KMC blues brothers on a mission from God!

I then asked David James (chair of outreach team) to visit Ivy Church at Parrs Wood, which he found to be very impressive and young! I also asked him to go to the Odeon cinema at Barons Quay to get a feel for what is happening there. David has kindly attended the cinema on a couple of occasions and has had very positive experiences. The cinema is available for hire by churches!

Dan has also been to visit HTB to meet their church-planting specialist Mark Elsdon-Dew who has currently overseen sixty-nine church plants! He advised of the challenges, such as the need for proper staffing and finance. The culture of the church plant is key and the vision has to be clear. "If the infrastructure isn't right, God can be in it, but it will fail," said Elsdon-Dew. HTB allow a budget of £50,000 and send fifty people! They are obviously operating in a slightly different league to us and are also London-based.

I then shared a review of our 2020s vision with both our morning congregations and shared more fully about the possibility of planting a church in Northwich, as all of the Methodist churches in Northwich had then been advised and our church council had received a letter from the Mid Cheshire Circuit inviting KMC to collaborate with them on this initiative.

The truth is that whilst I have shared the vision to start a church plant, the first phase will be to simply identify people who feel called to meet together to pray, to help shape and share a vision together. So the emphasis will be upon building a community of people who can do life together and be open with each other, so that values can be owned and a kingdom culture can be developed.

Yes, there will need to be grant applications made, an infrastructure developed, prayer letters circulated and permissions sought from church councils, circuit and district meetings, but the formal processes are almost secondary to the building of a kingdom community who are commissioned prior to the public launch, Easter 2018.

The target audience would be young adults and young families who do not currently attend any church, so it is not for those already attending other churches – but that does not mean that people will not prefer something more contemporary in worship style and culture. In developing a kingdom culture for young adults, it will no doubt also be appealing to those who are more mature.

The important thing is that a safe place is provided where people can experience acceptance, love and a sense of belonging to a kingdom community with shared values. There will be a branding process to determine the name of this kingdom community, which could be something like '*Tommy's* – a community for those who have their doubts, questions and need to touch and feel' or '*Zacs church* for those unseen individuals whom Jesus spots even when they are hidden up a tree!' It will be church – 'but not as you know it!'

As the vision develops, Dan describes the community in these terms:

> *The community will be known for <u>Loving out Loud</u>. I hesitate to use the word community, because for me it invokes a sense of forced altruistic duty that is bound by an obligation to a fleeting project. The word community could easily be replaced with group of friends, family, church or fellowship. The community pursues <u>a love centred faith that is found and expressed in the holistic incarnation of Jesus</u>.*[35]

This kingdom community will operate on the principal of BLESS, being a blessing to the people of Northwich and to each other. BLESS is a helpful acronym: <u>B</u>e prayerful, <u>L</u>isten, <u>E</u>at, <u>S</u>erve and <u>S</u>tory. This seems to fit the ethos and values that we aspire to. Being intentional in our prayers for Northwich and each other, it is so important that this whole initiative is covered by prayer. Listening to the community will enable us to hear about the local needs, but to also hear God's prompting. It is interesting to note that Jesus asked people ninety-six questions in the gospels, so that He could listen.

Eating together will enable a sense of community and trust to develop. Jesus ate with His disciples and the most unlikely of other people. Table talk can be so important. Serving the local community together builds trust and credibility, but it actually models the kingdom values of a Christian community. The Church has modelled this effectively through foodbanks, street pastors and much of the outreach work done in recent years and this is partly due to the challenge of Hope 08 to do so! Stories are powerful in sharing what is important to us and what makes us the people that we are.

I look forward to introducing these principals as part of sharing a vision for this kingdom community, but the acronym BLESS is also a

---

[35] Taken from the vision document '*A New Thing*' in Northwich.

helpful teaching device for every church preparing to engage the villages, towns and cities of our nation during Hope 2018.

It was a great experience filming a short four-session DVD course on *A Kingdom Community?* exploring our values, priorities and missiology based upon the book of Acts and the experience of the early church in the autumn of 2017 using some of *Hope in the Main Street* as case study material.

'If we do what we've always done, we will get what we've always got!' – So obviously, during Hope 2018 and beyond, we need to do and be Church, but not as we know it!

38

The Owl and the Blackbird, a Parable of Surprises

Carol and I decided to take our black Labrador Tammy for a walk on the heath in Knutsford and, as it was becoming quite dusky on a late winter afternoon on my day off, we decided to take her in the car before it became too dark. As we got out of the car, Carol noticed something up in the tree just outside Oakwood and the Beechwood accommodation. It was a large owl.

I crossed the road to where Carol was standing looking up into the tree. It was truly an impressive specimen even in the half light of a dusky winter's afternoon.

But then Carol said, "It's not moving much, if at all."

"Well perhaps it's asleep," I replied, "but it's strange that it is perched in such a public place. I've never seen an owl like this before." So I took out my torch and shone it up at the owl to get a better look at it.

Carol said, "It seems to be standing on a perch," which we both thought seemed a little odd, and then suddenly we both realised that it was just an artificial plastic owl!

Carol and I burst out laughing as we knew how foolish we had been to think that a large owl would be sitting in a tree just outside people's houses in Knutsford. But Carol was particularly disappointed that we had not seen the real thing; it was just a fake.

The following Monday I was taking a Communion service at Beechwood for the residents of both Oakwood and Beechwood. It was a re-launch of the service, having not met for a few months, after the co-ordinators John and Lesley Pamment had left their flat in the complex to relocate to Sunderland.

I had taken a carol service just before Christmas and had been encouraged by an attendance of over forty people. I had taken with me a small Open the Book team. This had been an experiment to develop a new project to share Bible stories in a creative way with a more mature audience. A number of us had thought that the project, which was so successful with local schools, would also work (with adaptions) in a very different setting with older people too. So the residents of Oakwood and Beechwood, alongside senior citizens attending our Christmas lunch club, were our guinea pigs! And it certainly worked on both occasions, but it had also provided me with the opportunity to invite the residents to our re-launched Communion service.

Previously I had met with five or six people, but with John and Lesley leaving I was not sure how viable the re-launch would prove as so many of the residents had hospital appointments to attend or were too frail to get down into the lounge. I was also aware of how busy my diary had become and that other tasks were awaiting my attention. And so, as a minister, you wrestle with yourself to try and work out the priorities in terms of time management and just how effective you are being. How many people do you need to attend a Communion service to make it viable? What had happened to my understanding of Matthew 18:20: 'For where two or three come together in my name, there am I with them'? Is my time so precious that I struggle to justify being with the few? Do I think that I am so important these days that I always need big numbers to listen to my talks?

In actual fact, at the time I visited Abbeyfields each month for a Communion service with only three, and at most only up to five, attending. Plus, the Communion service at Sharston House only had around eight or nine attending, some of whom were experiencing dementia and yet still appreciated our time of fellowship. Ash Court is slightly different in nature, because a number of our church members are resident and therefore we can have as many as sixteen attending. But then, the numbers attending are only one measure of productivity and significance in terms of the kingdom of God advancing.

There were seven of us at Beechwood who met for coffee, with Jack and Nancy Marchant hosting us and three people who had not been before, but I had met them at the carol service. So I decided to chat with them before launching into the Communion service and told them about Carol and me seeing the owl outside. Apparently, John and Lesley had been instrumental in helping to get an artificial owl fitted on a perch in the tree to scare off some pigeons which were sitting on the branch of the tree and messing up the cars parked in the car park below. We laughed together about how Carol and I had been fooled by the owl and it gave a really good, fun introduction to the service. Everyone was relaxed and seemed to thoroughly enjoy our time of fellowship together.

Jack then told me, "We may not have a real owl, but we do have a white blackbird!"

I was a little bemused by this comment and was not sure how to respond. *"A white blackbird?"*

"Yes," said Jack. "It has just the odd black feather, but apart from that it is all white, a white blackbird."

"But that's a contradiction in terms," I replied. "How can you have a white blackbird? Are you having me on? There's no such thing!"

All of the residents attending then joined in. "Oh, yes, there is – and it's got young ones. They sit in the birdbath."

I could not get my head around the thought of white blackbirds. So when I arrived home for lunch and told Carol, we looked on Google and found that white blackbirds are very rare but had been spotted in a Nottingham park. Having lived in Nottingham for sixteen years, we had never seen or heard of a white blackbird, but apparently birdwatchers travel for miles to see them.

I began to feel that the white blackbird could be something of a parable for me. Could it be a prophetic sign of something much deeper? God has a way of surprising us, just when we think we have got Him sorted out in our minds and put Him in a pigeonhole marked 'sacred' or confined Him in some way through our limited understanding. I want to say that there is no such thing as a white blackbird; logically, it makes no sense. In contrast, when I think I have spotted 'the real thing' and believe it to be amazing, in actual fact it's a plastic owl. I think I know what my priorities should be and how best to use my time, but God presents me with a white blackbird!

And so at the end of the Communion service, at a point when I was thinking of rushing off to write an article for the *Knutsford Guardian* before their deadline, Jack and Nancy asked if I had time to go upstairs to see an elderly church member named Margaret Squires. She was unable to get downstairs and had a nurse visiting her. So I went upstairs to be welcomed enthusiastically into her flat.

"Have you brought Communion with you?"

And we shared together in a simple act of worship, during which she was able to confess her sins, give praise to God and talk to me about the things that were on her mind. She also encouraged and was a real blessing to me. We shared an hour together talking through a number of things and sharing in fellowship together. My timetable for that day was completely out of the window, but I walked away feeling that I was on God's timetable, not my own.

The following week there was a coffee morning at Beechwood for all of the residents, when those attending the Communion service were telling the others what a marvellous time we had had together. A lady then said, "I think I will come to the next one and do you think it would be alright if I brought my friend?" Suddenly there was a woman who had never attended, who was going to do our evangelism for us by bringing others to the service! Jack and Nancy were thrilled to be able to tell of the conversations at that coffee morning. At a mature age, with their health issues and concerns, they were discovering a whole new ministry where they could effectively serve God. Nancy also began to write more meditations which she shares at each Communion service. God has not finished with them yet.

In fact, the Communion service at Beechwood, which I had thought might close, now has between sixteen to twenty people attending each month! God has certainly surprised me.

The white blackbird is a little parable of how God can surprise us with the illogical, unpredictable work of His Spirit in people's lives and of how God can do immeasurably more than anything we could ever think or imagine. I am looking forward to seeing some white blackbirds.

Who knows but God what He has in store for us? Could it be that a new ministry to the mature using storytelling and drama could be launched on the back of our experience at Beechwood? That could prove to be a very interesting white blackbird for many churches. A simple, effective idea might well produce results that will surprise us during Hope Together and well into the future.

39

Are You Martha or Mary?

Edith Mary Cotton (Mum)

Mary has chosen what is better, and it will not be taken away from her.

Luke 10:42

An important part of my story and life's journey is to reflect upon those people who have journeyed with me and made me the person that I am today. I have dedicated this book to my wife Carol who has been my partner in life, mission and ministry for the past thirty-six years and I give thanks for our children Sarah, Steven and Timothy who inspire us and are our greatest achievement and legacy in life. There have been others who have invested their time in me: ministers and friends who have trained me on placement such as Geoff Lear and John Hibberts, plus many friends who have prayed with me and worked with me in each of my ministerial appointments.

But amongst all others, I want at this point to give thanks for the life of my mum, Mary Cotton (née Wheeldon), who actually died some years ago now, back in 2002, but I still want to briefly write and remember the person that she was.

Mum was only sixty-four and in the weeks before her death I was sharing with a family about their loved one in preparation for a funeral; apparently, every time that this particular family had visitors, their mother used to be bustling away in the kitchen preparing a meal for everyone, but she would get quite stressed about it. So her husband used to quote a scripture verse to her because her name was Martha. He would say (quoting the old King James Version[36] of the Bible), 'Martha, Martha,

---

[36] KJV.

thou art careful and troubled about many things.' The New International Version reads, 'Martha, Martha, you are worried and upset about many things.' I guess it was a way of trying to get Martha to calm down.

But as they were talking about Martha, I was thinking about Mary, my mother Mary, bustling away in the farmhouse kitchen preparing meals for all the family and any *visitors* who would call at the farm. Maybe I was smiling to myself thinking of Mum looking after us all; picturing the AGA cooker with all the pots and pans on it, the glass door on the oven so that you could look in to see what was being prepared.

One visitor to our farm, Gordon Etheridge, like many other visitors was told to pull a chair up to the table and to "stretch or starve!" – an invitation to help himself to some food. When he went home to his wife, the comment was, "I'm not kidding you, there was so much food on the table, with all the family and workers around, it was just like that TV show *Bread*. The only thing that was missing was the pottery hen in the middle of the table!"

And later, when I left Martha's family, having prepared for her funeral, I was still musing about Mum in the farm kitchen. I thought that I could write a meditation about her – *Are you Martha or Mary?* – but of course I was very busy at the time, so it didn't get any further!

A couple of weeks later I had an urgent phone call to say that Mum had been taken ill. She had been really poorly with just a heavy cold and she woke up on a Saturday morning with a nose bleed which couldn't be stopped. So my sister-in-law Ann sent for the paramedics and I drove over to Staffordshire as quickly as I could, but ended up following Mum to the hospital.

We were told that something had been found in the blood. Mum had leukaemia. It was an incredible shock, though we visited the hospital and Mum seemed very positive and was about to start treatment the following week. But sadly for us, Mum died only eight days later on Mother's Day (of all days), which was an even bigger shock at the time.

It was only then that I knew why I had to write that meditation about Mum. Suddenly it made sense, almost as if God had been preparing me for that moment.

So I wrote a meditation which gave thanks for all the things that Mum did to support us, care for us and love us: taking us for the school bus, meeting us as we came home as children. Her apple pies were legendary, but for some reason she always called quiche lorraines "qwiche"; no matter how many times we told her, it was always "qwiche"! So I had to mention 'qwiche'. She was amazing at looking after little lambs who were virtually lifeless. Dad would bring them into the kitchen and Mum would somehow work her magic on them, rubbing them with some straw, feeding them some milk and keeping them warm on the AGA. We sometimes wondered as children if she was cooking the lambs! But more often than not, Mum would get them going and they would either be returned to their mothers, or if the mother had died we would all take turns at feeding the little orphan lambs!

The meditation was my thanksgiving for Mum and all my memories. I'm not going to quote it fully here, but the refrain was:

Are you Martha, or are you Mary?
Bustling away in the kitchen,
Or sitting at the feet of Jesus.
Because that's alright by me.
That's alright by me.

Mary chose to leave her sister Martha bustling away in the kitchen, and felt that the priority was to sit at the feet of Jesus, wanting to be with Him. Jesus said, "Mary has chosen what is better, and it will not be taken away from her."

You see, the priority in our lives is our relationship with Jesus, not all the things we do or are; it is our love of Jesus. And the good thing is that whilst Mum was great at bustling away in the kitchen and looking after her family, she also loved Jesus.

As hard as it was to have her die so young and to let her go, that's exactly what we had to do. We had to allow her to be with Jesus, to sit at the feet of Jesus. And that's alright by me. To know that my mum is with Jesus has been a great comfort and has enabled me to know His peace.

As we lose people and then give thanks for friends and loved ones, I think that our faith makes a very real difference to the whole experience of bereavement and grief, because in Jesus, as we trust in Him, we can have confidence and hope that our loved ones are with Him. We believe in the resurrection of the dead. Death is not the end; it's a new beginning with God in Jesus.

So as you read about my mother, Mary Cotton, I'd like you to think of your friends and family members, your loved ones sitting at the feet of Jesus, having a good old chat with Him. And whilst it can be hard to let people go, we can give thanks for all of our memories and we do commend them into God's loving care. As they sit at the feet of Jesus.

And for each one of us, as we trust in Jesus, He walks with us. In closing, I invite you to reflect upon that word 'Immanuel' – 'God with us' – and to know the truth and reality of that statement.

40

A Man on a Mission

Charles Frederick Cotton (Charlie – Dad)

It was early in the morning on 14th December 2015 when Carol woke to find a number of missed calls on her mobile telephone from the family farm in the Staffs Moorlands.

"You had better telephone David [my brother]. There must be something wrong if they've been trying to phone us in the night. It might be your dad!"

I quickly telephoned my brother, who didn't sound well, coughing as he answered the phone. "Have you been trying to reach me?" I asked. "We seem to have a few missed calls."

David began to respond, "Dad was taken ill last night at Cauldon Lowe Village Hall, at a carol concert. He was having a stroke and then had a heart attack."

I was preparing in my mind to race to North Staffs to the hospital to see Dad as soon as possible. But then the news suddenly became much worse.

"We tried to phone you, Rob, but we couldn't get any reply. I'm sorry, Rob, we've lost him!" At this point David burst into tears as he told me what had happened.

I was shell-shocked. I couldn't take it in.

I was mentally still preparing to race to the hospital, but Dad had died! I found myself apologising to David for not hearing the phone and not going to be with Dad at the end, but thankfully my siblings had all managed to make it to the hospital before Dad died.

Apparently, he had not seemed too seriously ill at first in the hospital, because he was talking lucidly, and when a nurse had asked him to push against her hands to check his mobility after the stroke, he had almost pushed her over! Dad had always been a strong man, working on the farm until quite late in life. When asked if he could lift his leg, it was almost an exaggerated high kick in the air. He seemed so well.

When test results returned, it became apparent that Dad had experienced a massive heart attack, that he would never be the same man again and that they could do no more for him. So he was brought off the sedation and allowed to talk with the family. My brother Andrew arrived just in time for Dad to hold out his arms and to give him a big hug, of which he was reluctant to let go. Dad died very soon afterwards.

Hearing the news of my father's death was an incredible shock. He had seemed so fit and well. It was a shock to all the family and to all his friends who commented about how well he had looked! In fact, in the last week of his life he had visited many of the senior citizens around the village of Whiston with Christmas cards and even on the last day of his life he had been to carol services at the chapel and also at St. Mildred's Parish Church. Then he visited Mum's grave with a wreath (which I certainly found very poignant later) before preaching at Dodsleigh and going to the carol concert with a brass band at a local village hall.

What a wonderful last day Dad enjoyed. If you could choose how to end your life, then it would certainly be doing the things that you most enjoy. But the shock for all of his family and for all his friends who saw him in the last hours of his life was quite awful. As I spoke to my stepmother Mauveen shortly after hearing the news, she related to me Dad's conversations in the hospital. "Your Dad knew where he was and he knew where he was going!" This was certainly a great comfort, which was helpful as I got my head around the shock of losing him so suddenly.

Alongside feeling devastated that we had lost Dad, I also felt really stupid and foolish for not even hearing the phone calls throughout the night! Whether it was that I was just so exhausted after a busy Sunday that I could not be woken, I'm not sure. But certainly, the fact remained that the one member of the family who is supposed to be available and on emergency call-out slept through the whole episode! I did feel that I had let Dad and the family down that night.

However, I then had to break the news to our children, which I found really difficult. Because actually talking about Dad's death somehow seemed to make it much more real and the emotions then began to get the better of me. It was particularly hard speaking to Timothy, as he was away in South Africa working as a volunteer for Hope Through Action. I wanted to stay strong whilst I told him what had happened to his grandad. But sadly, after a while, he knew that I was really upset and whilst he was also trying to be strong, it was hard to contain how upset he felt too.

My son Steven told me that there was no unfinished business between Dad and me, so I didn't need to necessarily speak to him before his death, which was certainly true and really helpful. Nevertheless, at first it was a struggle to get over the feelings of stupidity and anger with myself for not hearing the phone!

But actually, you do not have the luxury of wallowing in self-pity at these times, because there is a funeral to arrange and it became very clear early on that Mauveen (my father's wife of some six years) felt that Dad would have wanted me to take his funeral. Initially, that felt like too much of a challenge, but I knew that God would give me and other members of the family the strength to get through it.

My colleague Rev. Jackie Betts (superintendent minister at the time) had arrived at our door soon after Carol had rung her to bring her condolences and to give her support. I was in a bit of a mess at the time, I fear, and I will never forget her wonderful pastoral support. It was wonderful to be ministered to at that time, with Jackie listening and praying for us. I then prepared to visit Mauveen and the family.

We were all a little shell-shocked, but just being together felt important. On the Tuesday morning, Dad had organised a carol service at Leek Market in the cattle ring with Uncle Ab, Auntie Doris, Cousin Alison Fox, Auntie Beryl and Uncle Dave Stew amongst others. It felt right to continue and to host the Carol Service in Dad's memory. Carol and I were pleased to support this short act of worship, with our niece Rachael Shaw and Arthur Knobbs who had worked with Dad over the years standing next to us in the auction ring where one of my brother David's cattle would be later sold, and where Dad had no doubt bought and sold many cattle over the years. We later watched as four calves, once belonging to my brother Andrew and his wife Teresa, were sold in the auction ring next door.

Alan Sigley of Keate's Funeral Directors helped us to prepare for the celebration and thanksgiving of Dad's life and faith, but as I prayed about what to say and how to lead the service, I felt that the readings had to be from John 14, where Jesus spoke to his friends the disciples about his own death, and also from John 1.

What a wonderful passage of scripture John 1 is; it's a reading which is the climax of every service of Nine Lessons and Carols at Christmas and for me it's one of the most important readings in the whole of the Bible. I'll explain why in a few minutes. But that's why in many churches and schools you tend to get the minister or headteacher reading this passage – because it's one of our favourites.

My sister Catherine gave an excellent tribute to Dad at the funeral, particularly thinking of family and friends, which in some ways really put the pressure on me because she spoke so well. I then tried to focus a little on farming and faith. It was a bit ironic really, me speaking about farming, as apparently I told Mum and Dad that I didn't want to be a farmer when I was about eleven years old. The straw and hay dust had affected my nose and eyes at the time, so I thought I was going to go into banking, accountancy or sales, but God seemed to have other ideas!

Dad started farming at Blakeley Farm, Whiston in around 1957 when he and Mum first married. They had the Chasmar (Charlie/Mary) Pedigree Holstein Friesian Herd and certainly if the numbers of farmers, reps and auctioneers at his funeral was anything to go by, I think that he was always well respected for his integrity in farming. I still remember some of the names of Dad's cows as we grew up: Chasmar, Falcon, Pride, Daisy and Matty.

Dad always loved going to the market – *any* market. In fact, he used to plan his visits to see us in Preston around going to Uttoxeter Market and arriving in Preston so that he could go to Preston Cattle Market! He also worked at Uttoxeter Market with Bagshaws Auctioneers and met Jack Staley whom he then insisted that I visit each week whilst I worked with Refuge Assurance in Uttoxeter. When Uttoxeter Market closed he tried Derby, but didn't get on with the one way system, so he chose Leek as his favoured market. It feels very fitting that we were singing carols in the auction ring in his memory at a service he'd organised, just a couple of days after his death, and that there were posters around the market inviting people to share with us at his funeral.

Perhaps some of his friends remember that Dad used to go to Uttoxeter Market (or wherever) in his old battered Land Rover with the number plate 'COJ', which everyone at the market called 'Charlie's Old Junk!' But he loved his Land Rover.

Dad farmed well past normal retirement age which, no doubt, my brothers Dave and Andrew were pleased about. He only retired properly a few years before his death, when he said that he had decided to take life a bit easier and not get up at 5am every morning, so he had a lie-in until 6am! But he would still be across at Blakeley Farm to fetch his milk by 6.45 like clockwork!

In the last hours of his life in hospital, when asked what he did for a living, Dad said that he was a retired farmer. Dr. Chris Pickering who attended him said, "I've never met a retired farmer yet so I know you're lying!" But actually, apart from going to the market, looking after his hens, selling his eggs and taking an ongoing interest in the farms, he was enjoying his retirement with my stepmother Mauveen after they had met at Summerfire.

I had been given the privilege of conducting their marriage service a couple of years later and they had six very happy years of married life together at Daisy Bank Farm.

As we celebrated Dad's life and faith at his funeral thanksgiving, I told funny stories of him, because we wanted everyone to smile. We wanted the tributes to be honest and to say that Dad was a down-to-earth farmer, who loved his family, friends and farming, and he also had a faith. He loved his Lord Jesus and he loved the little chapel at Whiston in the Staffordshire Moorlands.

You see, some people might have thought that we should have had his thanksgiving at Cheadle where he had preached only a few weeks before his death, but that little chapel at Whiston was his spiritual home, where he taught in the Sunday school for many years and worshipped each week. In the last year of his life, Dad was like a man on a mission!

Dad had commented to me about improving Whiston Chapel, possibly with new chairs or something. But when there was the offer of some church furnishings from a church in Salford, Manchester that was closing, I asked the minister to let me know if no one else wanted them. I received a call shortly afterwards to see if I might find a home for them. After speaking to Dad on the telephone, Dad had a look at a photo of the church furnishings on the website with the folks at Whiston Chapel and obviously they very much wanted them.

So perhaps you can imagine the scene with me; because in true 'Charlie Cotton fashion', Dad, Teresa (my sister-in-law) and I set off with the Land Rover and trailer to fetch a pulpit, a lectern, font and Communion table from Salford and took them to their new home in Whiston Chapel. But not to be satisfied with that, Dad and the small congregation then redecorated the worship area and the Sunday school. They put in new kitchen units and a disabled toilet. And only a few days before he died, Dad was on the telephone again asking me, "We need a new ramp into the chapel. Do you think we should have it in concrete, tarmac or a metal one?" And he had obviously arranged for someone to give him a price. Dad was 'a man with a mission' to make Whiston Chapel the most welcoming and hospitable place that it could possibly be. He wanted to see the people of the village coming into church.

The new chapel chairs that people are now sitting on were bought from Swan Bank Mission, Burslem, but having got them he said to Uncle Dave Stew, "You'd be as well to get some for St. Mildred's Parish Church as well." So at Dad's funeral thanksgiving, people filled the chapel but they also filled St. Mildred's Parish Church too, and they were sitting on chairs that Dad had found! And alongside getting the £7,000 refurbishment work done with the congregation at Whiston Chapel, he had also written to anyone and everyone to give a grant to the chapel, whether they were from Kingsley Parish Council, Your Housing, Lafarge Cement, Alton Towers or wherever!

Dad's faith was very important to him and personally I have some great memories of Dad and my stepmother Mauveen going on two pilgrimages to the Holy Land with us. I think that one of my favourite photos of Dad and myself will always be of us standing in Shepherds' Field during our pilgrimage, where I had him reading to the other pilgrims about those first shepherds in the Nativity story as a modern-day shepherd himself. As Dad walked through Bethlehem he started a conversation with another man who asked if he, Mauveen and Carol would like to see his restaurant. They ended up having a lovely meal, but they also dressed Dad up in Palestinian dress so that he ended up looking more like Yasser Arafat! The next time we went on a pilgrimage in 2014, Dad was determined to find the same shop and restaurant, and each evening we ended up taking a group of ten or a dozen pilgrims for Palestinian tea and cakes and a dressing up session. It was one of the funniest highlights of our pilgrimage, all because of Dad!

Dad had a great life, he lived life to the full; he was a down-to-earth sort of guy and he had a wonderful last day at chapel, church, visiting Mum's grave, preaching at Dodsleigh and going to a carol concert afterwards.

Dad loved the chapel and even when he was taken ill at Cauldon Lowe Village Hall at the Brass Band Carol Concert that he really enjoyed, as Wendy Webster cared for him, he said, "If I don't manage to make it to the carol service on Sunday, will you go for me?"

Even in the last hours of his life he was inviting people to come to the chapel. In a very real sense, it is not actually Dad's chapel/church, it's God's church and it is also the church of the whole village. I wonder how many people Dad had invited to the church over the years. I also wonder how many people I have invited to church over the years too. As I think of Dad's life and what was important to him, his family, his friends, his farming, I also remember how central his faith was and what made him the man he was.

You see, that favourite passage from John 1 which Rev. David Watson read for us at Dad's funeral is important because, 'In the beginning was the Word, and the Word was with God, and the Word was God.' God was and is the Word! Then we read, 'The Word became flesh and made his dwelling among us.' In one version it reads that He made his tabernacle with us – in other words, He pitched his tent with us!

The Word became flesh, He became human, became one of us. He became, in actual fact, the human being that we know as Jesus, the baby Jesus. So if you want to know who the true God is, what God is really like, then take a long hard look at Jesus. Jesus is the Living Word of God.

You see, the reason that the reading from John 1 is so important, particularly at the more challenging times of life, is that we don't have some far-off remote God sitting on a distant cloud, tut-tutting or sighing when we get things wrong. We have a God who in Jesus became one of us, who was born in a stable, with a cattle feed trough as a bed. It most probably smelt a bit like a farmyard because animals had been living there – there was muck on the floor! Jesus was a down-to-earth man who worked with His hands in His father's carpenter shop. There was never any pretence with Jesus; He said what He thought whether religious people liked it or not. You certainly knew where you stood with Jesus. He experienced all the same things, feelings and emotions that we experience.

The very shortest verse in the whole Bible is just two words – 'Jesus wept!' Why did He weep? He wept when He heard of the death of a friend, a loved one named Lazarus. You see, in Jesus we have a God who understands what it is to grieve, who understands what it is to lose a loved one, a friend, and because of that I believe in a God who in Jesus knows how we feel when we lose someone and can bring us His comfort and a peace which passes all understanding! That's the God I believe in, and each Christmas, as we read John 1 in a Nine Lessons and Carols service, we remember that He became flesh, one of us! I commend that God to you, so that you might know His presence and peace in life too. As we have commended Dad into God's care and keeping, it's my hope and prayer that we can all be part of the legacy of Charlie Cotton's life, in learning from his priorities as we read about him. We may even become people of faith in Jesus. As a family, we give thanks for Dad's life – a man on a mission.

Appendix

A final thought to reflect upon:

The Church is the Body of Christ, and the Spirit is the Spirit of Christ. He fills the Body, directs its movements, controls its members, inspires its wisdom, supplies its strength. He guides into truth, sanctifies its agents, and empowers for witnessing. ... The Spirit has never abdicated His authority nor relegated His power. Neither Pope nor parliament, neither conference nor council is supreme in the Church of Christ. ... The church that is man-managed instead of God-governed is doomed to failure. A ministry that is college-trained but not Spirit-filled works no miracles. The church that multiplies committees and neglects prayer may be fussy, noisy, enterprising, but it labours in vain and spends its strength for nought. It is possible to excel in mechanics and fail in dynamic. There is a superabundance of machinery; what is wanting is power. ... To run an organization needs no God. Man can supply the energy, enterprise, and enthusiasm for things human. The real work of a church depends upon the power of the Spirit. The presence of the Spirit is vital and central to the work of the church. Nothing else avails. Apart from Him, wisdom becomes folly, and strength weakness. The Church is called to be a 'spiritual house' and a holy priesthood.[37]

A closing prayer for you as you finish reading this book, taken from Ephesians 3:16-21:

I pray that out of his glorious riches he may strengthen you with power through his Spirit in your inner being, so that Christ may dwell in your hearts through faith. And I pray that you, being rooted and established in love, may have power, together with all the Lord's holy people, to grasp how wide

---

[37] Excerpted from chapter 2 of *The Way To Pentecost*, a classic little book recently reprinted by Christian Literature Crusade. Samuel Chadwick (1860-1932), Methodist minister.

and long and high and deep is the love of Christ, and to know this love that surpasses knowledge – that you may be filled to the measure of all the fullness of God.

Now to him who is able to do immeasurably more than all we ask or imagine, according to his power that is at work within us, to him be glory in the church and in Christ Jesus throughout all generations, for ever and ever! Amen.

What Shall I Read Next?

Publisher's Recommendations

Life Begins When You Choose
Edited by Joyce Gbeleyi
ISBN 978-1-911086-01-7

These true stories of women in Manchester, each from a very different background, reveal lives transformed as they encountered Jesus through their church communities. The stories demonstrate how God can work through the church to bring others into a life of hope.

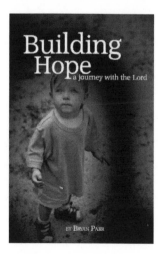

Building Hope
Bryan Parr
ISBN 978-1-907509-13-1

Bryan Parr had been a Christian for many years and was now retired. But one day, as he went through the motions of his Sunday church service, he found himself asking, "Is this all there is to Christianity?" His question led him to find ways to bring hope to the neediest in eastern Europe, using his building skills to create orphanages and work on other vital projects – to bring good news to the poor.

These books are available from all good bookshops and from the publisher:

www.onwardsandupwards.org